2(/0₅

MEDIA VIOLENCE and AGGRESSION
SCIENCE and IDEOLOGY

MEDIA VIOLENCE and AGGRESSION
SCIENCE and IDEOLOGY

Tom Grimes *Texas State University, San Marcos*

James A. Anderson *University of Utah*

Lori Bergen *Texas State University, San Marcos*

SAGE Publications
Los Angeles • London • New Delhi • Singapore

For information:

Sage Publications, Inc.
2455 Teller Road
Thousand Oaks,
   California 91320
E-mail: order@sagepub.com

Sage Publications India Pvt. Ltd.
B 1/I 1 Mohan Cooperative
   Industrial Area
Mathura Road, New Delhi 110 044
India

Sage Publications Ltd.
1 Oliver's Yard
55 City Road
London EC1Y 1SP
United Kingdom

Sage Publications Asia-Pacific Pte. Ltd.
33 Pekin Street #02–01
Far East Square
Singapore 048763

Printed in the United States of America

Library of Congress Cataloging-in-Publication Data

Grimes, Tom, 1951-
Media violence and aggression: Science and ideology/Tom Grimes, James A. Anderson, Lori A. Bergen.
   p. cm.
Includes bibliographical references and index.
ISBN 978-1-4129-1440-6 (cloth)
ISBN 978-1-4129-1441-3 (pbk.)
   1. Violence in mass media. I. Anderson, James A. (James Arthur), 1939- II. Bergen, Lori A., 1958- III. Title.

P96.V5G74 2008
303.6—dc22   2007014778

This book is printed on acid-free paper.

07   08   09   10   11   10   9   8   7   6   5   4   3   2   1

Acquisitions Editor:	Todd R. Armstrong
Editorial Assistant:	Katie Grim
Production Editor:	Sarah K. Quesenberry
Copy Editor:	Gillian Dickens
Typesetter:	C&M Digitals (P) Ltd.
Proofreader:	Ellen Brink
Indexer:	Molly Hall
Associate Marketing Manager:	Amberlyn M. Erzinger

Contents

Preface

We propose to examine a question that has hung in the air for over a century: Does media violence create psychological changes in most people, which harm society? That harm, since the 1970s, has been generally defined to be a rise in the level of social aggression. That is, media violence *causes* our nation's citizens to be more aggressive, more hostile toward one another. This, the advocates of this position argue, is a generalized phenomenon.

Those researchers who believe that there is an indisputable media violence/social aggression connection are pretty darned convinced by their position. For them, the data are in, the science is settled, the case is closed. For those on the other side, the data clearly suggest not a generalized phenomenon but rather a differentiated one, one in which media violence may affect psychologically ill people but does not seem to affect psychologically well people. Like arguments about global warming, there is at present an irreducible quality to the issue, which makes it irresolvable in one direction or another. Thus, we're often left with irrationalities—that is, things not scientific: Those who don't think there is a generalized media violence/social aggression link tend to eye-roll when the other side speaks. A kind of knowing look that we're dealing with zealots. That enrages the other side, of course, and lately some of the principal advocates of the other side have decided not to engage in the discussion at all. To paraphrase one such advocate of a causal connection between media violence and social aggression, L. Rowell Huesmann (a University of Michigan social scientist), continuing to debate the issue at this point, given that the science is settled, would just be "he said/she said" banter. Such discussions, he clearly believes, get us nowhere. We beg to differ. Debate and discussion, pursued in a civil, empirically grounded way, always gets us somewhere. To refuse to do so otherwise *guarantees* we'll all get nowhere. Therefore, this book was written with the intention of breaking past the recursive loop, that core, that irreducible entity that keeps both sides of the media violence/aggression debate spinning in circles.

In trying to make intellectual progress, we're mindful that a stalemate likely gives some measure of comfort to both sides because irresolvability builds a buffer against further assault. That is, at some level, both sides of the argument may find it comforting to embrace a stalemate and thus turn their backs on the hard intellectual work of figuring out how media violence does and does not affect society.

This discussion is not, as the cliché goes, just academic. The causationist position—that media violence *causes* social aggression—has inspired two decades of congressional hearings on the media, panicked calls for censorship by various special interests, and an entire industry of causationist scholarship along with a collection of comfortable professorships. The causationist position is said to have even had some influence over the outcome of the 2004 presidential and congressional election—that is, the election of Republican majorities that might "do something" about the proliferation of media violence and other "filth" invading the nation's mass communications (see Chapter 6).

This book is written for the policy maker and government regulator and their staffs as well as the student of media. But it's written in a way that will be easy for the layperson to understand. We've tried diligently to scrub the narrative of jargon, technical terms, and other literary devices that make these sorts of books generally difficult to read—even for policy makers and students who are the intended primary audience.

If this book is a success (sales notwithstanding), it will break through the core, the irreducible, that recursive loop that encourages both sides to bait one another, insult one another, and put the debate on that fatuous he said/she said plane of discourse. With this book, we want to try to do better.

We begin Chapter 1 with a fictionalized conversation—a montage of conversations we have had with policy makers, practitioners, and other scientists. It is intended to quickly place on the table the issues and the passions they invoke. From there, in succeeding chapters, we consider the history, theory, epistemology, cultural implications, evidence for causation, pathology of violence, methodological weaknesses of common protocols, and the constitution of the child, and we conclude with some policy problems and recommendations.

If this book is going to be used as a textbook for a media effects course, please note that we establish a position at the outset with a series of statements as to what we hold to be true and not true about the relationship between violent content and subsequent aggressive behavior and about media effects in general. We then go about the careful process of examining the evidence from history, theory, and scientific study to see if those positions are supported. The book is not a meta-analysis or an impersonal review, so students may need help in understanding the alternatives. But we believe that it is careful scholarship that leads to a deeper understanding of the field. As a textbook, it is written for advanced undergraduate and graduate students who come with a background that may well hold media effects as unproblematic. We hope that they will be more sophisticated in their assessments as a result of engaging this text.

As always, there a number of people to thank for their help along the way. The reviewers provided by Sage were invaluable in their comments, criticisms, and suggestions. We are particularly grateful to Janet Colvin for her contribution. She is the coauthor, with James Anderson, of Chapter 5's cultural analysis. That analysis also benefited greatly from a roomful of University of Utah graduate students and faculty who critically reviewed its methodology and conclusions following a colloquium presentation. We were able to clarify the argument as a result. Finally, we wish to acknowledge the thoughtful discussions we have had with George Comstock, Barrie Gunter, and John P. Murray, who may have disagreed with what we had to say at times but were always ready to join the conversation.

1

Setting the Stage

O ur topic is media violence, its role in the production of social aggression, and the possible social policy that should be developed concerning it. This topic is a complexity of issues, including First Amendment rights of producers and audiences; protections for children; freedom for adults; the significance of media violence as something warranting public concern; the evidence for and against the putative pathological effects on media violence from science; whose science to believe; what policies are possible, practicable, workable, and fundable; and what might be the unintended consequences of it all. Let us quickly set the stage with a bit of drama. What you're about to read is a mostly fictional but entirely feasible conversation between a policy maker (PM) and a team of three social scientists (SS) concerning the effects of violent content in the media. This conversation is a composite of conversations the authors have had with policy makers at various levels. Its purpose is to quickly establish the issues that will be dealt with in some detail in the rest of the book. It also intends to demonstrate the passion that attends the topic of media violence.

The Policy Maker and the Social Scientists: A Conversation

Policy Maker: (Following introductions all around) John, my Chief of Staff, tells me that you folks study media violence. I think that's good. There's too much violence in the media, and it's a big problem for society.

Social Scientist 1: I think a lot of people would agree with you.

PM: Sounds like you might not?

Social Scientist 2: We probably come at it from a different—we like to think more sophisticated—angle, which asserts that the presence of violence in the media is not a danger to most people in and of itself.

PM: Doesn't the presence of violent content in the media lead to violent crime?

Social Scientist 3: No, there is good evidence that this connection does not exist.

PM: But I thought that is why we had all those government panels?

SS3: Yes, when the crime rate took off in the 1960s and continued to rise for two more decades, there were several panels charged with studying the causes of crime. That period corresponded to the domination of leisure time by network television. It was natural to suspect it as a cause. Violent crime, however, has been on a decline for over 10 years now with no abatement of violent content—in fact, more content, more kinds of content, and more violent content are now available.

This column plays the role of expositor in a dramatic narrative—the individual who knows all the background information and the allusions referred to in the dialogue. Some readers prefer to read the conversation alone first and then come back to read the two columns together.

Violence inhabits all forms of human drama, but it had become a significant social issue by the end of the 19th century (yes, over 100 years ago) with the advent of technologies that could distribute it beyond the boundaries of the educated class.

There have been four major meta-analyses of the relationship between media violence and crime (Felson, 1996; Jensen, 2001; Messner, 1986; Savage, 2004). All four came to the conclusion of no relationship.

The National Commission on the Causes and Prevention of Violence (Graham & Gurr, 1969) concluded that social inequality was the leading cause of violence. This has turned out to be an unacceptable explanation.

Crime rates change for any number of reasons, including the median age of the population. The cell phone is the latest medium, however, to be suspected as a cause of a rise in crime both in

PM: Does the presence of violent content in media degrade our quality of life?

SS2: There is evidence that extensive viewing of violence is associated with higher levels of aggressiveness that ranges from a lessening of civility, a greater roughness of play, more difficult social relations, and the like. All of these conclusions rest on the definitions of aggression, civility, play, and social relations. This relationship may be causal. There is no evidence that its causal character is necessary or sufficient, which is the sort of evidence needed if controlling media content and its viewing is going to have an effect on the overall level of aggression in society.

There is evidence that extensive viewing of violence leads to desensitization to the effects of violence. Desensitization is a research construct that appears only in language-based measurement. That is, when people are asked questions by researchers about how they feel, they tend to generate answers that suggest they have been desensitized by the media violence they've seen. However, and this is an important *however*—we don't know if what these people report on questionnaires they're given in lab experiments has a real-world behavioral consequence or if it has any practical or social significance.

PM: Am I affected by violent content?

SS1: The greatest concern has been with children prior to age 12, based on cognitive development theory, which states that aggressive patterns can be fixed for life during that period. The theory is not clear as to what happens to adults. Researchers, for example, watch violent content with impunity.

planning/execution of the action and in documenting the bragging rights for having done it.

The softness of the definitions and measures of aggression have been a continuing critique of the media violence/aggression claim (e.g., Greenberg & Wotring, 1974). It is a claim that has been stoutly rejected by the media violence/aggression (MV/A) proponents (e.g., Carnagey & Anderson, 2004).

This concept was introduced as the "narcotizing dysfunction" (Lazarsfeld & Merton, 1948) to explain how individuals could ignore issues no matter how compelling.

Concerns about children occur in more than 50% of the literature (J. Anderson, 2006).

PM: Can a child who is not aggressive be turned into an aggressive child by violent content in the media?

SS1: Because aggression has multiple definitions, we would probably change that question to be, "Can a nonsymptomatic child become a symptomatic child through exposure to violent content?"

PM: So . . . ?

SS1: The answer to that question comes in least two parts, which draw on different theoretical perspectives.

PM: (Rolls her eyes.)

SS1: Yes, we know, we wish it were simple too. But let's start on the cognitive theory side of things. In cognitive theory, children can simply reproduce what they view, learn strategies and tactics from what they view, and/or develop attitudes and values based on what they view in an escalating hierarchy of consequences. But for anything to happen, they first have to view, and for the most severe antisocial effects, there has to be extensive viewing. The simple presence of content in the media is not enough.

Content is a resource for viewing, but it is not viewing. Further, extensive viewing is not ordinary viewing. Extensive viewing of any content type requires identifying and accessing the content, constructing the environment for viewing, and committing time, technical, and often financial resources to the viewing. All of this work to view extensively may itself be a symptom of some difficulty. (Watching 6 hours per week of golf may be symptomatic.)

PM: But isn't there a lot of violence available to be seen within the media?

The answer to this question all depends on where one starts. If one starts from a Freudian perspective that the natural child has to be repressed into the civilized being we want, then the child cannot be "turned." She or he can be delayed in maturation or regressed to an earlier stage but not turned. On the other hand, a strict cognitive scripts position (C. Anderson & Bushman, 2002a; Huesmann, 1986, 1988; Huesmann & Taylor, 2006) would suggest that human behavior is regulated by specific scripts and that bad scripts learned from media can replace good scripts (perhaps also learned from media). And on yet another hand, social action theorists (J. Anderson & Meyer, 1987; Bandura, 2001) would see us as agents of social practice—sometimes good, sometimes harmful.

The research literature is notably silent on the question of how "extensive viewing of violence gets done." There is a glimmer of a suggestion in Eron (1982) that parents support the activity of extensive viewing and, if not support, at least rationalize the aggressive behavior. Parental support for viewing and aggression changes the equation entirely.

An equally important issue might also be the environmental and social resources that have to be put into play to support the activity of extensive viewing. It doesn't happen by chance.

SS2: That depends on the medium and technology in use. It is actually fairly difficult to watch violence on broadcast and cable television. One has to spend an awful lot of time watching unrelated content. Here is a simple test: Turn on your television set and graze through the channels, stopping for three seconds on each one. More than 90% of what you see will not be violence. On the other hand, one can create an endless video loop of, say, the head-in-the-vice scene from *Kill Bill* (either volume). Media researchers often use such loops. Arcade, video, and computer games can provide a very high ratio of violence (at least aggressive behavior). Estimates suggest that two thirds of media content contains violence (Federman, 1997), but that simply means that there is one instance of some form of violence/aggression in the program (counted even if it is just talking about violence). Clearly, that leaves a lot of room for nonviolent content. And yet an arcade game may be entirely acts of violence.

PM: But if one made the effort, extensive viewing may be enough?

SS2: The evidence is controversial. We do not know if viewing alone is a *sufficient* cause of higher levels of aggression. The test would be if we could remove the violent content and aggressive behavior subsequently dropped in some portion of the respondents. That test has never been made. We do know that it is not a *necessary* cause of higher aggression. Individuals can be aggressive whether or not they view violence. Consequently, even if we removed all violent content, aggressive behavior would not disappear. Nearly all aggression researchers (see Huesmann, Eron, & Dubow, 2002, for an extensive review) agree that the causes of social aggression are multiple. The question here, then, is not the strength of the contribution but if the contribution of the media is unique.

PM: I'm reluctant to ask, but you said there were two parts. . . .

SS1: Like a moth to the flame, eh? Cultural studies would argue that your child doesn't even have to view to be affected.

PM: What?

SS1: It works like this: The media are a major distributor of images, symbols, performances, and cultural truths. Across a country like the United States with its great geographical distances and cultural differences, they are a common denominator. We know about popular shows, movies, songs, and the like even if we don't attend to them. The content of our media enter our society through gateway viewers who distribute the ideas in ordinary social processes. Your child is on the playground; another child says, "Let's play *Kill Bill*." Your child says, "What's that?" In the ensuing explanation, some form of the narrative of that movie becomes the basis of play. Your child is inducted into sword fighting, without having seen the movie. So, for the cultural studies analyst, once a narrative has been distributed (attended to) by a sufficient proportion of a society, its force will be felt throughout that society. Similar ideas are developed in information dissemination theory.

PM: This seems to mean that we are all affected by violent content.

SS1: The cultural analyst would agree but would go on to say that the *Kill Bill* narrative is but a current representation of the retributive justice narrative where the antagonists get their just deserts. The culturally significant part of this movie revolves much more around gender than violence. Your child knew the basic *Kill Bill* narrative well before the playground exposition but might have learned something new about women as killers. The other caution they might express is that a cultural marker is not the same as an individual performance. U.S. culture is considered by many as more aggressive than, say, Canadian culture, but an individual citizen can be of any sort.

PM: What are the implications here?

It is quite possible that we do not need the media to know the scripts of aggression.

Kill Bill may be a uniquely American movie.

6

...seen any vast now, I got to radian this other because viewing is not a necessary cause of aggression, removing violent content would not cause aggressive behavior to disappear from society and possibly not even to significantly lessen it. If viewing violent content is a sufficient cause for aggressive behavior, removing that content would affect the aggression of those individuals for whom viewing is the only cause of aggression but would not affect any individual in an environment populated with other sufficient causes for aggression. There are some emergent studies that *do* suggest that media violence may be a sufficient cause for aggression. But those studies clearly show that those for whom it is a sufficient cause are those who are emotionally ill. These disturbances appear to be enhanced or made worse by media violence. However, these studies also suggest that children who don't have an emotional illness don't suffer psychological damage from the violence they consume. These results notwithstanding, the adaptation of the cultural argument has been that because the media make violent content so widely available, the sheer scale of it must be affecting large numbers of individuals who would not otherwise be affected. The argument concludes that it has to be a significant negative influence on our society.

PM: And the problem with that is?

SS3: The problem is that you and I and we have to be affected as well as our children.

PM: Well, of course, you're a good person, and you raise your children properly, right?

SS1: You know the last major report was the "10 years later" report that came out in 1982. It was the first government report that said unequivocally that media violence is a cause of social aggression. But then it turned around and said, "Of course not all children are affected."[1] And now we see where this goes: It really is *those* people who are the problem. *Those* people and *their* children. It's never about us.

called for cannot be run with any suspected cause of aggression.

For instance, see Grimes, Bergen, Nichols, Vernberg, and Fonagy (2004).

Several issues are being addressed here: (a) All but the most reclusive of us has seen violent media content, yet we do not believe ourselves to be overly aggressive. We do believe that other people are overly aggressive, however. For a meta-analysis of this "third-person effect," see Salwen and Dupagne (2001). (b) It is an epistemological principle that good theory has to account for the exceptions (J. Anderson, 1996). There has been no accounting for why many children (in fact, most children) are not affected. (c) Personal probity such as good parenting practices has been

PM: OK, I admit, I am worried about *those* people and *their* children. By those people, I don't mean anything racially or ethnically, I mean those people who behave like idiots; who lie, cheat, and steal; people who raise their children to behave like animals; kids who drink, do drugs, have sex.

SS3: My point exactly, not you or your kids.

PM: No, not me or my kids; not that anybody's perfect.

SS2: How about the guy who flips you off on the freeway, or the guy who plays rough in high school football, or the kid who pushes your kid in the hall.

PM: That stuff doesn't bother me, and my kid can take care of herself. Is that what we are talking about?

SS1: A lot of it. Many studies consider those actions to be acts of aggression and use them as part of the measures of aggression.

PM: Hasn't that stuff been going on forever? I used to fight as a kid. Who didn't? And I flipped off a few crazy drivers in my day.

SS1: Maybe you should think about your media use. Seriously, some of those cultural studies scholars we talked about believe that as we have feminized the social sciences (we now have the highest percentage of women in the field), we have identified more and more masculine behavior as problematic. This is a very contentious issue as you might expect because it suggests that women can't be objective scientists. But if one reads the claim both ways, it says that men were not objective either in accepting masculine behavior as normal. In the end, what it says is that all social scientists are the product of their culture and socialization.

seen as the antidote to media violence. If one is aggressive, it must be a failure of the person or his or her upbringing. See Fowers and Richardson (1993) for a strong statement on the ideology of cognitive instrumentalism.

See McCormack (1978) for this sort of argument.

PM: So, you piss everybody off.

SS1: (Smiling) That claim is generally difficult for many, and your language might be considered aggressive.

PM: All right, but I'm not going to give up here. It just can't be good to have all that violent content available. I mean kids have to get the idea that violence is OK or they learn how to do stuff. And what about the kids who have to live in the slums or who have bad parents or are just disconnected from the right thing to do? They just shouldn't be watching violence.

Inadequate and even "bad" parenting is a consistent theme in the literature. See Hess and Goldman (1962) for an early representation and Scantlin and Jordan (2006) for one of the latest.

SS3: Children who are disadvantaged socially, educationally, and economically; who are victims of abuse; who have parents who are distant or noncommunicative; who have trouble maintaining relationships; and who are of a hyperactive temperament all are more likely to be aggressive. In fact, we can identify biological, individual, environmental, and sociocultural clusters of conditions that are associated with maladaptive aggression.

Both Sandra Ball-Rokeach (2001) and George Gerbner (n.d.) have raised the issue that it is not the individual who is the source of violence but rather a defective society. The causes of violence are in the distribution of wealth and in the social relationships of power.

PM: What do you mean "maladaptive aggression"?

SS3: Aggression as a concept is a problem for us. We applaud the aggressive police officer who captures the criminal; we want our soldiers to be aggressive; we want our children to fight for the ball on the soccer field; we want our lawyer to be aggressive in preserving our rights. We expect to get out there and "kick butt" at the office. The vice president of the United States drops the F-bomb on a liberal (Sen. Patrick Leahy [D-Vermont]) and feels good about it. Consequently, social scientists have to be able to distinguish between the aggressiveness we like and that which we don't. We don't like maladaptive aggression. As a term, it takes us inside the language of evolution. Maladaptive aggression leads us to fail as an individual and, more important, as a species but preserves aggressive behavior that is successful.

There has been no accounting for adaptive aggression.

This terminology allows us to consider aggression without any moral overtones—that a particular action is good or bad—it just works or doesn't work. In this way, social scientists can distinguish themselves from moralists and politicians and wrap themselves in objectivity.

PM: You don't sound like you like social scientists.

SS1: That's a problem; we are social scientists. And no, I don't think there's self-hatred here. We just study how we play the game. But to return to the children: We have identified multiple constellations of correlates of aggression—sorry—many conditions that are associated with aggressive behavior. Most of them sound pretty bad: child abuse; dysfunctional families; parental failure; the frustration of social, educational, economic disadvantage; racial injustice; and the like. And then we have violence in the media, which may be consequential when it is viewed at high levels. In the federal government, the Administration for Children and Families (ACF)—a bureau of the Department of Health and Human Services—is the parent of the Administration for Children, Youth, and Families (ACYF), which administers the programs that support children, youth, and families. ACF was funded for $49 billion for fiscal 2005 (by contrast, the current cost of the Iraq War by the end of fiscal 2005 was estimated at $204.6 billion). Within the ACF budget, $107 million is earmarked for grants on reducing child abuse and more than double that ($236 million) for abstinence-based sex education. The point is that we make political choices on what we are willing to spend money. Being against violence on television, holding congressional and regulatory hearings, and even funding a couple of million in research is a very inexpensive way of looking like we are doing something worthwhile without actually in costing us anything in money or privilege. It works well—very adaptive—which is why we have been in this pattern for over 75 years.

James Garbarino (2001) points out how singling out media (or any other individual cause) allows us to do nothing that would actually change anything.

PM: Well, maybe we are doing something worthwhile by being against media violence.

SS1: Maybe, but it all looks suspiciously too easy. Turn off the content (which, by the way, means that popular programs such as the *CSI* and *Law & Order* franchises and *Desperate Housewives*, not to mention nearly every award-winning program on HBO, would no longer be available for your viewing pleasure), and we will have a significant reduction in violence without spending a nickel more on child abuse, dysfunctional families, or racial injustice. What's that line about "If it sounds too good to be true?"

PM: I couldn't watch *Desperate Housewives*?

These were programs popular at the time of this conversation.

SS3: Don't worry (it's one of our favorites too), the first congressional hearings on violence on television were in 1952, which were preceded 25 years earlier by the congressional hearings on regulation of the movies and were followed in 1954 by the comic book hearings. A quick search of the 109th Congress dockets (the U.S. Congress of this conversation) shows 40 hits on hearings involving media violence. Despite the 75 years of congressional oversight, we have shown no political will to do much more than hold hearings on violence. We have established rating sys ems for the movies, television, and games, which have as strong a reverse use (oh, good, it's R-rated) as its intended purpose. And we have installed V-chips in every television set 13 inches or larger manufactured since 2000. The V-chip (regulation adopted in 1998) allows automatic controls on content based on a voluntary industry rating system. (It has been notable in its disuse by families.) All of these rating systems focus more on sexual content than on violence. Consequently, *Desperate Housewives* may be more at risk because of

W. D. Rowland (1982, 1997) has laid out the political forces that sustain the concern over media violence and aggression. His thesis is that it is the political capital of the relationship, not the scientific findings, that has sustained the question.

Cantor and Wilson (1984) report that the most common use of program ratings is to select programs, not avoid them.

its sexuality than its violence. In the end, if we do anything, it will have its major impact on the poor among us and not those of us who can buy access to any content we want. The V-chip, for example, made television sets more expensive by a few dollars, which was disproportionately felt by the poor. (It is interesting that the current target of Congress is not Fox Broadcasting, with its high ratio of problematic programming, but Public Broadcasting.)

PM: So what would you do instead?

SS3: With about one third of our families being single parent and about 60% of the two-parent families having both parents working, about 70% of all families have to use outside child care. Consequently, adequate infant and toddler care, universal preschool, as well as latchkey and summer programs (certified and regulated) seem to be obvious approaches. Children involved in educational activities are not watching violent television or movies, playing video games, or listening to violent music. The federal government budgets $6.8 billion for Head Start, serving a little more than 900,000 of the 24 million U.S. 5-year-old and younger age group. It is estimated that at least 17 million of this age group require child care during every workday—a need compounded during school recess periods, but about 8 million of these children do not have access to regulated care. On the other side of the ledger, the average wage for child care workers in the private sector is under $16,000 per year (poverty threshold is around $9,000). This combination of demand and inability of the private sector to appropriately respond is a strong indicator of the need for a federal intervention—an intervention that

All of this information was assembled from the appropriate governmental agency Web sites.

http://www.rand.org/news/press.05/12.15.html

will take at least $60 billion. Will the investment of our tax dollars be worth it? A RAND report estimates that universal preschool will pay for itself in higher educational achievement, lower welfare costs, and lower crime rates.

PM: And you think we will do that?

SS2: No, we don't. So far, at least, we have been more willing to build prisons to house over 2 million inmates—the largest inmate population in the "free world" both in total and in proportion—and of course to hold hearings than to do anything proactive.

PM: Well, because we won't provide adequate infant and child care or extended educational programs for youth, particularly for the disadvantaged, doesn't violent content pose some sort of risk that should be controlled?

SS2: It appears that you are asking us, "Because we won't do the right thing, shouldn't we be doing this other thing?"

PM: Whatever.

SS2: We accept that. Let's put some provisions in place. The primary push for content control is coming from cognitive theorists. Cognitivism is a particular form of psychological theory that holds that cognitive structures are formed in the mind/brain through socialization processes. The formation process goes on throughout life, but the significant structures that form the individual are thought to be developed during the first 12 years. These cognitive structures direct the behavioral choices of the individual. Consequently, the most at-risk population is the preteen, with the risk rapidly diminishing by age 25. Who we are and what we will typically do is

The form of cognitivism in play here is sometimes called cognitive instrumentalism. It is a combination of cognitive scripts (rules for behavior) and operant conditioning (behaviors deemed successful are repeated until extinguished). L. Rowell Huesmann, professor of psychology and communication at the University of Michigan, is recognized as the dean of this position (see Huesmann, 1986). Huesmann has participated in every major government initiative on the issue of media violence.

presumably pretty much in place by then, though it may be longer for men than for women. (For the moment, let's ignore all the critics of cognitivism, and there are many.) Cognitivists have also argued that we understand developmentally and experientially. Consequently, different age groups respond to the same content differentially. A 2-year-old may be oblivious to the meaning or implications of some content that is obvious to a 12-year-old; a 6-year-old is more likely to think something is real (literally true) than a 10-year-old. Children in the different stages of development are at different levels of risk (if you will) for the same content.

PM: So, a child's content risk profile changes as he or she develops or matures?

SS1: Exactly. Some cognitive theorists argue further that there are critical windows of development that open and close. The socialization influence that appears dominant at that period will have a disproportionate effect over all other influences for the rest of that person's life.

PM: Then a child heavily into a computer game might be influenced by its content just by virtue of its timing.

SS2: True developmentally and true critically, but. . . .

PM: Always a "but."

SS1: Indeed, the "but" here is that the child is not passive in the socialization process, and there are always other socialization influences present and active. The final outcome depends on all elements, not just the game content.

See C. Anderson and Dill (2000) or C. Anderson and Huesmann (2003) for this sort of argument.

A short review of this socialization literature is presented in Chapter 3.

PM: I get it. Children in the same developmental stage interacting with the same content may be affected differently, which might explain why some children are affected and others not.

SS2: But wait, there's more: Content is not a product of its facts but of its interpretation. The Coppertone suntan lotion service mark of the puppy pulling on the pants of a toddler to reveal the tan line may be a bit of sweet innocence to us, but it is reportedly a resource for the pedophile.

PM: What?!

SS1: Right, in the free-range interaction between content and the individual mind (and even in the constructed interaction of the laboratory), we cannot predict its meaning or the active elements or the outcome in the specific case.

PM: You mean we don't know violence when we see it?

SS1: We know the facts of the content, not its interpretation. We can count the drops of blood spewing out in the restaurant fight scene from *Kill Bill Vol. 1*, but you may consider it righteous, repulsive, fulfilling, stupid, ironical, comedic, metaphorical, or actual. Theorists claim that the interpretive frame makes a difference in the outcome. We'd be worried about the folks who saw it as righteous, fulfilling, or actual and not so much about those who saw it as repulsive or stupid.

PM: But there are still people you are worried about.

SS2: Yes, there are, and that worry extends far beyond the obvious. As writers, we are constantly amazed at the unintended meanings that are produced from something we have written.

PM: So, what is your conclusion so far?

Interpretation and its various modalities are taken up in Chapter 3.

15

SS2: First, we would argue that even the most egregiously violent content will affect a relatively small portion of individuals. Consider that the content has to be accessed, activated, and interpreted; it has to reach the individual at a developmentally appropriate stage and at a critical moment in that development; it has to compete with other socialization influences that oppose it and be reinforced by socialization influences of its own kind; and its behavioral effect has to be supported by (adaptive to) the behavioral context of the individual. Second, it may not be possible to produce any content that does not have a negative consequence for someone. The implications of these conclusions are that, for my part, I do not want my 5-year-old grandson (or anyone's 5-year-old grandchild) watching *Kill Bill*, but my concern does not have the same urgency as not wanting him to be on the roof. I am relatively certain that I can mitigate any consequence of viewing, but falling off the roof may be irreparable. At the same time, I was unprepared for his response to the hunting seal scene in the *March of the Penguins*. The repeated shots of the gaping, fang-filled jaws of the predator seal (penguins would probably support a baby seal hunt in Antarctica) caused problems that had to be believed. To protect him from those moments in which content might have negative consequences requires a level of surveillance that is impossible. The more you reduce one's experience with particular forms of content, the more effective is its simplest expressions.

PM: Wait, you said something interesting right at the end.

SS2: Faint praise. The unintended consequence of censorship (or protectionism if you will) is that the forbidden content becomes more powerful throughout its range even in highly masked forms. England's governmental censorship of the time was met with the Mother Goose nursery rhymes. This is the flip side of desensitization. The creative process

March of the Penguins was a narrative-based documentary of the breeding habits of emperor penguins in theaters everywhere in 2005. One year later, the boy had no trouble with the animated seal enacting the same scene in *Happy Feet*. He expressed great dismay, however, at the narrative of rejection in that film.

will press the boundaries no matter where you place them. And the most interested audience will always be there at the boundary line. One of my colleagues reports that his 7-year-old son sneaks down to the family room at two in the morning to watch cable movies. He was outed at a sleepover.

PM: Still you would ban *Kill Bill?*

SS2: That's not what I said. I said I wouldn't want any 5-year-old watching it. In fact, I would think that *Kill Bill* might represent a critical moment of risk for males from 4 to 25 who are either very young (4 years old) or who have emotional illnesses (the 25-year-olds). In the same way, it also might present a risk for females from 3 to 20, given the different maturation rates of the sexes. Further, there are some individuals, both male and female, involved in some pathologies who would always be at risk in viewing *Kill Bill.* I know I woke up thinking about the eyeball scene after watching *Vol. 2.*

PM: So, how do you achieve your goal of no 5-year-old watching it?

SS3: We have four approaches: We can prevent its production in the first place. We can limit its distribution by regulating its appearance or controlling its audience. We can educate the caregivers. We can inoculate the 5-year-olds. And to be most effective, we have to do all four. Despite the First Amendment, the government has seen some success in the first two of these in a process called intimidation. That is one of the purposes of the cycle of hearings—threaten legislation that will be worse than self-correction. The same technique has been used by regulatory agencies. The famed 1946 FCC Blue Book was never adopted as regulation, but it successfully shaped broadcast practices until it was overwhelmed by television. The global economy and the leveling effect of technology make it impossible to seal our virtual borders. Forbid production here and it goes underground and/or moves offshore. Limit distribution in regulated entities and it will move electronically. Still, it will remove the content from the least interested and the most disadvantaged. Remember, *Kill Bill* is out there and cannot be removed from the mediascape. It is in thousands of homes on video and DVDs. Stop the production and/or distribution of future *Kill Bills*, and the archive of *Kill Bill* becomes a cottage industry for everyone with a DVD burner. And on the effects side, the content of the sanitized sequel *Vex Bill* becomes as consequential.

Such was the history of "banned" EC comics, as documented in Chapter 2.

PM: That takes us back to education, doesn't it?

SS3: Yes, but we don't think my answer has been a setup. Education is fraught with its own fractures, starting with content and moving through delivery. It's pretty exciting to be in science education in this country right now, and that has nothing to do with the science. Think of how we might react to instruction on programs like *Desperate Housewives*.

PM: Don't mess with that.

SS1: Let me break in here to point out that just because it's hard to do is not a call to do nothing. On the other hand, you cannot justify the cost of any program that limits our political will to do something about the truly significant elements in the aggression equation. That means that we first take the lead on health care, economic opportunity, educational equality, and racial justice. Until we make significant commitments in these areas, media control and education will always be a middle-class project intending to protect middle-class privileges and nothing more.

This argument is taken up in Chapter 4.

PM: It sounds like you are questioning motives.

SS2: It does sound like that, but what we have done is to shift the level of analysis from the psychological (individual motives) to the sociological to

18

examine why we continue along this path of repetitive performance. Understand that the first media effects studies were conducted in the mid-1920s by some of the most significant individuals in psychological (Louis Leon Thurstone) and sociological (Hubert Blumer) research. The most common methodologies for analysis and the most agreed-on conclusions were established by these early studies. In the 80 years since, we have not added much new. What we have done is to continue to sound the alarm that the media are out of control, that content is perverting our children, that those affected children represent a threat to us and to our children, and that you should put us (the researchers) in charge. From a sociological level, all of this is very understandable. It is a cultural stratum taking care of itself. All of the major players in effect are and have been middle-class European Americans. (I know of no notable exceptions.) They bring that set of sensibilities to the table in the way they define *violence*, in the way they define *aggression*, and in the way they define *excessive*.

PM: And the problem with that is?

SS1: Because the practitioners cite one another, these class-based standards become normalized and are seen as objective. In this way, they speak for people who don't enjoy the same level of health care, economic advantage, educational opportunity, or experience of justice. Their efforts work to promote media as an agenda that distracts us from the responsibilities of sharing the privileges we have. So, "No we won't share our privileges, but we will limit your pleasures." We have been reminded of a speaker at a national media task force who was adamant about removing commercials for sugared cereals because poor children ate so much of those cereals. He, of course, was coming from a position that the poor were once again being victimized by the cereal companies promoting a product that was

These studies are known collectively as the Payne Fund Studies. The major report, *Movies and Conduct* (1933), can be accessed at www.brocku.ca/MeadProject/Blumer/1933/Blumer_1933_toc.html.

nutritionally suspect and way overpriced. But the subtext was that he knew so much better how to manage the breakfast table when there was not enough money, time, or energy, and furthermore, he did not want to be bothered by his children nagging him for those products. Again, in my case, I don't want my grandson watching something like *Kill Bill*, I also don't want to have to worry about him turning on the television set and finding that material, and I don't think any other 5-year-old should be watching that material either, but I don't trust those mothers and fathers, grandmothers and grandfathers to be as sensible as I am. So, prohibit it, Ms. Policymaker, then my world will be safe. I can always buy access to whatever the rules prohibit.

PM: My, my, the radical voice.

SS1: Certainly a voice in the wilderness. There are other parts of this sociological analysis. There is a symbiotic relationship between policy makers and scholars. Both of us have to make our mark, have to gain recognition. You have been appointed to the House Sub-Committee on Telecommunications and the Internet; I am a professor in something called communication studies. We ought to be able to make something out of that.

PM: It would be better if you were a psychologist or a medical doctor.

SS3: We all have PhDs; we can be doctors. That is one of the things we do now. We don't identify our academic department and call one another "doctor" as if our degree was based on clinical or medical training. Take a look at how it is handled in the *National Television Violence Study* volumes. It is a simple bit of puffery that is intended to raise the general level of importance of the work and of us.

PM: And you criticize us for spin.

SS3: Ah well, we learn from the best. And it's a good point; we do have to be careful not to become either cynical or personal. You are right to point out the deceit of the pretense of scholarly objectivity. All of us have to manage our way in a society using the tools and resources that the culture provides. First and foremost, I need to be successful in my chosen profession. At the Research One level (i.e., the nation's top research universities), the top level of success is generated by a grant-publication-grant cycle in which one always has an eye out for the next funding initiative or source. Funding agencies are a driving force in whatever is the current research agenda. For their part, funding agencies and their directors have to create impact out of their projects to justify their annual budgets to their revenue sources. The negative effect of media is a perennial favorite. (As a side note, does it strike you as strange that no one has funded a major longitudinal study on the effects of heightened [can't use the word *excessive*] prosocial viewing, though we have funded several on aggression? Are we not interested in knowing if media do some good?) And technology has helped us out. We moved our concerns from the dime novel, to the movies, to the radio serial, to the comic book, to broadcast television, to cable television, to the Internet, to the video game, essentially reproducing the same questions, the same methodologies, and the same answers in each of some slightly different content/technology combination. Gentle policy maker, are you amazed to find out that people can be informed, deceived, bored, incited, aroused, motivated, or persuaded that they can learn, will be imitated, overeat while using, be competitive, and take pleasure from the media? And do you really think that *those* people are so different from you?

PM: Well, certainly there is something of the Beltway Boogaloo in the hearings, but gentle researchers, you need to understand the pressures we face.

Frey, Botan, and Kreps (2000) discuss these forces on research.

And now I get to be the expert. We are constantly running for reelection. We need the media to be reelected. Our constituents on the right and the left complain about the media, more specifically about Internet porn, music, video games, and television, not necessarily in that order. The right complains about sex and liberal bias and the left about violence and cultural representations. Take Internet porn: The right hates it because people are naked; the left hates it because it is demeaning to women, and yet the greatest use of the Internet is for sexually related sites ranging from Paris Hilton videos to the subscription sites. (And no, it is not just men; Google Paris Hilton and you will get nearly 8 million sites—not just hits—that relate to her.) What galvanizes us as legislators is that those who complain are organized—though the right far more than the left—and those who just use it are not. I can always get the big media in my state to run a story on Internet porn. And hearings are one way I can get coverage in that story. Look at what Ted Stevens is doing over in the Senate Commerce, Science, and Transportation committee with his decency hearings and Bob Byrd connecting media violence to "the jihadists," as he called them. Wonderful press. On the other hand, I can't stop Internet porn, just as my colleagues cannot stop media violence. The political work that would be necessary would rouse the silent and scare the big media. I would be cast as a crusader, a religious nut, or a liberal idiot. Consequently, we make the .xxx proposal a big deal, saying that our government shouldn't support anything that suggests approval for pornography. That's a win-win issue. I'm on the side of the organized and haven't changed anything for the user. On the violence side, ratings regulations are the same kind of win-win for us. The average gamer is a 28-year-old male. More often than not, when a game is purchased, an adult is either the buyer or is the parent paying for it. So is all this just too politically crass for you?

Paris Hilton declared herself the "Marilyn Monroe" of the early 21st century.

This political activity is called symbolic politics (Edelman, 1971).

The policy maker is referring to the then-current proposal to have .xxx as an Internet protocol suffix for sexually related sites. The arguments for it stated that it would clearly identify such sites and allow for more effective controls, but it failed. Some legislators argued that having that suffix was an admission that such sites existed.

SS3: Surprisingly honest, we would say, and very well informed.

PM: That's what all those hearings are for.

SS3: Have you been sandbagging us?

PM: A little. You consider yourselves educators, but I bet I spend as much time educating people as you do. I educate people on the art of what is possible. Most of the time, when I see researchers such as yourselves, they are on some crusade or another. "We have to remove all violence; we have to change the way this group or that group is presented in the media" or some other impossible thing. They seem to have no concept of the economics of media content or of how government works or of small niceties like the First Amendment or case law. They have not done risk/benefit or cost/benefit analyses. We kill 45,000 people on the highways every year because we believe the benefits outweigh those costs. The one cost/benefit ratio that my staff has been able to extract from different studies on violence in the media (yes, we study this stuff too) is that 31% of social aggression—mostly issues of incivility and explicitly excluding violent crime—could be made less serious were we to remove 57% of the current content of television. How much less serious, we don't know. So . . . is less pushing in the schoolyard really worth that much governmental control of content? Especially when it doesn't affect violent crime? Bye, bye, *Desperate Housewives*.

And even if we were to all agree that media violence has some widespread negative social effect, the researchers have no plan for how to deal with it. Just look at you three: You say there are no measurable outcomes, no mileposts, no follow-up. What if all the perpetrators migrate to other sources, or what if researchers are just plain wrong in assuming that violence in television works

The 2001 Surgeon General's report on youth violence (http://www.surgeongeneral .gov/library/youthviolence/ chapter4/appendix4b.html) states, "The preponderance of evidence indicates that violent behavior seldom results from a single cause; rather, multiple factors converging over time contribute to such behavior. Accordingly, the influence of the mass media, however strong or weak, is best viewed as one of the many potential factors that help to shape behavior, including violent behavior." It also concludes, "Most youths who are aggressive and engage in some forms of antisocial behavior do not become violent teens and adults" (both quotations from Appendix 4-B: Section I).

by itself to heighten aggression? It's "My research shows this, you have to pass a law." And if we do, it turns out like the V-chip regulation where, as you point out, most people can't be bothered or won't bother because they don't (apparently) believe in the various calls to danger in the first place. And the researchers return saying that we have to automate the V-chip—make it people-proof. Such arrogance.

And then you come in asking for $60 billion.

SS1: It's a simple request.

PM: Indeed, and actually the money's fairly easy. It's everything else that is hard. The total budget for the Department of Education is somewhere around $72 billion. Now you want to take a program that is three levels down in the Department of Health and Human Services and fund it at, what, 80% of that total. Do you see the dislocation problems?

SS2: Well, uh. . . .

PM: Right. The $60 billion you propose is based on the current funding of $6 billion for ACYF's Head Start programs. But those programs are well established. That $6 billion is maintenance money. You have not calculated the front-end startup costs, which could easily double the amount of money needed. Where are you going to house 8 million preschoolers? Where are you going to find their teachers, the teachers of the teachers? Where are you going to find the evaluators for these certified programs?

SS3: Well, yes there will be some ramp-up needed.

See Scantlin and Jordan (2006) for a study on parental noninterest.

PM: Have you thought about the impact on the private sector? What is its role? We have over a half million persons currently employed in the preschool and child care industries. What happens to them when you drop a program of this size, at this funding level, into the mix? And why do you think that the private sector responding to market forces rather than academic theory won't provide these services with more attention to parental needs and interests? Have you thought of the consequences of a huge federal bureaucracy thrashing about in early childhood education? Do the states' complaints about "No Child Left Behind" ring any bells? What about the curriculum—do you really think that it would be nonpolitical or rather just your politics? You seemed to know about abstinence education. What do you think we could do with 8 million preschoolers? Do you know that under the guise of better child care, your federal government advises cohabiting couples with children to get married for the children's well-being?

SS2: Couldn't you just give out grants?

PM: Sure, no strings attached. You probably make fun of local school boards and their occasional penchant for unenlightenment. But at least you can vote them out. Can't vote out a bureaucrat. And what's your rationale for this now $120 billion behemoth? That children won't be watching TV or playing video games.

SS3: Oh, come on, there are lots of very good reasons for supporting these programs.

W. D. Rowland (1997) calls the funding bureaucracies the hidden government and considers them responsible for advancing certain agendas, including the media violence/aggression agenda.

25

PM: Yes I know, but you haven't made the case. You haven't networked with educators and providers. You don't know how to get from Point A to Point B. You want it all, and you want it now. Sorry, it doesn't work that way.

You know, you don't even have the evidence that time spent in educational activities will mitigate the consequences of participating in media consumption.

SS2: That might be difficult research to conduct—control issues and all that. But we ought to be able to look at those in educational programs and those not—with proper funding, of course. But isn't your job to develop this legislation?

PM: I have a law degree, and you want me to design universal preschool education? Get me a demonstration plan that I can attach as a rider to an appropriations bill and that speaks to my constituents and that benefits my district. If you can convince me that it is money well spent, that your plan has promise, I'll get your money. But it's baby steps, not pie in the sky. Now, if you'll excuse me, gentle researchers, I have to attend a hearing.

As J. Anderson points out, media education or media literacy interventions have been on the record since 1905. His research (J. Anderson & Ploghoft, 1981) showed that there was little transfer from the classroom to ordinary media use.

Plan of the Book

The modern era of media effects can probably be traced to the French bicycle manufacturer Louis Lumière's invention in 1895 of the familiar projection system we call motion pictures. But in truth, the print medium as well as speech had long been under the scrutiny of scholars and authorities alike for their social consequences. There is a nearly continuous history in human affairs of a concern over what is presented in the public sphere. One can reach back over 250 years to the theatrical licensing act in Great Britain and well over 2,000 years to read the complaints of Plato in the *Republic*. In our own country, one of the principal contributing factors of the Revolution was the suppression of speech and printed communication, by British governors, within the colonies. These were British overlords who believed speech could undermine their authority and lead to social unrest.

In all of this scrutiny, the official concern has been about the putative ruination of society, whether in the decline of morality, the standing of its public officers, or the civility of its citizens. The complaints of the past 100 years have been little different. One notable difference has been the enlistment of science into the battle. The social sciences are barely 150 years old, yet they have been involved in the social movements instigated by mass communication from the beginning and, indeed, mass communication's instigation of the study of media effect 80 years ago (Thurstone, 1926).

During those 80 years, media effects has become, if not a business, at least a cottage industry (J. Anderson, 2006), funneling millions of dollars into panels, institutes, and professorial hands. All of this effort and money has been expended toward the effort of finding the definitive (read scientific) causes for multiple social ailments not in society itself but in the media.

In the chapters that follow, we will take a close look at this amalgam of science, politics, technological imperatives, social engineering, academy economics, firebrand crusaders, children advocates, careful scholars, dedicated public servants, and opportunists of every stripe. In the next chapter, we take up a short history of effects that helps us understand why we have continued to rehearse the same questions and methodologies for this eight-decade span with no scientific or political resolution and why we will continue to do so. Chapter 3 looks at the epistemological work that grounds the enterprise. Chapter 4 takes up the pathology of aggression and the value system that undergirds much of the research about media effects. Together, Chapters 3 and 4 clearly show the limits of the science involved and why sound social policy cannot be derived from it. Chapter 5, through the means of a special research report (written by the second author and a colleague), considers the cultural roles that the continuing repetition of this science serves. Chapter 6 considers the politics of the debate and the evidence for convergence in the present research literature. Chapter 7 returns the focus to the child. Chapter 8 looks at the psychopathology of aggression and poses an alternate hypothesis. Chapter 9 takes a careful look at the protocols of causation. And the final chapter, Chapter 10, considers the policy implications of it all.

The work that we do in these chapters has some unique resources attached to it. Your authors have just completed editing a special issue of *American Behavioral Scientist* that brought together media researchers George Comstock, Barrie Gunter, and John Murray; criminologist Joanne Savage; psychiatrists Stuart Twemlow and Tanya Bennett; and philosophers of science Bruce, Clark, and Maria Glymour. Their work and online discussions enhanced this book tremendously. In developing his contribution to that issue, Anderson, building off the work of Pecora, Murray, and Wartella (2007), assembled an effects article bibliography of more than 1,000 entries, coded them by type and content, and then did a close analysis of the claims, methodology, and cultural language and location of a stratified random sample of entries to develop an intimate knowledge of the literature. That work is referenced here as *the archive,* and it undergirds much of the critical analysis that we present. Tom Grimes brings professional experience and an extensive record of media scholarship to which he added a fellowship in psychiatric studies at the Menninger Clinic, and Lori Bergen has had a professional lifetime interest in the social construction of the child.

Ludwig Wittgenstein, the 20th-century Austrian/English philosopher, provided an intellectual legacy that, frankly, only professional philosophers can understand. He was a logician who applied tediously crafted principles of logic to the formation of language, among other study areas, in philosophy.

Wittgenstein did distinguish himself, however, in one way that everyone can understand. In the late 1920s and early 1930s, when his work was at its most influential—when an entire philosophical movement, logical positivism, was building around it—he renounced the work he had produced up to that point, claiming he had made serious logical errors. He eventually introduced work that addressed those errors. Our point is that his faithfulness to the truth, no matter how much reputational damage he sustained, still stands, in all its power, as one of Wittgenstein's lasting moral and intellectual achievements.

We are not comparing ourselves to the great Wittgenstein, of course. But we stand ready to renounce, in the twinkle of an eye, what we advocate here when, or if, empirical evidence surfaces that reasonable men and women would consider a credible refutation of our position. Indeed, we *hope* our arguments in this book motivate our critics to prove us wrong. If they can do that, then don't we all benefit? An early reviewer of this text called this claim into question (actually she or he called it bull****), but it is at the heart of Karl Popper's (1959) critical rationalism, which describes how science should advance. The literature of media effects research provides convincing evidence of its authors' attempts to silence critics and suppress alternative voices even to the extent of telling us not to believe ourselves. Here's what we mean. Sparks (2006), in an attempt to explain why it may not appear to some that media violence provokes social aggression, states,

> One possibility is that the conclusion from personal experience is valid for one-self but not for others. The fact that violent media might not trigger aggressive behavior for one individual does not necessarily mean that media violence functions the same way for everyone. Another possibility is that one's impression about being invulnerable to media impact is simply incorrect. Perhaps the effects of media violence are difficult for people to detect in themselves—even though the effects are definitely present. (p. 3)

Foundational Principles

Both of those possibilities may even be possible, but the argument serves to bulletproof the body of media effects research from the questions of the rational, reflective individual. We hope you will consider these two possibilities in light of your own experience and perhaps those of your children or of your childhood.

The writing here is easily recognized as contrarian (we like to think of it as skeptical realism), but it is not without its own position. From our over 100 years of collective work in media and media effects, *we hold to the following to be true:*

- Media effects exist. They are multiple and manifest. Even the choice to watch or read something is a media effect.
- Children and adults *can* use media in ways that result in personal and societal harm. That is, if there is an intent to harm someone through manipulation of a media message, it likely can be done.
- Media content does not determine the use children and adults will make of it. That is, the simple fact that violent media content exists doesn't, in itself, have any important meaning. Viewers must *do* something with that content.
- Media content works through interpretation, and interpretation begins in physiology, moves through cognitive processes, but in the end relies on social processes for its consequences.
- The presence of violence in our media may present a potential for "doing something about it/to stop it/to censor it." However, whether we, as a society, decide to censor it or whatever depends on various social processes that interact with violent media content, not on simple exposure to the content in and of itself.
- The way we behave does not develop independently of the social processes that provide for the development and sustain the behavior once learned.

- Certain well-recognized, catalogued mental illnesses most likely account for the majority of the correlational data that claim media violence causes behavioral aggression.
- The layperson can reliably consult his or her own experience with the media, but as with all examinations of one's own life, it requires systematic effort.
- There is a rich panoply of theory that goes beyond strict, narrow, and technical psychological explanations that should be used to develop policy for children and the media.
- Much of what passes as recommendations for policy is fear-mongering.
- Much traditional media effects research is a party—perhaps unwitting, perhaps not—to a political process that holds out simple solutions to social problems that do not involve a restructuring of privilege.
- The commitment to adequate resources to social justice, economic opportunity, and educational equality is the first and most effective line of defense against violence in society.

There are also some points that must be intercepted as false. *We hold the following to be false:*

- It is not true that exposure is all that is necessary for a life-forming effect to occur.
- It is not true that theory that explains the empirical findings is well developed and provides a good understanding of how exposure works.
- It is not true that our rejection—or anyone's rejection—of models built exclusively on media exposure (i.e., mere exposure can result in psychological harm/ increases of aggression in society) is not the same as claiming that there are no effects.
- It is not true that there are no useful theories of media effects other than narrowly focused psychological explanations.
- It is not true that all children are at risk from the media.
- It is not true that banning content will reduce violence, social aggression, and incivility in society.
- It is not true that the layperson cannot recognize the effect or lack thereof of media exposure in his or her own life.
- It is not true that the interventions proposed to break whatever connection exists between exposure to media violence and aggression/psychological harm in society are simple to implement, are without predictable harms, and will have no unintended consequences.
- It is not true that media violence research is the only objectively conducted science that is independent of politics, devoid of moralizing, and free from class-based ideology.

We now turn ourselves to the development of the justification for what we hold to be true and what we hold to be false about media violence and social aggression.

Note

1. National Institute of Mental Health (1982).

2

A Short History of the
Concept of Effects

In this chapter, we will see how the arrival and diffusion of new media—
comic books, motion pictures, radio, television—led to early 20th century concerns about moral depravity in society. By the mid-20th century
that concern became a hook upon which politicians could hang their aspi-
rations for higher office as Senator Estes Kefauver did in the 1950s. The
latter part of the 20th century saw the media violence issue become
"science-tized" in that the politicians who held hearings on media violence
also provided the money to research its putative negative effects on society.
Then came the rush of scientific papers, generated by media researchers—
self-styled "child advocates"—who crusaded for the suppression of media
violence by the government. Their research was largely funded by the very
politicians whose hearings produced the hyperbolic mix of fear of media
violence and calls for its suppression. Nonetheless, scholarly inquiry begat
studies that concluded that media violence raises the level of behavioral
aggression in society. Thus, we see a body of scientific work whose origin
derives less from empirical evidence than it does from political opportunism
(on the part of legislators who have something with which they can launch
a crusade) and the committed advocacy of a scientific position (that is, a
position generated the research, funded by legislative interest in media violence and its effect on society).

❖

Robert Davis, in his 1965 analysis of the social rhetoric generated by each successive introduction of new media, demonstrates that the social concerns surrounding media have been the same from the dime novel of late 1800s forward. We are concerned about the conduct and values that the content of those media might promote. Writing in the middle of the communication technology revolution, Sidonie Gruenberg (1935) summarized the concerns well:

> Looking backward, radio appears as but the latest of cultural emergents to invade the putative privacy of the home. Each such invasion finds the parents unprepared, frightened, resentful, and helpless. Within comparatively short memory, the "movie," the automobile, the telephone, the sensational newspaper or magazine, the "funnies," and the cheap paper-back book have had similar effects upon the apprehensions and solicitudes of parents. (p. 123)

A Record of Scientific Concern

Parental fears have been matched with scientific concern as each new medium has generated studies concerning its content, its effects, and the mitigation of those effects. Charles Peters, writing in the *Journal of Educational Sociology* (1933) to report his objective evidence on the matter of morality in the movies, commented,

> There has been a vast amount of argument regarding the extent to which commercial motion pictures are in conflict with our standards of morality. Many persons have been charging the movies with "the vilest and the most insidious immorality," while a few others have condemned them on the ground that they are as timidly conventional in morals as were the old-time Sunday School library books. In this agitation neither side has been able to appeal to objective evidence, either as to what constitutes morality or as to the amount of conflict by motion pictures with it if defined. On the contrary, the discussion has been emotionalistic and propagandist in character and has turned upon each individual spokesman's personal interpretation of what constitutes the demands of morality. (p. 251)

Peters (1933) reported that his "plain folks" evaluators were concerned with sexuality in films, particularly the depiction of sexually aggressive women (limited to kissing, however). But violence in the motion picture was the topic of much critical review as well. In an opening statement that would presage the modern concern with television written when motion pictures were still silent, A. T. Poffenberger (1921) reported,

One of the surprising things about the wave of crime which is reported to be raging throughout the country is the large number of very young persons found implicated in crimes of all sorts. Much attention has recently been given to the matter in newspaper articles and editorials, and blame is placed rather frequently upon the motion picture. (p. 336)

Even print media came in for similar criticism. Holmes, in his 1929 collation of criminologists', judges', district attorneys', and police chiefs' opinions on the role of newspaper crime reporting, concluded unequivocally the following:

Newspapers are guilty of inciting to crime, of aiding criminals in the commission of crime by furnishing them more or less exact information as to how to commit crimes, of showing criminals how profitable crime is, of aiding them in their escape from apprehension, of thwarting justice by "newspaper trials" and otherwise making a travesty of the administration of the law, of the actual court proceedings themselves, of preventing the securing of impartial juries, of making of the offender a popular hero, one to be emulated, and by omission at least of thwarting whatever deterrent effect there may be in present penal methods. (p. 52)

And in line with the contemporary claim that exposure leads to aggression, he also found that "prison inmates spent much more time in reading the daily papers than [did] university students," and these inmates "read the more sensational types of papers" (p. 53).

In the1920s, estimates vary but reasonable figures suggest that the paid circulation for newspapers was around 42 million, approximately 22 million motion picture tickets were sold each week, and in 1922, there were 400,000 radio receiver sets in the United States (in a population of 122 million). By 1936, radio had grown to an estimated 33 million sets (N. Miller, 1939). It was not a surprise that radio was the next target of concern. Pediatrician Mary Preston conducted a study with 200 normal children and found that 57% of them had a severe addiction to radio crime drama (regularly listening to three or more of such programs), and another 19% had mild to moderate addiction (Preston, 1941). Her work, published in the *Journal of Pediatrics,* concluded that the children "continue to think about the horror in bed: they dream about killings and have fears of kidnappings. Daydreaming, in addition, is filled with thoughts of crime in which most children identify themselves with criminals" (p. 155).

H. Rowland, in his 1944 content analysis of 20 radio crime dramas, offered the premise that "crime and violence in drama lose their cathartic value when there is a constant habituation to overdoses of these ingredients which not only results in jaded taste in children but may contribute to those frustrations which bring about aggressive behavior" (p. 214).

He goes on to offer what has become a typical laundry list of characteristics of the overexposed child:

Case studies of children indicate that addiction to crime stories is most acute among those children who have experienced the greatest amount of frustration in their attempts to reconcile the conflicting cultural patterns of adjustment to parental authority versus acceptance in the gang or play group. This frustration is greatest among children who are oversized or undersized, who are markedly retarded or markedly precocious; who suffer from extreme overprotection or extreme neglect by their parents; and children who are subjected to marginal or conflicting cultural contacts such as the Negro child living in a predominantly white neighborhood or the child from a foreign home living in a neighborhood of settled American families. (p. 216)

The modern comic book arrives in the mediascape in 1933. By 1946, the monthly circulation is reported as 40 million (Cavanagh, 1949). Perhaps history has taught us what to expect, and Agatha Shea (1948) brings the familiar invocation: "Every now and then, when tragedy enters into the life of some boy or girl, investigation leads back to the youth's reading of the comic books and their incitement to crime" (p. 163). But it was Frederic Wertham, often described as "a prominent New York psychiatrist," who, more than any other, raised the cry about the effects of reading comic books. His best-known work is *Seduction of the Innocent,* published in 1954, though he had regularly published in the popular press prior to that date. In her somewhat sympathetic review, Anita Mishler (1955) begins her review by noting Wertham's 7-year interest and public testimony on this issue. She then summarizes his position and offers her support:

Dr. Wertham claims that comic book addiction has contributed to the rise of juvenile delinquency by making criminals and criminal acts attractive, by presenting techniques of violence, by the advertisements in the comic books making available the very instruments of violence such as switch blade knives, whips and similar "toys." Legitimate doubts can be raised as to whether the comic books alone can cause a child to become delinquent. But this aside, there are hundreds and thousands of children who read ten and twenty comic books a week and are reading nothing else. Surely we must agree with Dr. Wertham that a child's view of the world is influenced by such a consistent atmosphere. The child learns from these sources that the world is amoral, that might is right, everyone is potentially corruptible, that relationships between men and women are merely exploitative, and that "inferior" peoples can be used and violated with impunity. (p. 116)

The Government Considers

Wertham is a useful figure in this transition because he served as a consultant to the 1954 Senate hearings on the effects of media on violence, often seen as the watershed of the many hearings that followed. It may seem surprising how late Congress took up the issues of media content. But perhaps there was no need.

Congress had passed the racially toxic Sims Act of 1912, banning boxing films in response to African American boxer Jack Johnson's crushing of more than one great white hope (Grieveson, 1998). And in 1915, the U.S. Supreme Court denied the motion picture any First Amendment rights, declaring film to be commerce pure and simple (Jowett, 1989). Thereafter, it was to be entertaining, instructive, and harmless. As it grew more entertaining and perhaps less harmless, there was some subsequent interest in a national film commission designed to govern content, but that was effectively co-opted by the mid-1930s by the Motion Picture Association's Hays code and the formation of the Legion of Decency. Individual state boards of censorship were very active, further lessening federal interest.

Radio broadcasting was under the aegis of the Federal Communications Commission (FCC) and was rising rapidly as a mass medium of social significance as the war loomed. World War II, of course, gave the government far more important things to consider through the decade of the 1940s. The political value of attacking the media was discovered very shortly after, however.[1]

The first of the congressional hearings was conducted in 1951 under the authority of House Resolution 278 (U.S. Congress, 1952), which directed the House Committee on Interstate and Foreign Commerce—the committee that had oversight for the Federal Communications Commission—to

> conduct a full and complete investigation and study to determine the extent to which the radio and television programs currently available to the people of the United States contain immoral and otherwise offensive matter, or place improper emphasis on crime, violence, and corruption. (p. 1)

Little public effect was generated by this hearing, but that was not the outcome of the Senate hearings that followed. The Senate hearings of 1954 were chaired by Senator Robert C. Henderson, Republican of New Jersey, but it was Senator Estes Kefauver, already identified as a crime fighter and a possible 1956 Democratic nominee for president, who gained the most politically from of the hearings that covered the relationship between juvenile delinquency and film, comic books, and television. When the Senate reorganized following the 1954 election, Kefauver chaired the remaining hearings and formed a national conference on juvenile delinquency using organizations from his political base. That is when his campaign for his presidential nomination began in earnest.[2]

Hoerrner (1999) considered the national prominence that Kefauver gained in the process to be a success story that set the stage for the many hearings on violence in the media that have followed. There were hearings in 1962, 1964, and 1968 and, by Hoerrner's count, "nine congressional hearings on television violence in the 1970s, seven in the 1980s, and five in the 1990s." Her conclusion is that the hearings are a game as in economic game theory of symbolic politics (Edelman, 1971), in which political capital is gained by the investigators, and threatened constraints on the industry are deflected. The result for Hoerrner is that "the public is assured that both Congress and the industry are concerned about children. No further action is attempted by either side, however."

A similar fate seems to have befallen the three major governmental initiatives into the scientific study of media violence and aggression: the 15-volume 1969 report of the National Commission of the Causes and Prevention of Violence, the 1972 report of the Surgeon General's scientific advisory committee on television and social behavior, and the National Institute of Mental Health's 1982 report on television and behavior. These three reports have a linked history and similar findings relating to the media.

The National Commission appointed by President Lyndon Johnson was a response to the social unrest of the 1960s and more specifically to the assassinations of Martin Luther King, Jr. and Robert Kennedy. Charged by the president "'to go as far as man's knowledge takes' it for the causes of violence and the means of prevention," the commission produced a prodigious synthesis of research within its short 18-month lifespan (Milton Eisenhower, in Baker & Ball, 1969, p. iii). Among its conclusions were the claims that the United States has both a history and tradition of violence in its society, that the primary source of this violence is the inequitable distribution of wealth, that the solution was a massive social program to eradicate poverty, and that "there is sufficient evidence that mass media presentations, especially portrayals of violence, have negative effects upon audiences" (Baker & Ball, 1969, p. 381).

Despite the commission's call, Johnson's War on Poverty was mostly disbanded by that time, and suppression of protest rather than redistribution of wealth became more to U.S. liking. In 1969, Senator John Pastore—perhaps influenced by the commission's conclusion on media, perhaps playing to the newly inaugurated Nixon administration—called on the Surgeon

General to mount a research program on the effects of media violence on children and aggression. The Surgeon General's Scientific Advisory Committee on Television and Social Behavior was embroiled in controversy from the start. Seven researchers, including Albert Bandura and Leonard Berkowitz, were blackballed from the panel, and industry insiders participated in the final selection of committee members. One inexplicable result of this process is that researchers associated with the catharsis hypothesis (that viewing violence reduces aggression) were apparently systematically excluded from the panel (Boffey & Walsh, 1970).

The committee ended in controversy as well when a week before its report, *Television and Growing Up: The Impact of Televised Violence,* was to be submitted, the *New York Times* scored a scoop by running an article on the findings. The *Times,* however, reversed the major finding that some children were harmed by running a lead that the majority of children were found to be unharmed by televised violence. Although true, it was not the story the committee wanted told. The Television Information Office quickly distributed the version by the *Times* ("Low Blows," 1972).

Although individual studies from the five-volume staff report have shown legs, the report to the Surgeon General itself (there never was a report from the Surgeon General) seemed to have little impact. Its temporizing finding that some children are at risk was nothing new and in fact had been (and still is) the default assumption of most researchers and social policy experts (Bogart, 1972–1973). Nonetheless, the political value of the question remained, and in 1979, the Surgeon General was again convinced to revisit the issue in a 10-year retrospective funded by the National Institute of Mental Health (NIMH). The funding paid for 24 literature reviews and their subsequent meta-analysis. No new, original research was funded. The conclusions, however, were markedly different. Gone was the conclusion that *some* people watching *some* programs under *some* conditions will be harmed by media violence. In its place was the causal claim that media violence causes aggression. The primary author of that claim was L. Rowell Huesmann, suggesting something of a palace coup in this directorship of NIMH under David Pearl. Once again, there was very little response to the study other than a lengthy and technical review appearing in *Public Opinion Quarterly.* But then the decade of the 1980s was marked by a substantial die-off of funding and interest in media violence/aggression research, just as the causationists and cultivationists were in their political ascendancy (J. Anderson, in press; Gerbner, n.d., Part II, para. 4). It would take nearly 15 years for them to regain their footing.

How far they moved from the political center became apparent in the most recent (and predictably not the last) Surgeon General's report that appeared in 2001. The preface of the report attributes the impetus for the panel's work to the tragedy at Columbine High School in Colorado and, more generally, to the "tide of serious youth violence that had erupted in the early 1980s," following the standard of crisis politics. Many of the 15 "participants" (a category that will become understandable below) in the development of the 2001 report (as listed in the acknowledgments) had worked on the 1982 NIMH report, the majority were media effects scholars, and nearly all were immediately recognizable as coming from the causationist point of view. Nonetheless, there was no chapter in the report on media violence and aggression. That coverage was relegated to Appendix 4-B, albeit that its strength and complexity clearly suggest that it was not intended to be an appendix. Clearly, the reason was that it expressed a countervailing point of view from that of the main body of the NIMH report. Furthermore, many of the conclusions were strangely muted, given the evidence presented in the argument and the other writings of the participants. We have seen the one example:

> Violent behavior seldom results from a single cause; rather, multiple factors converging over time contribute to such behavior. Accordingly, the influence of the mass media, however strong or weak, is best viewed as one of the many potential factors that help to shape behavior, including violent behavior. (http://www.surgeongeneral.gov/library/youthviolence/chapter4/appendix4b.html)

This language undercuts the importance of media as a factor in youth violence and explicitly signals that the notion of influence is problematic. Later in the report, it concludes its analysis of the flagship longitudinal studies of the causationist argument with an ending that mollified the majority of the participants who put the report together:

> In summary, these longitudinal studies show a small, but often statistically significant, long-term relationship between viewing television violence in childhood and later aggression, especially in late adolescence and early adulthood. Some evidence suggests that more aggressive children watch more violence, but the evidence is stronger that watching media violence is a precursor of increased aggression. (http://www.surgeongeneral.gov/library/youthviolence/chapter4/appendix4bsec2.html)

This tacked-on ending was too much for at least 8 of the 15 who later appeared in print[3] (C. Anderson et al., 2003a, 2003b) to give what, in their minds, should have been concluded. They appeared under the masthead of an editorial that reported on their consternation (Ceci & Bjork, 2003):

Given that they had been selected precisely for their expertise and knowledge in the domain of the report, the authors were stunned by the substantial alteration of their writing and conclusions. Ultimately, they indicated to Delbert Elliott, a distinguished criminologist and the editor of the overall youth-violence report, that they were not willing to have their names associated with the altered report. Key members of the panel met with Elliott in an attempt to resolve the conflict and to develop a draft that the committee members would be willing to sign. However, Elliott subsequently reported that the Surgeon General's staff had decided (against his advice, according to the authors) to drop the media-violence section from the youth-violence report and, instead, simply to discuss media violence in another section of the overall report as one risk factor to be considered. The authors concluded that the staff of the Surgeon General's Office did not want to include any relatively uncensored report on the effects of media violence in the Surgeon General's broader report on youth violence. (p. ii)

The moral, of course, is that in government-funded science, one lives by the staff and dies by the staff.

Congressional and Regulatory Action

There is surprisingly little congressional and regulatory action to point to during the 50-year period from the first of the congressional hearings. Perhaps congressional activists were chastened by the landmark Supreme Court decision of 1952 that finally brought film under the protection of the First Amendment after 50 years of state regulatory oversight waning though it had been. Perhaps film, comic book, and broadcast industry codes worked to preempt direct legislative or regulatory action. Regulators did use their bully pulpit to move broadcasting particularly to restrict content, beginning with the FCC 1946 Blue Book programming proposals that were never adopted but served to influence broadcast programming nonetheless, to FCC chair Newton Minow's (1961; http://janda.org/b20/News%20articles/vastwasteland.htm) vast wasteland speech to his successor Richard Wiley's campaign for a family viewing hour (1975) to the development of a rating system for broadcasting (1993) and one for video games (1994). The election of Ronald Regan ushered in the start of the contemporary era of deregulation that shifted political action to such interest groups as the National Coalition on Television Violence, the National Council of Churches, and any number of organizations with *family* in their title and away from the regulatory agencies.

Nonetheless, there were some pieces of legislation that were attempted and two that actually passed in the 1990s. Of the latter, Senator Paul Simon, Democrat from Illinois, sponsored legislation to exempt media industries from antitrust laws so that these industries could jointly draw up guidelines to reduce violence. The intent was to remove the competitive impetus to show violent programming always considered popular with audiences. The bill, amended to include illegal drug use and explicit sexuality, passed with near-unanimous support of both the Senate and the House. The media industries refused to participate.

Through the mid-1990s, there was a growing interest in restrictions on both sexual and violent content during the so-called children viewing hours. The Third District Court of Appeals had upheld FCC regulations that prohibited patently offensive sexual material from the airwaves from 6 a.m. to 10 p.m. (but did not ban it altogether). Bolstered by that ruling, Senator Ernest Hollings, Democrat from South Carolina, introduced legislation to similarly regulate violent content. He was immediately attacked by broadcasters and civil libertarians. Under his legislation, the FCC would determine both what constitutes violence and when it could not be shown. The bill was later passed without those provisions as the Parental Choice in Television Programming Act of 1996. That act established the requirement of a ratings system connected to V-chip technology that could be used to block the selection of programs by unauthorized viewers.

The result, therefore, of 50 years of hearings on violence in the media has been two legislative acts, some regulatory action on sexual content and its time of presentation, and highly publicized but, in the long run, mostly ineffective industry self-regulation. The presentation of violence in our media has continued unabated and, across all media, has grown in viciousness and explicitness. There has been a continued chorus of social critics, medical professionals, and social scientists who have decried its presentation as each new medium reached a threshold of mass distribution. Yet the political will for action has not held.

The Force of Technology

If the will for political action has yet to materialize, the time for effective political action may well have passed, given the relentless force of innovation in media technology. The 20th century has been a remarkable era in the communication field. Entertainment and information industries have developed in motion pictures, sound recording, print serials, radio, television, computers, video games, and the Internet. Each of these is now universally available and distributes any form of content imaginable.

Content, itself, is devolving into smaller and smaller units, evolving into collaged and montaged presentations, and being liberated from distribution constraints. Fewer than 10 years ago, if one wanted a single song, one bought a $12 to $15 album. Now that person can sample 30 seconds for free and purchase that single song for less than a dollar. Audiences routinely construct their own content from multiple sources both serially with the remote control and simultaneously with picture-in-picture capacities. Cable and satellite companies provide multiplex channels that allow a child in your house the ability to watch one show while maintaining surveillance on six others at the same time. Time shifting using VCRs, DVRs, or TiVo makes industry-distributed content available whenever wanted. Peer-to-peer file exchanges easily distribute content outside authorized distribution channels. Content, therefore, has moved from the characteristics of vertical control by the producer and/or distributor to the horizontal control of the audience. What, when, and the final character of content are now determined at the point of reception, not at the point of distribution.

But wait, as they say, there's more. Advances in devices and reduction in prices have distributed the technology of production into the hands of nearly everyone, if not in direct ownership then in community-funded (mostly) library programs. It is now possible for a disenfranchised group, such as the homeless, to achieve international distribution of content and to garner worldwide recognition as a result (see, e.g., http://thehomelessguy .wordpress.com/).

And in this first decade of the 21st century, we are witnessing the final erasure of *the medium* as convergence makes the distinction of motion pictures, television, and other media merely an academic exercise. One's television viewing can be entirely of motion pictures delivered to a cell phone, iPod, or wireless laptop. The content delivered can be from Hollywood, Bollywood, Japan, or Mulholland Drive.

The significance of these characteristics of the 21st century is threefold: First, it is no longer possible to address the contemporary situation from studies conducted as little as a decade ago.[4] Such studies were located in a mediascape that no longer exists except in pockets of nostalgia, and certainly they do not describe the world of contemporary youth. Second, it is no longer possible to address the *effect* of any particular medium or content in any meaningful way as if it were distinctly separable. The effect of television is nonsensical when it is available anywhere and everywhere, with or without traditional television technology. Third, and last, it is no longer possible to effectively control media or their content. One may, indeed, still remove designated programs from broadcast television or relegate designated cable programs to particular hours or subscription channels, should the political will for it ever appear. But that will not deter an audience that wants those programs.

In this regard, the history of the horror comic book is instructive. The 1954 Comics Code Authority that resulted in part from the Kefauver hearings caused a great disruption in the horror comic book publishing industry, although perhaps it was already set for television's executioner's blade. William Gaines, publisher of EC comics, the premier horror line, was forced to abandon his entire list. (He turned to publishing *Mad Magazine.*) The means of the success of the code was its influence on the means of distribution. Horror comics did not disappear from the marketplace (estimates suggest that some 300 horror publishers survived the code), but they did from the corner drugstore. Driven underground, small press comics resurfaced in record shops, comic book specialty shops, and counterculture venues that replaced the drugstore comic book rack. Ironically, the entire EC horror line was republished beginning in the late 1970s, and boxed sets now sell on eBay for around $50 (accessed January 16, 2006). DC Comics has since returned to the genre, and of course, the Internet can provide for all your horror comics needs 24/7 (see, e.g., Demiseofthedamned.com).[5]

At best, the victory of the social reformers was short-lived. At worst, it was no victory at all—simply a change in the way the market did business either by substituting television or moving around the code. As always, its primary effect would have been on the poor and disadvantaged who could no longer easily get the entertainment they desired (and what we, the elite, considered so dangerous in their hands). This consequence is a continuing and troubling refrain throughout all of the effects history.

Social Science Paradigms and Social Power

Social science considered globally, from the earliest figures to the present time, has evidenced a number of irreducible tensions over its foundational units, objects, methodologies, and lines of argument (see, e.g., J. Anderson, 1996). That history is extensive and, from the standpoint of academic warfare, rather bloody. Both ideas and careers have been casualties. In their review of this history and present practice, J. Anderson and Baym (2004) conclude that the differences across these foundational issues are so great that social science practitioners "occupy the same disciplinary space only by administrative convenience" (p. 590). Writing from the field of communication, Anderson and Baym divide the social sciences into different philosophical domains. The concept of "effect" appears most clearly in their domain marked foundational, modernist, empirical, metric, individualist, and causal. Space does not allow the full development of the implications of those markers. For this purpose, it is sufficient to note that multiple alternatives (realities?) exist for each of them, and those alternatives appear within different communities in the domain of social science. Most often, as one moves across those communities, the concept of effects fades or disappears entirely. This part of the history, then, concerns the success of one of those communities, which was able to command the resources of a nation, to construct a social reality, and to become, for a short time, the singular voice in the field of media studies.

Let us go to the decade prior to World War II. During this period, as in the decades before but not as much in those to follow, higher education and certainly the social sciences were under the financial influence of the philanthropic foundations. Considering this decade, Hollis (1940) called the foundations "the most powerful external influence these institutions [of higher education] had known" (p. 177). During this period, the Rockefeller Foundation, under the presidencies of Max Mason and Raymond Fosdick and the section directorship of John Marshall, began to heavily fund the social sciences with the intention of creating centers of excellence in this field. The goal of developing these centers, as described by Simpson (1994), was to discover a "'democratic prophylaxis' that could immunize the United States' large immigrant population from the effects of Soviet and Axis propaganda" (p. 22). Brett (1996) argues that the initiative "helps impose theoretical coherence and a 'scientific' research paradigm on this inchoate area of interdisciplinary inquiry" (p. 126). One person's "inchoate area" is, of course, another's vibrant diversity. The era of the 1920s and 1930s was one not unlike that of the 1980s and 1990s, with active methodological disputes over metric versus interpretive empirical approaches to the social sciences (J. Anderson, 1996; Smith, 1994). The difference between the two eras is that social scientific measurement was the new kid on the block in the 1920s, and interpretive was the comeback kid of the 1980s.

What took social scientific measurement to its ascendancy was a weak federal government creating a vacuum, which a strong private agenda—with money— would quickly fill, in this case, by the Rockefeller Foundation–sponsored discussion group commonly called the Communications Seminar (even communication's concluding "s" is instructive[6]). Brett (1996) argues that the seminar defined the approach that "was foundational in the intellectual history of the field" (p. 126). The seminar participants developed over long months of debate the fundamental communication model—who? said what? to whom? with what effect?—that would govern communication research well into the 1970s and is still the underlying model of effects research today. It was this direct, linear model (very much like a mathematical equation), with no space for context, culture, or sociology, that allowed *effects* to appear. Presumably, by these theorists, were one to add to the equation the ecology of reception—that is, the ways in which people use the media they consume, the idiosyncratic interpretations of communities that view identical messages differently, personal interpretational differences, and the way different people behave in response to what they drink in from the media environment—then effects would disappear or be unclear.[7] So, with all of that messy sociology disposed of, all it would take at this point would be a constituting theory and a revealing methodology. As chance would have it, both were developing during the decade of the 1930s as well.

This part of our history does not end with the Rockefeller seminars, however, because as Brett (1996) points out, "By the end of 1940, each of the established media projects [of the foundation] had been tied into some security-related research" (p. 143) as part of "the emerging national security state" (p. 145). Simpson (1994) comments that dozens of prominent social scientists entered the governmental agencies to help win the war. They were the names familiar to any historian of the field: Cantril, Roper, Likert, Doob, Schramm, Lazarsfeld, Stanton, Paley, Becker, Mead, and Lasswell (Simpson, 1994, pp. 25–27).

They carried with them and put into place the framework that directed congressional sensibilities and agency funding for the next three decades. Simpson (1994) shows the consequence by stating,

> Federal agencies such as the Department of Defense, U.S. Information Agency, and Central Intelligence Agency and their forerunners provided the substantial majority of funds for all large-scale communication research projects by U.S. scholars between 1945 and 1960. (p. 9)

He goes on to state that

> the government allocated between $7 million and $13 million annually for university and think-tank studies of communication-related social psychology, communication effect studies, anthropological studies of foreign communication systems, overseas audience and foreign public opinion surveys, and similar projects that contributed directly and indirectly to the emergence of mass communication research as a distinct discipline. (p. 9)

They also created what Nathan Maccoby called "one of the best old-boy (or girl) networks" that provided an "open door to most relevant jobs and career lines" (qtd. in Simpson, 1994, p. 28). This network was the governance of the field. We need not go to any sense of conspiracy theory, but consider the circumstances of a nascent field dominated by a group of individuals bonded in a successful war effort and directed by a set of strong personalities who held a set of common beliefs about media and their messages. In this atmosphere, effects are surely to be found.

As Carey (1983) remarked, "The student of the 1950s [had] two options . . . one could be either a certain kind of psychologist of communications or a certain kind of sociologist of communications." And he notes that the options were two sides of the same page: "These two options were jointly oriented toward resolving the question of the effects of mass communications" (p. 311). What is surprising is that much of the field moved on even if the funding did not follow. There is good reason for both of these outcomes. The field moves because one cannot sustain the belief in a direct and linear relationship between content and behavior in the face of one's own experience and the overwhelming evidence that life provides. Funding continues in its previous mode because that is an institutionalized process. What we see from the 1960s to the 1980s is the repeated funding of the same study. It has different settings and different contingencies, but the theory and methodology (and consequently the results) remain mostly unchanged. And it is to that theory and methodology that we now turn.

The Constituting Theory and Revealing Methodology of Effects

Media effects claims are composed of four elements: (a) a content/medium combination such as violent television or magazine advertisements, (b) a focal audience (often children), (c) some consequent in behavior or cognitive formation such as aggression or attitudes toward men, and (d) some theory/methodology combination by which to generate evidence and constitute claims such as cognitivism and attitude scales. Figure 2.1 presents the typical forms these elements take and their relationships.

The concepts of media violence, effects, and aggression all depend on the kind of social science one uses to approach them. In the field of media effects, the social science most closely allied to the effects literature is that of cognitivism. We will take up a fuller analysis of cognitivism in the next chapter. Here, it might suffice to say that cognitivism is built on the premise that mental structures develop primarily through the socialization process and primarily in the formative childhood years that direct the behavior of the individual. In the effects literature, one of the principal arguments is that media content is an important socializing influence for the child and can shape adult behavior.

In the overall history of cognitivism, the theory has adopted an increasingly complex view about how this process works. It has moved from a "one-size-fits-all" approach to a careful examination of the multiple elements and processes that lead to the performance of human behavior. As the theory has matured, its practitioners have become more sophisticated in determining the conditions

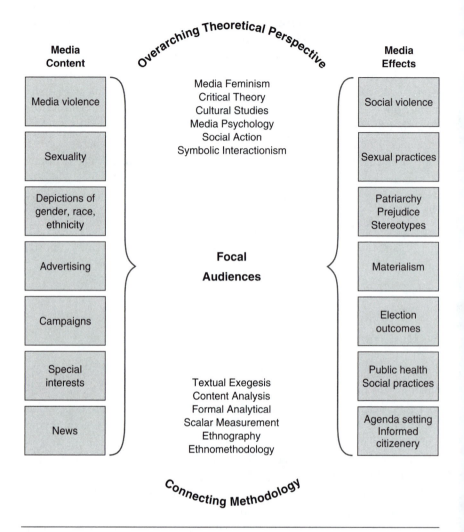

Figure 2.1   Overarching Theoretical Perspective

under which cognitive formations might influence behavior. For example, in the attitude change and formation field, contemporary research is delving ever more deeply into the conditional circumstances that predict attitude formation and change, such as with the cognitive response model (Lutz & Swazy, 1977). This model could be called the "it depends" model because the variables of attitude formation and change are dependent on the individual's cognitions rather than the simple qualities of some outside influence. There are a lot of if/then/may calculations performed in the application of the cognitive response model in sharp distinction to the message-centered models of the 1930s and 1940s.

A good portion of the history of the media violence/aggression issue, however, has moved in quite the opposite direction. Historically, researchers started on the conditional side of things. Blumer's (1933) conclusion from *Movies and Conduct* stated,

> It is insufficient to regard motion pictures simply as a fantasy world by participating in which an individual softens the ardor of his life and escapes its monotony and hardships, nor to justify their content and "unreality" on this basis. For too many the pictures are authentic portrayals of life, from which they draw *patterns of behavior, stimulation to overt conduct, content for a vigorous life of imagination, and ideas of reality* [italics added]. They are not merely a device for surcease; they are a form of stimulation. Their content does not merely serve the first purpose, but incites the latter result. What might be intended to have the harmless effect of the former may, on occasion, have the striking influence of the latter. (p. 196)

The phrase that we italicized nicely sums up the issues of the archive over the next 70-plus years. It was echoed nearly 30 years later by Schramm, Lyle, and Parker (1961), who concluded,

> For *some* children under *some* conditions *some* television is harmful. For *other* children under the same conditions, or for the same children under *other* conditions, it may be beneficial. For *most* children under *most* conditions, *most* television is probably neither particularly harmful nor particularly beneficial. (p. 1)

The conclusion we draw from this early literature and these analyses from the archive is that the scientific questions concerning the role of media in aggression were answered by the end of the 1970s by the social learning theory represented by Bandura, the neo-associationist arousal theory represented by Berkowitz, excitation transfer theory represented by Zillmann (1979), and the cognitive process theory represented by Collins (e.g., Collins, Sobol, & Westby, 1981). Together, they provided the answers to the "some/some/some" conditionals of effects, which Schramm et al. (1961) refer to. Media content can provide the resources for learning aggressive behavior, attaching positive value to aggressive behavior, and motivating one to aggress, just as Blumer (1933) warned us and Schramm et al. concluded.

The Contributionists

We might call these researchers contributionists in that they hold that media content can contribute to a lifestyle or an immediate response. They are a diverse lot. They include Joanne Cantor (from whom we draw the term) and many of her graduate students in fear research, as well as Elihu Katz and Alan Ruben in uses and gratifications; John Hartley, Gunther Kress, and John Fiske, who are collectively known as the semioticians; U.S., Canadian, and British critics and sociologists; David Riesman, Harold Innis, Raymond William, Richard Hoggart, and Stuart Hall, who are identified with cultural studies; and many others. Contributionists, in general, hold that media are potent among the vulnerable, but good parenting, good education, a good society, or even good choices can reduce one's vulnerability to a manageable state.

But the contributionist answer was not the answer that many wanted. The some/some/some conditionals established media effects as a case-by-case analysis under the control of an actively participating audience member. A major social issue was thereby reduced to a matter of personal probity and science to the role of the educator. The preferable answer in the generalized claims of science is not somebody but "anybody." Anybody who gets "too close" to the sun of media violence will be sure to fall.

The Causationist Project

The cultural project represented by the mosaic of the science and political activism of contemporary causationists such as C. Anderson, Bushman, Huesmann, or Strasburger has been to move the effects of media from a set of conditionals to a generalized pathology of behavior. No longer are we concerned about media violence because one might choose to use it for some antisocial ends. Now we are concerned because media can turn the good toward the bad. As Craig Anderson testified in 2000 before the Senate Commerce Committee hearing on video games, "Children who are exposed to a lot of violent media learn a number of lessons that *change* them into more aggressive people" (C. Anderson, 2000, Section 4, para. 1, italics added). He goes on to claim,

> The developing personality is like slowly-hardening clay. Environmental experiences, including violent media, shape the clay. Changes are relatively easy to make at first, when the clay is soft, but later on changes become increasingly difficult. Longitudinal studies suggest that aggression-related knowledge structures begin to harden around age 8 or 9, and become more perseverant with increasing age. (C. Anderson, 2000, Section 4, para. 2)

This position is advanced by the causationists without a trace of doubt. L. Rowell Huesmann, quoting a letter he and Anderson wrote to the Federal Trade Commission, he claimed the following:

There is virtually no divergence of opinion among legitimate media violence experts concerning the basic factual question of most concern to the general public: Does exposure to violent entertainment media increase the likelihood of aggressive behavior by youthful consumers? The simple answer to this basic question is "yes," and we know of no legitimate media violence research experts who disagree with this statement.[8] (L. Rowell Huesmann, personal communication, 2004)

Huesmann has a well-known[9] reputation as the enforcer on the media violence/aggression causality hockey team. He is also a brilliant and well-respected researcher (who has apparently forgotten that he participated in concluding that "aggressive behavior seems to occur most often when there is a convergence of a number of these factors during a child's development [Eron, 1982], but no single factor by itself seems capable of explaining more than a small portion of the individual variation in aggression" [Huesmann, Lagerspetz, Akademi, & Eron, 1984, p. 746]). He draws his current hubris from the fact that the historical and contemporary field of media research has, with consistency, found evidence of a relationship between the content of the media and the behavior of its audiences. But what he fails to mention is that the field (even his corner of it) has argued about the meaning of that relationship with even greater consistency. That argument takes many forms. Barrie Gunter, a widely published media researcher (Gunter, 1985, 1988, 1998) writing to his fellow contributors of a special issue on media violence and causality, provided this latest example:

It is clear from some of the discussion in this collection of papers, as well as from other literature that parental examples, disciplinary practices, peer groups, local living conditions, financial circumstances, and so on can all contribute as preconditions that render individuals more or less likely to behave in an aggressive manner in different situations. Some individuals—partly through the nature of their genetic makeup and partly through learning experiences—have little impulse control, while others have considerable self-control.

How do experiences with mediated violence add to the mix of factors and in what ways? Does media violence represent a profound influence upon the "development" of impulse control or upon the "erosion" of established impulse control (and these are not the same effect)? Does the degree to which either of these effects takes place depend upon the broader makeup of the individual?

Or can media violence represent a "tipping point" effect whereby added to the right cocktail of other factors it can push the individual's state over a threshold beyond which impulse control is temporarily lost?

For us, so far, the research literature, despite its size and methodological diversity, has lacked clarity of thinking in relation to these core concepts. (Barrie Gunter, personal communication, 2005)

What is not argued in the field (and probably could not be argued by anyone in the field) is that media content has no effect, no consequence, or no participation in the behavior/action/performances that are evoked, that we produce, or in which we appear. We are left then with a continuing responsibility for understanding media in society, but with the freedom of association to choose the community of thought that will direct how we discharge that responsibility. For the optimistic contributionist, the move is to interventions that develop parenting skills or cultivate sophisticated audiences. For the more pessimistic of the social reformers, the move is to some redistribution of social resources, and for the causationists, simple and outright censorship will do.

Lessons of Our History

What this history of effects tells us is that the process is not simply a disinterested science quietly going about its business of discovering facts about the world. Historically, the actual process has begun when society has been required to accommodate a new, rapidly diffusing form of entertainment. That new form raises societal concerns in its own right because it is quickly connected to the ongoing and often intractable problems of that society. Politicians and their hunt for social ills they can exploit for political gain, in turn, further elevate the significance of what is now *the problem*. But happily, these politicians often provide the funding for the science that follows. That science has a mandate to solve *the problem*, and *the problem* is a now a media problem. Consequently, the issue gets framed as the effects of the media.

We can summarize this process in more academic language as: An effect as a social/scientific construct appears when socially contested forms of content are distributed widely in a popular medium through controllable channels to an audience that is heavily populated with children (or others considered to be vulnerable) and that represents the Other. (The Other, in this instance, is a population of which I'm not a member, a population that is lower—or I perceive to be lower—on the socioeconomic ladder than the population/race/ethnic origin/religion to which I belong. *Therefore,* this is a population about which I must be concerned because that population is vulnerable to the media's pernicious effects.) Those circumstances constitute *the media problem,* and science is invoked to provide *the solution,* which is found in the control of effects. In this way symbolic politics becomes symbolic science.

When we examine the various elements of this relationship—between problems and solutions—we find that (a) the content of concern is both secular and commercial, whether it is found in the serial publication, over the air, through a wire, or on a recording medium. It is (b) content that is not under the purview of the ideological apparatus of The State, The Church (whatever its denomination at the time and place), and The School. The content is (c) industrially produced. There is (d) some threshold of distribution that will lead to a "problem": Radio is not a problem at half a million but a serious one at 33 million. There is (e) an arc of popularity that plays into the constitution of an effect. The grave concern over the motion picture photoplay rapidly becomes film theory when television captures center stage. That is, as a medium fades, such as movies in comparison to the hugely popular medium of television, then that fading medium becomes quaint. It helps immeasurably if (f) the channel of distribution can be controlled. Newspaper reportage of crime disappears as a cause of juvenile delinquency when local police censorship boards are put out of business. And (g) the audience is rarely us. (This is where the Other comes into play.) It is an audience of lesser ability marked by youth, race, and immigrant status. The "We" of the social critic and the researcher are interestingly immune. That is, if *I'm* exposed to media violence, it won't affect me, but it might harm *you*.

These characteristics come together to create the social importance that is the engine that drives the funding to research the problem of media violence. That, in turn, drives the studies that are the currency of an academic economy. Into that crucible of money, careers, and social legitimacy one adds a compliant methodology to carve out an effect from the panoply of influences and cultural ideologies that is everyday life. The simple solution of what ails us is nicely packaged in science and social concern.

Notes

1. This description draws heavily on the work of Keisha Hoerrner (1998, 1999, 2000).

2. Information reported here came from a search of ProQuest Historical New York Times, with the search terms *Kefauver* and *juvenile delinquency*, between the dates of January 1, 1953, and December 31, 1954.

3. Craig A. Anderson, Iowa State University, Department of Psychology, Ames, IA; Leonard Berkowitz, University of Wisconsin, Department of Psychology; Edward Donnerstein, University of Arizona, College of Social & Behavioral Sciences; L. Rowell Huesmann, University of Michigan, Institute for Social Research, Department of Psychology; James D. Johnson, University of North Carolina, Department of Psychology, Wilmington, NC; Daniel Linz, University of California at Santa Barbara, Department of Communication and Law & Society Program; Neil M. Malamuth, University of California at Los Angeles, Department of Communication/ Speech; and Ellen Wartella, University of Texas, College of Communication, Austin, TX. Affiliations are those listed at the time of the publication.

4. One consequence of this convergence is that there will be a new rash of effects studies.

5. DC Comics (no longer a subscriber to the Code) released *Seven Soldiers: Frankenstein #2* January 11, 2006, with the following story line: "The Monster's on Mars, following a trail of death and human misery to the demon-haunted Tombs of B'aal B'zaar and the largest seam of gold in the solar system! Carnivorous horses, a new kind of slave trade, the secret origin of Melmoth the Wanderer and the unstoppable menace of Red Zombies await!" (http://www.dccomics.com/comics/ ?cm=4727). There has been no public outcry.

6. The study of communications (messages) is different from the study of communication (a discipline), just as the study of medicines (drugs) is different from the study of medicine (a discipline).

7. For a more thorough discussion of this period and its consequences on the field of communication, see the *Journal of Communication* symposium titled "Tangled Legacies" and edited by John Durham Peters (1996).

8. There is an interesting line between cause and contribution that gets walked here. Joanne Cantor (2002) draws it by stating, "The question is not, of course, whether media violence *causes* violence, but whether viewing violence contributes to the likelihood that someone will commit violence" (http://www.joannecantor.com/ montrealpap_fin.htm, Section 2, para. 1).

9. It is also a well-deserved reputation as he answers every critique with sharp reply—for example, "such serious errors of reasoning" (Huesmann, Lagerspetz, et al., 1984, p. 747). Beyond serious error, he has accused critiques of sloppy scholarship (Huesmann, 1973), being antiscience (Huesmann, 1993), and being disconnected from reality (Huesmann & Taylor, 2006).

3

The Epistemology
of Media Effects

I n this chapter, we will develop the theoretical foundations for the social
science argument that sustains the traditional "media effects" claims and,
more particularly, the media violence/aggressive behavior connection. Media
effects claims are composed of four elements: (a) a content/medium combination, (b) a focal audience, (c) some consequent in behavior or ideas that
might motive behavior, and (d) some theory/methodology combination by
which to generate evidence and constitute claims.

Any theory in any science is a way of knowing something. It gives names
to objects and actions, sets boundaries around them, defines their properties, indicates the relationships among them, and connects to some methodology for doing all that. The study of how all that gets done is called
epistemology. This section of our history, then, is an epistemological field
trip through the domain of the effects of media violence.

A final note before we proceed. This is a difficult chapter to read.
Although formal principles of logic aren't presented here, we do deal with
logical "difficulties" that the causationists have gotten themselves into.
The causationists' argument is predicated on assumptions about necessary
and sufficient conditions needed for media violence to affect certain outcomes of human behavior. Those assumptions simply don't hold water.
Teasing out these assumptions is, at times, tedious. But we ask you to
bear with us. If you can stay with us during the presentation of this
chapter, we think you will better understand the profound flaws in the
causationist argument.

The Foundation in Behaviorism

The concepts of media effects, in general, and media violence and aggression specifically depend on some theory of mind/brain that provides the linkage between the content as cause and the following behavior as effect. The first theory that provided that causal linkage was behaviorism. Behaviorism may be best known from canine experiments at the turn of the 20th century by Ivan Petrovich Pavlov, in which dogs developed a "conditioned reflex" to salivate at the sound of a bell because that response was reinforced by the presentation of food. But it was John Watson (1913) who took Pavlov's reflex protocol and developed it into the foundation of behaviorism. Behaviorism reached its U.S. apogee in the 1950s through the work of Clark Hull and in the writings of B. F. Skinner and his famous (or infamous) Skinner Box.

In the behaviorist paradigm, a stimulus is a change in the environment that elicits a response, a response is any behavior under the governance of a stimulus, and reinforcement is any change in the environment subsequent to a response that raises the probability of that response (for an explanation of terms, see Dinsmoor, 2004). For example, a light goes on (stimulus), a rat pushes a pedal (response), and a food pellet drops into a cup next to the rat (reinforcement). The next time the light goes on, the rat will be much quicker in pushing the pedal (proof of the stimulus, the governance of the response, and its reinforcement).

For behaviorists hewing to Morgan's requirement that explanations must be at the simplest physiological level (Morgan, 1894), none of this requires any reasoning on the part of the rat. The rat does have to be hungry (food deprived in behaviorist terms), however. Reinforcement, therefore, requires a connection to some fundamental state of the organism. These fundamental states (or unconditioned reinforcers) are the basis for all other reinforcers. It all goes back to the biology of the organism. This position was in sharp contrast to Cartesian rationality and participated in the mind/body arguments that are yet unresolved.

Behaviorism was an attempt to objectify the study of behavior of all sentient organisms within a causal paradigm of stimulus-response-reinforcement. Human behavior was no different from that of a dog; both were to be devoid of internal "mentalist" functions (there was no need to posit an "expectation of food" inside the mind of Pavlov's dogs) and disconnected from any act of the will or agency. Behaviorism took a very mechanical and strictly causal view of behavior. Consequently, it stood in theoretical opposition to contemporary introspection theories of Wilhelm Wundt and pragmatism of William James. This opposition, between behaviorism and those who promote the existence of internal cognitive processes, was close to the origin of the argument over the location of the controlling agent of human behavior. Is the controlling agent external in the stimulus (content) or internal in the mind of the receiver (one's interpretation of the content)? This direct versus moderated effects argument is still debated.

Behaviorism was an egalitarian theory. Behaviorism held that we all started out relatively equal and that differences developed through the happenstance of conditioning. It should then be possible to produce superstars of all of us given the appropriate conditioning regimen (Skinner, 1953). As such, it was in cultural opposition to the eugenics movement of the turn of the century, which focused on heredity. The nature/nurture argument that also continues today is a manifestation of the tension between behaviorism and theories about the internal, unseen mind.

Behaviorism lost its place on center stage because it could not offer satisfactory explanations for the complexities of behavior that seemed to involve a foundational difference in ability, the reading rather than simple reception of the stimulus, an interpretation of meaning, and choice making based on that interpretation. As appears always the case in ascendant theories, behaviorism contained the seeds of its own destruction. Its dependence on concepts such as the conditioned reflex, the stimulus, and its reinforcement as well as the surprising diversity of responses[1] kept raising questions, the search for the answers of which drove theoreticians to the interior of the mind and cognitive processing.

The Comfort of Cognitivism

The historical reaction of cognitivism to behaviorism appeared early, fewer than two decades after Watson's 1913 behaviorist manifesto (Tolman, 1930). It was based on the interest of returning intention and desire to the study of human behavior and, as such, was a partial recuperation of ideas from Wundt and James while retaining the basic format of behaviorism. If behaviorism was the study of the context of behavior's appearances, cognitivism was the study of the "design of the internal machinery through whose functioning organisms are capable of behaving in context" (Schnaitter, 1987, p. 2). The causal linkage between stimulus and response was modified by slipping the operation of the organism's internal machinery in between. That linkage now became stimulus-organism-response-reinforcement, with the organism playing a determining role in the character of the stimulus, the choice of response, and the qualities of reinforcement.

The internal machinery of cognitivism has developed into a panoply of recognizable concepts that we currently use to explain a person's behavior.

Concepts such as personality, aptitudes, traits, attitudes, values, schemata, and scripts are all from this field. Each in some way is a mental structure that mediates the stimuli of the outside world, maintains and moderates the behavioral response of the organism, and designates the value of outcome (reinforcement) of the response.

Cognitivism declared itself the victor over behaviorism at the 1960 American Psychological Association convention (Hebb, 1960). (It was a little like a fraternal twin declaring a DNA victory over its sibling.) Its victory secure, it fell into a long, slow decline to its "dominant but dead" reputation within contemporary theory. Dominant-but-dead means most experimentalists use it as a theoretical backdrop to their work, but dislike much of what is inherently—and frustratingly—ineffable about this episte- mology. Thus, many experimentalists "put up" with cognitivism, flawed as it may be. That notwithstanding, nothing has risen to take cognitivism's place (Gibson, 2000; Robbins, Gosling, & Craik, 1999).

Media effects found the perfect partner in cognitivism. The relationship between media effects and cognitivism developed very early. L. L. Thurstone (Peterson & Thurstone, 1933; Thurstone, 1929, 1930) formulated the basic cognitivist media effects protocol in the late 1920s, using it to study the effects of motion pictures. His pre- and postexposure measurement of attitudes has remained the methodological mainstay of effects studies to this day.

Not all cognitivism serves media effects equally well, of course, because cognitivism is not a singular formulation but varies, importantly, across two dimensions: First, variants of cognitivism differ on whether the "internal machinery" is physiologically encoded or developed through socialization processes in a reprise of both the nature/nurture argument and the mind/ body dispute. Second, they vary across the character of the "stimulus." Does the stimulus literally make someone behave a certain way? Or is the stimu- lus subject to individual interpretation, which, if this is so, would determine how each individual responds to that stimulus (e.g., Tryon, 2002)?

And finally, there is one other argument—older than cognitivism or behav- iorism: Does consciousness, in and of itself, determine behavior independently of the stimulus? An effect such as a behavioral response must necessarily have a cause outside of itself, but an action—from some perspectives— can be its own cause. The question is simply stated: Can I act because I choose— without influence—to do so, or must there always be an agent of my actions? The question, of course, strikes to the heart of the meaning of an effect or the response of the individual (Levy, 2003).

This review of cognitivism leaves us with three issues hanging: (a) Is our cognitive development primarily a function of our genetics or widely adaptable to social processes? (b) Are the external stimuli received by us in the literal form of delivery, or do we somehow reconstitute them within our minds? (c) To what degree, if any, do we have conscious intentional control over our actions apart from whatever influence the stimulus might have? We will add two more to that list: the role of reinforcement and the force of the stimulus. We visit each of these contentions briefly.

Physiology or Social Development

In the physiological formulation (nature in the nature/nurture argument) of cognitive development, much (and ultimately nearly all) of the internal machinery is genetically predetermined, secure, and stable. Changes in the environment do not produce changes in the internal machinery but do produce predictable responses. In the early days of cognitive theory, these were called instincts and were considered hardwired prior to birth.

That concept still remains but much in the background. What replaced it were the concepts of imprinting from ethnology, "critical windows" from the acquisition of language, and the "perfectible brain" from human development. All three of these positions suggest that there is an open period, ranging from a few days to as many as 8 years, during which the brain completes its development in the critical areas of sexual orientation, language acquisition, and the formation of personality. Once these critical periods close, one cannot change the outcomes, although conscious overlays (such as learning a second language) can be achieved. For the physiological cognitivist, the essential or core person has been formed by age 12 or so. Social influences cannot undermine the core, and behavior that runs counter to it is considered temporary and unstable.

In the social developmental formulation (nurture of nature/nurture), the internal machinery is both formed and subject to reformulation through socialization processes. The work of completing "the person" may never be done and may always be at risk for, or open to, the possibility of change. Developmental cognitivists vary across the degree of openness to change available. Some adopt a critical period viewpoint and limit major change to childhood. Others believe that major change can and necessarily must occur across life's stages.

The social developmental formulation is the preferred position in media effects studies (see Figure 3.1).

In Figure 3.1, material practices of socialization operate on the brain/mind to produce an internal cognitive structure that is the proximal agent of some behavioral outcome. The empirical barrier to demonstrating the actual existence of a cognitive structure is noted, as is the range of cognitivist thought on this matter.

One can easily see why. If media are to have their most meaningful effects, then they have to participate in some way in the configuring or reconfiguring of the structures or processes that are the proximal cause of behavior. If those

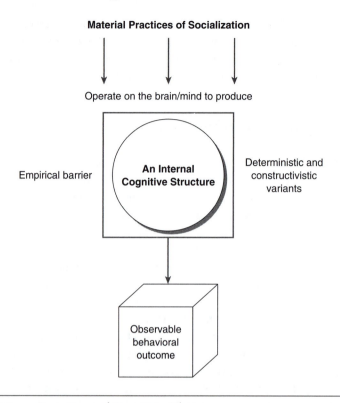

Figure 3.1   Basic Form of Cognitivist Theory

structures were entirely the results of physiological development rather than social development, then the long-term effects of the media would disappear, leaving only proximal, unstable effects. With respect to aggression, it means that media content might cause an immediate aggressive response but could not change the fundamental character of the individual. In the most open world of social developmental cognitivism, exposure to content becomes one of the agents of cognitive development that creates this fundamental character. Not only can content cause an immediate aggressive response, but it also can create a natural born killer as well.[2]

The Role of Reinforcement

There are two ways in which this cognitive development can perform as the proximal cause of one's behavior. One is in the process of reinforcement; the other is the force of the stimulus. Reinforcement is an issue of physiological or social development, and we will address it here. The force of the stimulus is a control issue addressed in the next section.

Cognitivism retains the behaviorist concept of reinforcement—the notion that there has to be a consequence to a response (action) that sustains the response or extinguishes it when there is no consequence (e.g., Tierney & Smith, 1997). But cognitivism does not pay much attention to the process of reinforcement in either its theorizing or in its analysis. The presence of predicted behavior is sufficient evidence that reinforcement has occurred. Where reinforcement does come into play is in the cognitivist concept of value structures. For the social developmental cognitivist, value structures are configurations of the mind that register the worth of something else (e.g., Nordlund & Garvill, 2002). They are internal reinforcement centers that govern the course of action by determining its value. In social behavior terms, a maladaptive value configuration supports the inappropriate action of the individual in ways that, for example, can disregard the stimulus (disconnected behavior) or be without regard to other consequences (e.g., empathetic failure; see Grimes et al., 2004).

If value structures are the product of DNA rather than socialization processes, the media scholar doesn't have much to say about the media's social influence on society. That influence would be slim to none. If people are both aggressive and enjoy watching violent content because they come from a long line of aggressors (remember that physiological connection requirement of behaviorism), what we do in the media is substantially less interesting. So it's understandable that media effects scholars always fall on the social development side of reinforcement.

There is a cost to that position, however. That cost requires three payments: The first is that media effects must differentiate across different socialization processes. The same content cannot have the same effect on everyone because not everyone is socialized in the same way. Consequently, if there are risks in content, those must be greater for some and lesser for others. That differentiation has left media effects scholars open to charges of racism, classism, and sexism. This charge is clarified when we consider first- and second-order risk. The first-order risk of media violence is that the viewer will become more aggressive. The second-order risk is that that viewer will aggress against me or mine. Media effects scholars do not fear for their own psyche. We do not fear our own; we fear the other—the poor, the disadvantaged, the less educated.

The second cost comes in understanding how media messages are shaped by the culture in which they emerge. What is it, then, that promotes the conditions under which this formation can develop? That set of circumstances, whatever it is, is more important than the media. The inconvenient implication for the causationist is that we should be focusing our time, money, and research expertise on those conditions rather than on media content.

The third cost involves the competitive strength of media content to operate as a socializing agent. For our concern about media content to be at its highest, a content form must be a strong competitor in a field of multiple, prospective socializing agents themselves fully capable of providing adequate—but different—resources for cognitive development. In that sort of figuration, certain content becomes inherently dangerous. If, on the other hand, the socializing force of media content is weak, or must have the support of other socializing agents, or only functions in the absence of other adequate socializing agents, the importance of content recedes. Media effects scholars contain that threat to their social importance by boldly and baldly dismissing other socializing agents. Huesmann, Lagerspetz, et al. (1984), for example, simply claim with no citation of evidence that "the mass media, especially television, have become socializers that compete in importance with home, school, and the neighborhood" (pp. 746–747).

Indeed, media scholars must hold to some such belief even in the presence of consistent evidence to the contrary (presented in a later section of this chapter). Consider what happens if they do not: The results across any of these three conditions are that media effects cannot be consistent and/or stable across large populations because both the processes and the content of socialization differ widely within these populations. In the first two conditions, the social environment is more important than media content as media content operates only in concert with a noncompetitive or reinforcing social environment. The third case requires the absence of other effective socializing agents—no parents, no peers, no other institutions that can effectively intervene. Again, that condition seems far more important to investigate than media themselves.

Traditional media effects scholars are the last of the mass media breed. They hold their theorizing fixed in time when the world of media could be adequately described as three networks reproducing the derivatives of each other's content. In that moment, they surrendered the central tenet of cognitivism's revolt against behaviorism: internal control of the stimulus's effect. Technology has clearly passed that "mass media moment," but its legacy lives on in the refusal of media effects scholars to consider the mise-en-scène of media consumption or to consider any form of interpretation as an intervening process. The ecology of consumption is addressed in the next chapter. It is to the location of control to which we now turn.

The Force of the Stimulus: External Versus Internal Control

The mechanism by which the stimulus results in a response is where the control argument centers. This issue can be identified as the force or the character of the stimulus. In the behaviorist realm, a stimulus is any change in the environment recognized by the organism. Recognition is demonstrated by the organism's response or change in behavior. To establish a light as a stimulus, all the behaviorist has to do is vary the characteristics of the light (e.g., color, duration, intensity) until the rat does something different. The rat, by generating something deemed to be a response, is considered to be under the external control of the light. It does not matter to the behaviorist what the light meant to the rat.

Depending on where she or he sits on the external/internal continuum, the media effects cognitivist has a different task. To begin with, we are no longer dealing with a simple on/off stimulus but rather a complex narrative text that is coded first in the deep structures of human semiotics and then in the multiple terms of a linguistic cultural group, its societal expression, its local social appropriation, and finally its immediate context of reception. (An example of the multiple positions on this issue can be found in the comparison of Zubov, 2004, and Brockmeier & Harré, 2001.) None of this matters for the strict externalist as long as the media text can be objectively specified and it elicits the expected response. For the strict externalist, the force of the stimulus is entirely encoded in the properties of the stimulus. It requires no processing by the individual, just as the rat did not have to think about what the light meant. From this perspective, the researcher can also vary the objective qualities of the text to elicit different kinds of responses—no different, really, than using, say, different light intensities to cue the rat to push a different pedal. The researcher holds that the characteristics of the text have objective qualities and that those qualities are the agent of the response. Control is firmly external to the respondent. Or, in that colorful behaviorist language, "the skin doesn't matter."

The skin starts to matter the moment the researcher holds that the text has to be "read" (interpreted) in some manner by the respondent. At this moment, control is shared and begins its movement to the internal side of the continuum. This march usually begins with some discussion of literacy. Literacy requirements are most clear in written texts, where if one is illiterate, the content cannot be accessed. But every medium carries its own literacy requirements (e.g., Kellner & Share, 2005; Potter, 2004). For example, the experienced video gamer can pick up the latest release and quickly discover the powers and abilities of friend and foe alike and begin immediately to participate in the game's narrative flow. For the inexperienced, there is no narrative flow, only a series of bewildering graphics and seemingly random events. The latter player does not know the means and conventions of play or the signs and portents of the display. She or he is illiterate. To become ideologically connected to the terms of the narrative, she or he will first have to become competent. Different media have higher or lower competency demands, but all have some (Norton-Meier, 2005).

Literacy, however, only opens the door to a full interpretive process that addresses the surface and extended meanings of the text, to its coloration by the technology of its presentation; to the ironic, comedic, and other configurative modalities; to the master contracts, genres, forms, and conventions that govern its construction and interpretation; to the development of close, implicative, and critical reading abilities; and to the extraction of the textual resources for improvisation, innovation, and invention in the performance ecology of the participant (J. Anderson & Meyer, 1987). At this point, we are a long, long way from the externalist position. In this full-blown internalist position, the response of the media participant is connected to the text in the same way that the architect is connected to the brick maker.

Media effects scholars have been criticized for their failure to deal with the critical interpretive skills that can be brought to play in the engagement of content (Couldry, 2004). Some defense can be mounted on their behalf by pointing out that much of the work (51% in the archive) has been directed toward children where there is at least some reason to believe that these critical interpretive skills may not be as highly developed. Nonetheless, most effects work shows little sophistication in accounting for interpretation, choosing to spend the time on what its critics consider to be scholastic definitions of content.[3]

It seems clear that both the strict externalist and strict internalist positions are untenable as the full-time understanding of how we engage media texts. We all have daily experiences where the same text has different consequences for different people,[4] and if everyone's interpretation were unique (using the word in its absolute form), there would be no common ground on which to communicate. The result is that research practice occurs in the big muddy field in between. That practice is opportunistic. Researchers will claim that content *is* of a particular kind that *will* produce a particular effect and therefore should be regulated (externalist position) and then recommend that children be enrolled in media literacy classes to provide them with the critical skills by which *they* can *control* the *consequences* of engagement (internalist position).

From Conscious Control to Agency

Given the demand of science for causality and media scholars' need to be seen as scientific, the acceptance of content as a direct cause of some large sociological process on their part is at least understandable. We can offer further unwanted sympathy if we consider the deus ex machina solution that cognitivism has had to build. Cognitivism, remember, moved the causal framework of behaviorism to behind the eyes and out of sight (the empirical barrier of Figure 3.1), where it could better represent human complexity. In the process, however, the theory lost its observable character and fell into constituting metaphysical structures (personality traits, values, attitudes, motives, schemata, scripts) to reach that complexity (Uttal, 2000). And when that didn't entirely work, it introduced latency, salience, activation, value-conflict, automaticity, and a host of other modifying conditions that would fill the explanatory holes. Cognitivism began to approach a chaos theory of the mind. At some point, it became easier for many theorists to revert to behaviorism and to effectively abandon internal control. It also occasioned a few theorists to say, "I think he did it because he wanted to. He willed it to be so." Whether we call it active interpretation, conscious control, or agency, any loss of causality is a problem for the scientific modernist. But it may be a matter of fact. Let's see if we can sort through the circumstances where we are willing to accept causality and those where it is more difficult to do so. We will do so by looking at immediate, long-term, and "ambush" effects, taking up immediate effects—immediately.

The Immediate Effect

For the animal behaviorist, the evidence for an immediate effect of a stimulus is relatively clear: A rat is introduced to an environment that has, among other things, a light (that is off), a food trough, and a foot pedal. During an initial period of acclimation, the rat investigates all the elements and, through trial and error, learns to push the foot pedal. In the conditioning period, the light goes on. The rat responds to the changed environment with rehearsed and unrehearsed behavior and, if the planned conditioning is to occur, pushes the foot pedal. A food pellet drops into the food trough. The next time the light goes on, there is much less unproductive behavior. The response latency (time between stimulus and response) declines rapidly. The rat's behavior has been conditioned as a response to the light.

The human cognitivist sets up a somewhat similar protocol, but with different evidentiary requirements. Respondents are introduced to an experimental setting and given a pretest that measures one's cognitive position on a topic. (Note that both the rat and the human respondent are in a controlled environment with few choices over stimuli or responses.) In the laboratory, the television set goes on, and a video clip with content relating to the pretest topic is shown. The pretest measurement instrument is now administered once again. Differences between the two administrations that are appropriate to the video content are attributed to respondent viewing. The cognitivist is not interested in the observable behavior of the check mark, however. The cognitivist wants to claim that the cognitive machinery— usually called attitudes—that motivates the check marking has been changed. To continue the parallel, it could be said that the respondent's attitude structure has been conditioned to the video clip.

Would we accept this evidence as a response caused by the content of the video? We think so. Let's simplify the example: At time one, you ask me, "What time is the movie?" I answer, "I don't know." You hand me the movie section of the paper, which I read. You ask again, "What time is the movie?" I say, "1:15." Unless I was lying in the first case or being inventive in the second, we have evidence of a direct effect of the media. Has there been a change of cognitive state? Certainly, the state of my knowledge about the movie time has changed.

Well, of course, this is obvious. So what raises our concern in the cognitivist example? Certainly, we can see that if the question is, "Is it OK to hit someone who is bothering you?" and the pretest answer is no but the posttest answer is yes, then the social implications of the change become worrisome. Furthermore, there is an added level of concern. That concern revolves around the issue of whether the immediate response is predictive of future responses. The cognitivist argument is that the cognitive machinery— one's attitude—has now been set, like the register of a computer, to respond to this generalized class of behavior (aggression) in a particular way. The response that the cognitivist is interested in is this preset attitude.

Are we willing to accept that response? Let's return to the simplified example: In that example, I changed my state of knowledge about the time of a movie by reading a newspaper. The change, however, is specific only for the circumstances of the question. I do not believe that all movies start at 1:15, and if you ask me about the starting time of another movie, I may well return to my initial state of "I don't know." Shouldn't the consequences of the attitude change hold only for the circumstances underlying the experiment? Shouldn't each respondent be free to behave in preconditioned ways outside of those circumstances? Those questions are unanswered by the experimental protocol.

How could we reasonably answer them? Let me seat you in a movie theater. The person next to you is making disgusting mouth noises while you are trying to enjoy the film. Immediately before you came to the theater, you participated in a communication experiment that showed a video clip demonstrating that it was OK to hit someone who was irritating you. You changed your pretest answer from no to yes on the posttest. Now in the movie theater, do you hit him? Do you hit her? The person sitting next to you is a 2-year-old child. Do you hit him? Do you hit her?[5]

Very likely, whatever the circumstance or the person, your first response will not be to strike the irritant without warning. You will shift uncomfortably in your seat, sigh obviously, glare at the person, and finally actually say something in an irritated voice. Might the ensuing exchange escalate to fisticuffs? It might, given supporting circumstances, but we bet the irritant throws the first punch. (Hope you win, but you both will be thrown out of the theater.) Whatever the case, your posttest answer is not a magic talisman that can predict what you will do. From the very beginning of attitudinal testing, the evidence has consistently been that results of a particular test do not generalize to other specific events. That is why we earlier noted that attitude formation and change research could be plausibly called "it depends" research: A lot simply depends on a multitude of variables.

The result is that we can accept changes in cognitive states from time one to time two. We can, by attending to media content, learn, opine, imitate, feel happy or sad until we forget, change our minds, adopt new behavior, or level out. Such changes, indeed, may be the reason why we are there in attendance. But we need not go beyond these transitive states. And because we are not starving rats in a cage or credit-hungry college students in an experiment, we may be in charge of when those transitive states do move into the future.

Long-Term Effects

Accepting immediate changes does not mean that we must accept a claim of response generalization or that we must accept that we have been preset to behave in a particular way in a long-lived fashion. The immediate effect of change may be an immediate effect and no more. Indeed, if a single, brief media presentation could affect long-term consequences, it seems that it would last only as long as the next presentation. Both response generalization and long-term effects require the formation and the hardening of some cognitive structure. This "hardening" must occur if a message's effect reaches beyond its initial presentation and sustains its consequences over time.

For most media scholars (e.g., Huesmann, Moise-Titus, Podolski, & Eron, 2003), long-term effects require repeated and extensive exposure to a message with respondents who are in a critical period of cognitive formation (generally 8–12 years old).[6] These requirements show up in longitudinal studies in which viewing behavior in the fourth to sixth grades are regressed against performance measures as an adult. In many of those studies, the evidence is present that children whose viewing history included extensive exposure to media violence report higher levels of adult social aggression as well.

Should that be a reason for concern? Might be, but let's consider the following. First, let us note that we will not take the usual critique of such studies. That critique engages the problem of demonstrating causality from correlational studies. That critique, in this case, is an irreducible "t'is/t'ain't" argument, which we can't settle. Correlational studies of media violence and adult social aggression will never reach the gold standard of causal evidence and can always be dismissed because of that failure. And the studies that we can run in this area that reach for the gold cannot extend into the future:[7] We cannot ethically constitute a research environment that we believe will take a child and create a social aggressor, just as we could not force a child to smoke to see if cancer develops. Interestingly, ardent advocates for causality have made the comparison to smoking and cancer. Those arguments of causality between smoking and cancer, however, were extensively supported by animal studies in which the operative chemicals in tobacco smoke were shown to be cancer agents. There is no such body of literature here.

Whether it is just a marker of a third variable or evidence of a cause, the correlational findings raise some interesting policy questions, but perhaps not the ones immediately apparent. To restate, the relationship is one in which extensive viewing in the formative years leads to reports of higher social aggression in adult years. During those formative years, then, some system must be in place that allows extensive, repeated viewing of particular content to occur. We may consider most media attendance to be a low-quality diversion, but any viewing is work; extensive viewing is extensive work. What is it that allows the child or even makes it worthwhile for the child to spend considerable time and effort in the attendance to media violence? And, at the opposite end of the correlation, what is it about the environment of the adult that makes social aggression an ostensibly successful strategy? These are fair questions because not every child views violence and not every adult who did view violence reports higher levels of social aggression. And this is where we again come under the watchful eye of the social critic because the answers to those questions almost always entail cultural circumstances that are not like our own. We are going to do something about media violence because those people do not supervise their children's viewing or because those adults do not live the life that we do, but we fail to ask the crucial question of why.

There is no question that media can play a part in developing knowledge—even knowledge that we consider wrong or false. It should not be surprising that narratives of violence can be a part of that knowledge. Some may believe the narratives to be true and behave accordingly; others, however, will hold them false and behave accordingly. No one will have media as the sole source of their knowledge because knowledge occurs in the interaction between the individual and the environment. There are other sources, and there are consequences. For one to hold something to be true in a nonpathological fashion, therefore, there will be a supporting matrix of sources, and the environment will reflect the consequences of that truth. It is truly a symptom of some pathology if a person adopts a position that has no support in that person's matrix of relationships and that fails to return an appropriate reinforcement from the environment. In fact, the strongest predictor of aggression is living in an environment where aggression is common (Huesmann & Malamuth, 1986).

The question for policy makers is not whether media content may play a part in creating an environment that supports aggressive behavior. Of course it can, and from oral traditions to classical myth to Punch and Judy to Grimm's fairy tales to comic books to movies to television to video games, it consistently has the resources to do so. The question is whether it is an appropriate focal point for social policy. We provide our answer near the end of this chapter.

Ambush Effects

Media scholars have developed a third class of effects that has appeared in their public writings and testimony. We will call them ambush effects. Ambush effects can be short or long term, though the evidence for them is always based on immediate-response change measures. Ambush effects occur when an individual is unexpectedly exposed to some content to which he or she would otherwise not be exposed. The ambush can also occur when the individual seeks certain content but is not prepared to manage that content (e.g., such as the shock of a seeing video or a photograph of a bloody car accident).

An example of an ambush effect warning—albeit for sexual content— appears in *Men's Health* (October, 2005, p. 48) in an article run directly underneath a picture of bikini-clad twins with the headline "Talking Dirty." The article reports a study published in the *Journal of Sex Research* (Taylor, 2005) in which college students were shown clips from TV comedies recognizable for their sexuality.[8] Respondents' attitudes were shown to be more permissive after exposure to the shows. (Note the standard, paper-and-pencil protocol.) Realistic sexual dialogue was said to be more influential than images and to be more influential for women than men. The article quotes the study's author as saying, "Talk about sex tends to slip past our parental radar more easily than sexual behaviors do. Fathers need to watch for both kinds of content."

We suspect that the concern expressed here is an extension of the findings to populations for which sexual behavior would entail considerably more risk—that is, much younger viewers in the 8- to 12-year-old category. The population typically tested by this research—college-aged students—would not seem to be vulnerable to the ambush. Many of them are sexually experienced, with the rest being not easily sexually impressionable—their attitudes toward sex having been formed.

In recognizing this anomaly, the author of this particular study does two things: First, because there were no significant main effects in the study, he implies that change may not have been possible because the respondents were "sexually experienced" (Taylor, 2005, p. 135). But, second, when partial support is found for one hypothesis, the researcher does not question the attitude change but concludes that it should have an even greater effect on younger viewers (Taylor, 2005, p. 136; and then ends with the ubiquitous call for more research). In other words, the theory cannot be falsified.

Second, increased permissiveness in this case means an average difference across 49 respondents of less than one unit of measurement on a set of multiunit rating scales. Interestingly, despite *Men's Health* reporting that attitudes "shifted toward permissiveness," there is no evidence of change because this is not a pre/post protocol. The scale, consequently, has no anchor in the particular because we do not know its nontreatment value for these 49 respondents. Equally interesting, the same respondents' estimates of their peers' sexual activity did not vary across treatments. Our conclusion is that where there is an external, empirical register to be evaluated rather than a transitory state of mind, the content has no effect.

Effects studies are replete with this flippant attitude toward cognitive theory. On one hand, we are to be concerned that socialization by the media creates long-term socially significant effects through the production of stable cognitive structures that consistently influence behavior. On the other hand, these same researchers continually produce evidence that these same cognitive structures can be changed in a single short session of exposure to selected media content. The evidence presented in support of the media as a socializing agent is also evidence that there either are no such cognitive structures (e.g., behavior is much more opportunistic and much less teleological) or that the structures themselves are not stable.

The respondents in this study were recruited from an introductory communication class and rewarded with extra credit. In this process, they entered into a social contract with the researcher—do this work, get paid in credit. What is the work? Can I do it? How do I do it well? These are all natural questions that get answered when the respondent sits down to fill out forms that are similar to multiple-choice tests. Some respondents then view sexy television and are subsequently asked to identify their position on a set of five items. The programs from which the treatment segments were selected are among the most popular for college-aged viewers. It would be more than remarkable if this respondent group was unfamiliar with or had not attended to the content on several occasions prior to the experiment. The content presented is successful because it connects to human sexual arousal—beautiful young people talking about sex, talking about wanting sex, talking about the joys of sex. In the process of viewing this content, the respondent has indicated that she or he believes it to be realistic and is now asked for her or his position. All of these are cues for what the social contract requires, what social scientists call a demand effect. Clearly, we have to admit to the possibility that the social context of the research protocol may be participating in the outcome even if in unknown ways.

Of course, if sexually charged dialogue from a television comedy (e.g., *Friends*) can significantly alter sexual behavior, what will witty, slightly salacious conversation on a dinner date accomplish? (Who knows, but at least the young lovers are being careful about it as teenage pregnancy rates are now at their lowest since record keeping began in 1940.) It often seems as though media researchers presume that people have none but a life in the media. People hang out, hook up, and live in face-to-face relationships every day.

Finally, the *Men's Health* article clearly implies that daughters are more vulnerable and of greater concern. Are we not concerned if boys are more permissive? Or are the *Men's Health* editors reproducing gender stereotypes that boys will be boys? In all of effects studies, one will find these interesting intersections of science and moral judgment. Taylor (2005) clearly believes that being more permissive is a problem, just as other researchers believe that more vigorous play in a field hockey game is a problem. From a pure health standard, being more permissive (which may simply mean being less negative about permissiveness) may not be a problem. Whereas engaging in sexual activity without adequate safeguards certainly would. It is, of course, this extension from the socially trivial to the socially important that gives media effects studies their standing by association. Something it cannot seem to gain by the facts of the case.

This effort to heighten the consequence of an ambush is furthered by coupling the effect with a "drug" metaphor that is used to underscore the danger to children. That argument goes something like this: (a) Children are at risk because violent content is inherently attractive. (b) Violent content shows effective strategies of living in the world to an otherwise naive and inexperienced child. And (c) the narratives of violent content appear to transfer as effective performances in one's environment when in fact they are dysfunctional.

The possibility of ambush by a recreational drug like content has been the justification for calls for suppression of content, for the regulations that developed the V-chip technology now available on all television sets (13 inch or larger), and, most recently, for television remotes that would only tune to family tier programming (rtsp://video.c-span.org/15days/e121205_decency.rm).

In response, the critique of ambush effects is its own list: that the concept requires (a) the presumption of a naïveté in the respondent, (b) a *Pleasantville* social context for that respondent, (c) an absence of real-life modeling experiences, (d) the absence of exposure to content that is commonly available, (e) the instantaneous formation or reformation of cognitive structures that support some negative activity, and (f) the lack of correctives within the ecology of action. Can we be ambushed by content for which we are not prepared? Of course. It is a commonplace happenstance in the media, in the classroom, in an ordinary conversation.

Summary

Media effects and cognitivism are celebrating nearly 80 years of marital bliss. This relationship is a textbook example of how one's theory and methodology constitute the object of analysis. Cognitivism allows us to posit an effect of great social significance based on socially trivial behaviors. In nearly 80% of the studies investigated here, the measures of aggression were paper-and-pencil reports—often simple check marks on a scale. It is the cognitivist theory that allows us to translate these check marks into mental states that are the precursors of the targeted behavior. There are few studies that investigate whether the predicted behavior actually occurs (and those few studies indicate that it does not).

One can easily see why. If the standard of analysis was that the researcher had to trace the consequences of exposure to forms of content to actual behavior in social contexts, the methodological requirements would be prohibitive given the current economic climate of media research. It would take years to conduct such research, and it would be beyond all but the most sophisticated and well-funded of researchers.

Social science is always a product of the social milieu. If one applied a "freakenomics" analysis to media research, one would find the convergence of technology, cognitive theory, and methodology; the post–World War II, explosive growth of the university; and first the fears of the liberal community and now the fears of the conservatives to be driving forces—and more will be discovered—behind the continued, repetitious, and, in the actual social practice of media use, virtually ignored studies of media effects.

Notes

1. It is not unusual in animal behavioral studies that up to 50% of the animals will not adapt to the trial.

2. And for the traditional media effects scholar, it is one that apparently outperforms the family, the peer group, the educational apparati, and other ideological systems such as church and sodality. Or, at least so it would seem, as the typical longitudinal effects study (e.g., Huesmann et al., 2003) does not provide controls for such influences.

3. One of the keys to these definitions has been the "intent to harm"—it's not violence without that intent. What happens if the participant does not read that intent or if the participant inserts that intent in the text?

4. One could, of course, argue that the differences in ostensible meaning are variations caused by different socialization processes and that, for a given socialized class, the stimulus is still evoking the response. Differences in what something means are merely reflective of different socializations.

5. If at this point, dear reader, if you are thinking, "I wouldn't, but I know people who would," you have taken yourself into the characterization of the Other. In your mind's eye, what does that "Other" look like?

6. This claim of a modulated relationship is true of Huesmann's scholarship but not of his public pronouncements in which he has been known to claim that every exposure to violent content raises the likelihood of social aggression.

7. It is generally accepted that experimental studies are the gold standard for causal claims. The typical experiment, however, does not meet the "Greene Test" (Greene, 1984), in which both the cognitive structure and the manner of its performance have to be demonstrated.

8. Laramie Taylor, PhD, is a member of the Aggression Research Group at the University of Michigan under the directorship of L. Rowell Huesmann.

4

The Social Scientific "Theory" That Never Quite Fit

A s we learned in Chapter 3, theories, whether in the social sciences, natural sciences, or biological sciences, help us better categorize and come to better understand how the world works. Theories, then, are supposed to make the world more explicable, more understandable, less confusing. However, some of the theories generated by the causationists have done the opposite. Their theories seem to confuse things more than they elucidate them.

Theories in the social sciences are often formulated through laboratory research. But that's only one way to develop a theory. There are other ways that don't rely on some sort of stimulus-response model that's replicated in a lab. And, without giving away the punch line just yet, we think most causationists' emphasis on laboratory research, as well as the claim that media violence research is strictly an empirically based, objective, numerically quantifiable, wholly dispassionate endeavor, is where things begin to get off track. Let us explain.

Any theory that scientists use to explain the world has four components: It must define the reality, context, environment, or domain in which it operates. Therefore, if we were to develop a theory of crime, we would likely be looking at the context or environment in which people who commit crimes live. Oftentimes, they live in a troubled, panicked world. They are "at wit's end," "at the end of their tether"; name the cliché. And whatever cliché one chooses, it denotes a desperation, a just-barely-able-to-control-the-situation denotation. That state of affairs can define one's reality, one's perceived place in the world. In any event, this area of study is usually known as the *ontological,* the study of being, of what it means to be in the world, what that person's reality in that world is like. In research analysis, it is concerned with definitions such as media violence or aggression.

We're already discussed in the previous chapter the second component, which deals with issues of how we know what we know so that we can decide, commit, and eventually act. That, of course, is *epistemology:* the study of knowledge. The third component is the study of the way in which people behave or otherwise act on what they think or believe. That is, how do they put into practice their fear of something, desire for something, dislike of another person, and so on? That's known as *praxeology:* the study of the engagement of a belief with the intention of acting on that belief.

The fourth component is the study of values—the way in which the predicted behavior (predicted by a theory) affects one's surrounding environment on the dimension of value. That is, if media violence causes social aggression, then what does that behavior imply for society? What will become of society with respect to social values if aggressive behavior is allowed to run rampant in the culture? This part of theory development is known as *axiology.*

The media effects literature is dreadfully inconsistent and contradictory with respect to these four components—thus the specter of confusion rather than elucidation. That, then, that theory generated by causationists (in particular) seems to confuse matters more than elucidate them. That stipulated, what has been reasonably consistent has been the finding of a statistical association between some conditions of viewing media violence and gross forms of behavior labeled as "aggression" at least by research psychologists but not necessarily by ordinary folk (Kane, Joseph, & Tedeschi, 1976). No theoretical position or methodology of which your authors are aware denies that viewing/using/participating in media violence can be associated with forms of social aggression (everything from having a mild argument to threatening one's father with a club; Belson, 1967). But it is the character and significance of that association that has been and still is hotly debated.

Certainly, causality is a central tenet of science. Random events are only so in appearance, which reminds us of that famous phrase in philosophy: Somewhere a butterfly has flapped its wing (and, through a long chain of connected events, a hurricane eventually results). Spontaneity as an explanation is frowned upon by scientists, and the individual's freedom to intervene in the causal chain of events and change things is either ignored or outright rejected. That's because individual actions, which are not locked in a casual chain, have the fragrance of randomness, spontaneity, and thus unpredictability—a condition with which scientists are quite uncomfortable. The struggle over causality in human behavior is still in full engagement. In his September 20, 1971, *Time* magazine cover story (http://www.time.com/time/magazine/article/0,9171,909994,00.html), the behaviorist B. F. Skinner claimed that there was nothing special about him. Anyone starting with the same genetic resources and given the same history of behavioral conditioning could have achieved whatever greatness he had. He was a fully caused being in search of being the cause of the behavior of others (Skinner, 1948).

Skinner may well represent the apogee of causality as the explanation of human behavior as 50 years before, James (1890) had represented its perigee in the arc of psychology by allowing for an individual's free will to act. These two theorists clearly anchor the poles of causality and the freedom to act independently in the sphere of human theory. On the one side of this arc, aggressive behavior is a necessary consequent that is inexorably driven by exposure. On the other, aggressive behavior is a possibility, but not guaranteed or otherwise fixed, outcome, one in which media content can be used as a resource. Both of these interpretations can be supported by the very same data.

The intriguing question for an epistemologist is, How does the scientific argument of effects change its predominance from the Schramm et al. (1961) position that it is children "who use television rather than television that uses them" (p. 1) to the Anderson/Bushman/Huesmann causationist claim, which asserts that television can change the otherwise psychologically well child (Grimes et al., 2004) to an aggression pathology? We believe the strength of the causationist pathology argument comes about because of some technical issues that pertain to the research and some cultural issues that pertain to the media and its audiences. We visit these in turn.

The Technical Issues

As we pointed out in the previous chapter, cognitivism cannot be engaged empirically. Cognitivism and theoretical physics share the same metaphysical weakness: One must infer outcomes in both; directly observed outcomes are not possible. In both cases, we are left to read tracks and tracings that reach their clarity only inside the theory that motivates the observation to begin with. It is the measurement device itself that creates the empirical event that can be directly observed. In crass terms, what the media cognitivist needs is a measurement protocol that will reliably change values in, say, a preexposure, postexposure analysis. Given that, the theory will assign the change to an unseen cognitivist concept such as intentions, values, attitudes, scripts, or schemata, all of which function in the same way to predict subsequent behavior.

As noted earlier, the protocol that provides for the cognitivist argument came very early on the scene. Thurstone (1928, 1929, 1930, 1931) and Peterson and Thurstone (1933) developed the "attitude scale"–based protocol that, in its Likert simplifications (i.e., **Good** ___/___/___/___/___/___/___**Bad**), remains as the foundational measurement scheme. It is a preexposure, postexposure design with respondents indicating their agreement or disagreement on each of 100 statements drawn from the content of the motion picture to be viewed. Peterson and Thurstone (1933) note,

> The experiments reported in this paper include studies of the effect of a single motion picture on attitudes, the cumulative effect of two or more pictures pertaining to the same issue, the difference in the effect of a motion picture on groups of different ages, and the persistence of the effect of the motion pictures. (p. xvii)

This is the basic way of doing things for the cognitive analysis of immediate, cumulative, and long-term effects reported in the cognitive studies in the media violence/aggression archive.

This way of doing things has become so ingrained that it has become the unquestioned and unquestionable method of gathering knowledge in this research area (Latour, 1987). Potter (1988; both a causationist and interventionist) calls it axiomatic:

> It must be assumed that individuals have attitudes, that they are aware of their attitudes, and that they are able to express their attitudes accurately to researchers. We may feel uncomfortable accepting these axioms from a philosophical point of view, but we must accept them if we are to conduct social science research. (p. 36)

Potter's claim represents the typical parochial perspective of cognitivist effects, parochial because there are several approaches through which we can conduct social science research—psychoanalytical, semiotic, uses and gratifications, symbolic interaction, and social action, to name just five— that depend on none of his three axioms. The problem for Potter's epistemic community is that the axiomatic standing of the way it does things precludes that community's critical examination of itself. If it's axiomatic, then that ends the discussion ipso facto. The result is that the findings tell us nothing about the cultural or social conditions of what constitutes the reception, interpretation, and subsequent cognitive formation and behavioral outcomes that also determine people's behaviors.

Definition of Aggression

The second technical issue involves the definition of aggression. We will take up this issue extensively in the next chapter. Let us presage that work with the following discussion: To measure a person's aggressive tendencies for the purpose of doing media violence research, aggression has to be defined as a cognitive structure rather than a behavioral expression. In cognitivism, behavioral expressions are only the surface representation of a controlling cognitive structure. C. Anderson and Huesmann (2003) summarize the achievement of this definition: "Like most psychologists, we define human aggression as *behavior directed toward another individual carried out with the proximate (immediate) intent to cause harm. . . .* Actual harm is not required" (p. 298). Although seemingly behaviorally grounded, what this definition does is to allow the researcher to measure the *intent to cause harm* to another as that which is the distinguishing feature of the behavior. The definition fits hand in glove with the typical paper-and-pencil cognitivist measurement protocol. Changes on a scale of intent to harm are sufficient evidence of increased aggression.

The result of the intent-to-harm criterion is that the literature is replete with creative solutions that offer surrogates for violence, everything from children punching a bounce-back toy, to college students delivering ostensible shocks as grades for English themes, to middle schoolers' field hockey play, to young children "having more aggressive thoughts." Creative as these solutions are, they raise a number of questions about the components, conditions, and behaviors that fall under the terms *violence* and *aggression*. Savage (2004) states unequivocally that "the body of published, empirical evidence on this topic does not establish that viewing violent portrayals causes crime" (p. 123). Cantor (2000), on the other hand, although acknowledging that measures range from the trivial to the serious, holds that it is well established that media violence leads to higher levels of *antisocial behavior*. So what are we actually talking about? It appears that we are talking about nearly anything that can be considered "not nice," from "hostile thoughts" to "flipping off" one's fellow drivers to more active play in a contact sport.

Paik and Comstock (1994; both are causationists) provide two important insights here: First, the strength of the relationship between viewing and aggression decreases as the aggression measures become more realistic and the aggression more severe. Second, observing even staged aggression has more consequence than viewing mediated aggression. These two insights strike at the social significance of the media violence/aggression issue.

What the media effects field has not done (and its funding agencies have failed to advance) is a systematic analysis of the construct of aggression to arrive at a coherent protocol of measurement that is predictive of behavior. The result, as we have seen, is that aggression is defined by whatever operational definition researchers can convince their peer reviewers stands for, well, aggression. Furthermore, the operational definitions are not ordinarily themselves the behavior they purport to measure. They are, rather, paper-and-pencil measures that are interpreted by researchers to identify such behaviors. In substantive epidemiology studies, such as smoking and cancer, the criterion measures were actual deaths from cancer and confirmed diagnoses of cancer. They were not higher scores on self-report items such as "I believe I have lung cancer" or in peer reports such as "I believe he is sicker than I."

Until some better way to measure aggression is agreed to (a better way that we will suggest in this book), traditionalists among media effects scholars are simply engaging in exercises in abstraction. And that's the problem: At a sufficient distance in the abstract, all things, however disparate, converge to a single point, a single explanation.

Definition of Violent Content

The third technical issue is the definition of content violence. The behaviorist lineage of cognitivism requires that the properties of the content stimulus be objective and that its engagement be literal. The National Television Violence Study (NTVS; Federman, 1997) concludes, "The most critical aspect for any study of television violence is the definition that is employed to identify acts classified as 'violent'" (p. 41). It reaches this conclusion after declaring that "there is no single commonly accepted definition of violence in the research literature" (p. 37). It then goes on to offer its own definition that is composed of three parts: "credible threats of violence, behavioral acts [of violence], and depictions of harmful consequences of violence" (p. 55).[1]

Neither objectivity nor literal engagement is achieved in this language-based definition. Obviously, you and we could disagree on what might be a credible threat of violence. What is credible? What is a threat? And still yet, what is violence? Both objectivity and literalness are achieved in the coding process in which coders are brought into agreement as to what represents violence and are trained in interpreting that representation in particular ways. Consequently, you, we, and a coder might disagree on what is a credible threat of violence, but the coder's decision would count and ours would not.

Because you and we were not trained as coders, we still do not know what constitutes any of the elements of the definition. We are left in the reading of the report to substitute our own practical definition of what these elements might be. The problem arises when our very work-a-day definition has little correspondence to the very technical definition of the researchers.

We would argue that the technical definition grossly inflates what is considered violent programming. For example, the typical opening of a courtroom drama, where a dead body has been found on the gritty streets of the city, would be constituted as an incidence of violence under the third component of the definition (see, e.g., Federman, 1997, p. 55). The presence of this one coded act also codes the whole program as violent (p. 85), leading to the NTVS's conclusion that 57% of the sampled programs are violent. But that opening scene may represent less than 5% of the total program content. To classify it as violent in the same way that we might classify *Kill Bill* as violent makes little practical sense but a great deal of sense to the causationist project. The more violence that is found, the greater the threat, and the more important the work.

We see the pressure of this social significance in the work done for the NTVS by the University of Texas at Austin group. Charged with studying violence in "television programming which represents or purports to represent the 'real world'" (Federman, 1998, p. 54), this group modifies the definition to include "talk about violence." Why do they do that? Because they are studying news programs that do not ordinarily show the dead bodies they talk about. The irony of this definition is that should the researchers report their findings on some television news program, their segment would, of course, be coded as violent. Again, we see that the prevalence of violence in fictional or reality programming depends entirely on the manner in which violent content is defined.

The economics of scholarship, which demands social significance, disciplinary legitimacy, and individual achievement, forces the definitions of both aggression and violent content to expand. Such a demand would be fine *if* there were empirical correlates to those definitions. But, without an empirical evidentiary base, matters quickly get out of hand. Definitions of aggression and media violence proliferate without the benefit of the economics of scholarship to intervene. Just as classical economics basically relies on the scarcity of wealth, as well as the demand of society for access to that wealth, the economics of social science demands the same. Not every behavior can be defined as "aggressive," not every media presentation as "violent." But without a fundamental scarcity of class membership in that which is "aggressive" or "violent," proliferation of membership explodes. And with it, meaning disappears. The fact that we will continue to trumpet grave concerns about the media violence/aggression connection without any reference to a decade-long decline in violent crime is good evidence as to why we ought to heed the restraining economic forces of science.

Together, the definitions of aggression and violence and the protocol that connects them form the center of a practice of science that is firmly under the control of the researcher. In its bizarre ontological and epistemological purview, it will nearly always work such that the occasional failures can be easily understood as the failure to properly draw up the items for the scale, not the absence of an effect (J. Anderson, 1996). The continuing work in a normalized science field is that of accretion—the steady effort to find the scope and exceptions of the known operation. And so we see in the archive the repetitive application across technology, media, content, and subject groups. Each variation provides a new opportunity for the reproduction of research.

Post Hoc Theory

The final technical issue has to do with the manner in which theory has been articulated and applied from the cognitivist position. We begin this comment by noting once again that the protocols for associating the viewing of media violence with some ostensible measurement of aggression have existed at least from the Payne studies reported in the early 1930s. In this regard, the empirical side of the issue has been reasonably stable. What has been very unstable has been the theorizing that has attempted to understand the finding. Eron (1987) traces those attempts across the 22-year longitudinal study he conducted with his colleagues:

> Over the course of a 22-year longitudinal study, it has been possible to interpret and reinterpret findings in light of the current and developing advances in behavior theory. For example, although our original hypotheses, methods, and findings in the middle and late 1950s were couched in terms of Hull-Spence theory (Eron, Laulicht, Walder, Farber, & Spiegel, 1961), by the early 1970s our findings were interpreted to fit a Skinnerian model, and our conclusions and recommendations were cast in behavior analytic terms (Eron, Walder, & Lefkowitz, 1971). In the mid 1970s, the relevance of social learning theory became apparent, especially learning by imitation, and it was possible to interpret the findings and make suggestions for child rearing according to that model (Lefkowitz, Walder, & Huesmann, 1977). Now, in the mid 1980s, we explain our findings in the light of a more cognitive framework (Huesmann, Eron, Lefkowitz, & Walder, 1984). (p. 435)

Eron (1987) goes on to state that he does not expect the current theoretical orientation of the study to be the final one. One begins to suspect that this is the pattern of an empirical finding in search of an adequate explanation. Apparently, it has yet to be found. C. Anderson in Anderson and Dill (2000) presents the general affective aggression model (GAAM), claiming that

> the model integrates existing theory and data concerning the learning, development, instigation, and expression of human aggression. It does so by noting that the enactment of aggression is largely based on knowledge structures (e.g., scripts, schemas) created by social learning processes. (p. 773)

GAAM itself doesn't last very long. Barely born, it quickly loses its affective dimension. C. Anderson explains in Anderson and Bushman (2002a):

> Specifically, we have dropped the "affective" part of the earlier general affective aggression model, based on the new and broadening definitions of the proximate and ultimate goals of aggression elucidated in Bushman & Anderson (2001). (p. 33)

One way to interpret this flow of theory is to hold that theory development is progressive. That it makes a continually better approximation of reality and each theoretical development is an improvement over the past. The reader can certainly see that position in the language of the quotations. To adopt that position, however, one would have to say that the progress of science in this one field has been breathtaking. Another explanation, the one that we have used, is that there is no material anchor for the theorizing—that it represents one metaphysical failure after another. What we do believe to be present, nonetheless, is a continuing struggle to contain the finding to that of one-directional causation. Anderson and Colvin (Chapter 5, this volume) have found that the majority of experimental studies in their sample reported that any relationship in media effects was at least conditional on other variables, and often the relationship was multidirectional.

But it would appear that those findings are not acceptable. One can read the history as showing that theories that allow conditional or limited effects are discarded until a universal, one-directional effect can be theorized. That achievement is reached in Huesmann et al. (2003): "We need to be aware that media violence can affect any child from any family. The psychological laws of observational learning, habituation/desensitization, priming, and excitation transfer are immutable and universal" (p. 218). Perhaps such laws are immutable and universal (though they may also be a surprise to other members of the field), but at least we suspect that they do not operate in the way Huesmann et al. expect, as our analysis of the media as a socializing agent suggests.

Media as a Socializing Agent

In our tour of the epistemological foundations of media effects, we found that media scholars would have a necessary preference for social processes as the basis of cognitive development. Contrary to what is common in social theory, cognitivism has not been able to conventionalize its position on the requirements of a socializing agent that brings about aggression in the presence of media violence (thereby failing to do what seasoned, mature social theory does). As a result, researchers have a great deal of freedom in making claims about the constitution and power of any possible influence agent. There are some limitations, however, including (a) the limited power of a single agent, (b) the reciprocity of the socialized, (c) the predispositions and psychopathologies of the socialized, and (d) the social constitution of interpretation. Let us explain to what each of these, (a) through (d), is referring.

The Single Agent Problem

A given socializing agent does not stand alone but works in concert or in competition with others (Kochanska & Aksan, 2004; Schecter & Bayley, 2004; Vandell, 2000). The most effective socialization will occur when multiple sources are in agreement as to goals and behavior. Kiesner and Kerr (2004), for example, as editors of their special issue on adolescent problem behavior in the *Journal of Adolescence,* show that it is the "reciprocal influences of parenting practices and deviant peer process [that] combine [with institutional opportunities] to create individuals [who exhibit problem behavior]" (p. 493).

Because effects scholars pay almost no attention to the provenance of parenting, peer processes, and institutional influence (J. Anderson, in press), the subtext of effects is that of a child stolen from an otherwise loving family by the irresistible influence of media violence. Lee (2001) describes this as "panic about the disappearance of childhood," which he goes on to describe as a panic about the inability of adults to control and censor the childhood of their children and (perhaps particularly) of the children of others. We will address this issue in a later chapter on the "moral panic" that society envelops around childhood. And in that insight, the movements to control and censor media become better understood.

Reciprocity of the Socialized

Child development literature has consistently shown that socialization proceeds with, if not the consent, then at least the participation of the socialized (Martin & Ruble, 2004). Bell (1979) has shown, for example, that even before the onset of language, children are making their requirements known and resisting the attempts to shape behavior in particular directions (see also Potegal & Archer, 2004). Clearly, the aggressively motivated may have their aggressive tendencies reinforced by the media and may well learn effective expressions of aggression from the media. On the other hand, those not so inclined are unlikely to be "turned" to aggression (Grimes & Bergen, 2001; Grimes et al., 2004). For the meek of heart, the content neither makes sense as a lifestyle nor is there a pattern of performance in which the content can be activated.

But is the fact that the aggressive of us can feed our aggression and learn techniques sufficient to raise the media to a level of social problem? The answer to this question—and one of the most important points of this book—lies in whether the media provide a *unique resource* for those ends. And here we have to consider the attraction of media as a singular influence. If media are a unique influence that stand above, or are as important as, the social, economic, and educational levels of the family, peer processes, the community in which one lives, and the social constructs of the larger society, then at least some part of the problem of violence (declining as it is) can be solved with no effort toward social justice, economic opportunity, or educational equality. In other words, media violence lets us off the hook: Whatever we might do to change society with respect to equity issues—economic, educational, whatever—it all comes to naught because of the ubiquitous—and pernicious—mass media. So . . . why try?

Predispositions of the Socialized

Media effects scholars have been surprisingly simplistic in their approach to the respondent in their studies. Few studies investigate the individual predispositions toward aggression or the psychopathologies that support deviance. Grimes and Bergen (2001) have pointed out that most studies work from the presupposition of the normalcy of nonaggression—a sort of extension of the Lake Woebegone convention where all children are not only good looking and above average but also of the temperate kind.

Clearly not the classic Freudian picture of the child being the pure expression of the pleasure principle. Nor is it the conclusion of U.S. developmental psychology (Bremer & Fogel, 2001; Ehrler, Evans, & McGhee, 1999; Grigsby, 1994; Teglasi, 1998). J. R. Udry (1994) quite directly concludes that biologically based predispositions have greater predictive power in assessing deviant behavior than the social or environmental factors that shape the manifestation of that behavior. Children start out differently with different consequences for who they become and how they behave.

We can immediately recognize this position as part of the continuing nature/nurture debate that has been in the human conversation for several centuries. But the argument also moves forward in development to where nature and nurture have worked their stuff to constitute the individual personality. That personality now becomes part of the resources of interpretation. And, according to Ehrler et al. (1999), that personality makes a difference in predicting children's deviant behavior (see also Brook, Whitman, & Gordon, 1981; MacDonald, 1984; Roe, 1995).

Social Constitution of Interpretation

The epistemological theory that is the foundation of the causationists (J. Anderson, 1996; Nagel, 1961) is the theory that holds that all explanations must emanate from the individual. An effect of the media, then, must be entirely explainable as a person-by-person consequence of each exposure. There can be no social nexus that provides the fundamental basis of action.

Niklas Luhmann's publication of *Social Systems* (available in English translation in 1995) marked a significant call for the reconceptualization of the variable "social influence" (Vanderstraeten, 2000). Luhmann, a systems theorist, argues against methodological individualism. He states in his *Essays on Self-Reference* (1990) that communication "is produced by the network of communication not by some kind of inherent power of consciousness nor by the inherent quality of the information" (p. 3). What Luhmann is arguing is that mass communication's *effect* on a culture is measured by myriad social influences that move a *society,* not necessarily an individual.

But "inherent quality of the information" is indeed, as we have seen, the stock and trade of the effects scholar. The concept of violent content must not vary between or among individuals if it is to serve as an agent of aggression, according to the causationists. If this is so, one has to believe in the doctrine of literal meaning. And in that doctrine, content has to control any individual's interpretation of it.

Is that the case? Consider three 12-year-olds watching *Pulp Fiction* (a film well marked by graphic violence but described on John Travolta's official Web site as "a sometimes violent but always entertaining film" [www.travolta.com, accessed January 26, 2005]). One of the viewers says, "Oh, that's gross. I love watching that kind of stuff." Another, "Oh that's gross. I want to do that to my teacher." And the third says, "Oh that's gross, I don't want to watch this anymore." Each viewer interprets the content as "gross," but the consequences of that interpretation (and consequently its meaning) are quite different. The necessary conclusion is that we can agree on the characteristics of content (even Travolta's publicist thinks it's violent), but its meaning—its consequent—remains indeterminate.

It is not in the effects scholar's best interests to problematize meaning. If meaning is handed off to some other process than attending to kinds of content, the effects paradigm falls apart. It becomes some form of uses and gratifications or—weaker still—active audience and activated text argument. Both of these cast the politically active effects scholar as some sort of latter-day temperance unionist when clearly the role they are auditioning for is the objective scientist, one coolly testifying to what, of course, is true.

When one does argue for multilayered meaning making—as Luhmann (1990, 1995) argues we must—that moves meaning making outside content characteristics and individual consciousness. That, in turn, means we have to find meaning as social processes—that "network of communication" of which Luhmann speaks. When social processes are used to explain how messages are decoded, that suggests a message is not in the individual's decoding of it but in the social practices that are accorded to it. There is nothing inherent about violent content or in the desire to "do that to my teacher" that leads one to be aggressive.[2] Just as the socialization of the individual depends on the concert of a constellation of influences, so too does the meaningfulness of a message depend on the sociological framework of interpretation.

This conclusion leads us back to what is permissible, which is made possible by community standards and practices. What behavior is allowed in the schoolyard, on the sports field, during the commute to work? Are the standards and practices that define acceptable behavior the necessary element that constitutes the media violence-aggression relationship? If they are, then much of what we look at in the research on media violence is a cultural clash between those who have voice, which allows them to be definers of standards, and those who do not. Topics we take up next.

The Cultural Issues

The analysis of cultural issues starts with the assumption that science is a message among messages to be put to use within the separate purposes of different cultural stakeholders. And so the argument that we would advance is threefold: First, the media-as-dangerous arguments, which have reigned for more than 80 years, are class based. Second, the causationist argument allows us to understand the bully and the criminal as a failure of the family (not ours, of course, but those allowing these 8- to 9-year-old children to consume violent media) and to understand the media as singular threats to "family values." And third, both the causationist and contributionist arguments allow us to deflect social reform from the much more difficult issues of racial justice, economic opportunity, and educational equality.

Class-Based Sensibilities

Georges Bizet's 1875 opera *Carmen* is full of violence and sexual intrigue, and it ends with the enraged murder of a beautiful woman. Though filmed a number of times and currently available on DVD, we have yet to find it—or any other opera for that matter—as an object of concern in an archive of more than 1,000 media violence/aggression-related journal articles now under a cultural-analytic study at the University of Utah (J. Anderson, in press). This notation of its absence is both playful and serious. It is playful because we would never expect opera to be a cause for concern in contemporary U.S. society (though it has an uproarious past). And it is serious, just for the same reason. We are not concerned about opera because of our vision of its audience as highly educated, moneyed, high-class, cultured people who would never consider mugging someone on the street. It is the persistence of these class-based fears that provides the sociological motivation for the persistence of research work that had long before completed its contribution.

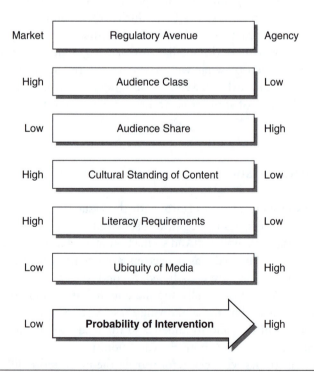

Market	Regulatory Avenue	Agency
High	Audience Class	Low
Low	Audience Share	High
High	Cultural Standing of Content	Low
High	Literacy Requirements	Low
Low	Ubiquity of Media	High
Low	**Probability of Intervention**	High

Figure 4.1   Conditions of Intervention by the Academy

Our preliminary examination of the archive on this issue indicates that there are six dimensions that predict scholarly concern over the media: the avenue of regulation, audience class, share of that audience, cultural standing of the content, the literacy requirements for engaging that content, and the availability (or ubiquity quotient) of the medium. Concern over the media will be highest when the class of the audience is low (mass media are the media of the masses, after all), the cultural standing of the content is low (popular culture), the literacy requirements for engaging that content is low (any child could participate), the share of the audience is high, the ubiquity of the medium is high, and the regulatory avenue is agency based (such as the Federal Communications Commission [FCC]). Figure 4.1 on page 82 shows that relationship.

Clearly, the nearly four decades of broadcast television, starting in the early 1950s and extending into the late 1980s, when cable passed the 50% penetration mark, represent the perfect conditions for the academy's call to danger. Culley, Lazer, and Atkin (1976), writing in the mid-1970s, present a good representation of these calls:[3]

> Television appeals to small children as no other medium can. Movies, books, even comic books and magazines, are all relatively inaccessible to the young child. He ordinarily cannot enjoy them unless an adult is willing to put out some time, effort, and probably, money. But the television set is an experience in independence. Always present in the home, it costs neither the child nor the parent anything, and a toddler learns early to manipulate the dial that starts the whole thing going. While a radio produces only music and talk, television turns on a live world of pictures and sound, and sometimes color. (p. 3)

This quotation puts nearly all of the predicting elements together (the rest of the article adds regulatory avenue). But it is the phrase "and sometimes color" that intrigues us. Culley et al. (1976) were writing at the tail end of the black and white television era. Sales of color television sets had surpassed black and white just 2 years earlier, but 75% of U.S. homes had at least one color television (A. C. Nielsen, 1976). The pricing of new technology ensures a rough distribution of it by economic class (consider the distribution of flat-screen television). Most homes represented by Culley et al. would have had color by 1976. The "sometimes color" phrase references the Other of social, economic class.

The Other Family

The second cultural issue is the failure of the *other* family. The family argument is not newly minted in the archive, although it certainly has gained new prominence in the current conservative turn and explosion of special interest groups with "family" in their names. We can reach back to the arguments of the late 1960s and early 1970s to find the staff of the National Commission on the Causes and Prevention of Violence (1970) huffing, *"Parents should make every effort to supervise their children's television viewing and to assert their basic responsibility for the moral development of their children"* (p. 175).

The media's inherent threat to the family is nicely captured in the "problem section" of an advice column by Strasburger (n.d.), who warns, "In any survey of adolescent attitudes, parents are always listed as the #1 influence in teens' lives. But the media plays [sic] an unquestionable role, and the material being 'covered' on television must be 'covered' first by you. This is, in fact, an issue of family values. Whose values do you want your children to learn? Yours, or those of the characters they see on TV"? Of course, Strasburger is a pediatrician whose job is to give advice, and he has to give it from what he holds to be true. His text, however (not necessarily he), connects the causationist science to the panoply of the "family values," constituting yet another voice in that social movement. In that movement, children are continually at risk from the media.

But, of course, it is not just any families or any parents. The commission had also pointed out the following:

> Television is a particularly potent force in families where parental influences and primary group ties are weak or completely lacking, notably in low-income areas or where violent life-styles are common. In these instances, television does not displace parental influence: it fills a vacuum. The strong preference of low-income teen-agers for crime, action, and adventure stories means that they are constantly exposed to the values of violent television programs without the ameliorating moral influence of their parents. (p. 170)

We can readily agree that violent content is more likely a resource of aggression when we view it as being within the communities and conditions that produce and support aggressive practices (Proctor, 2006). Parents of families in such communities, however, may not have the luxury of worrying about the media content that family members are watching. But the less challenged in other communities appear to worry about those family members, in a sort of "finger-pointing" way. Ethnographic studies (J. Anderson & Meyer, 1987; Fisherkeller, 1999; Mayer, 2005; Meyer, Traudt, & Anderson, 1980), as well as the studies on the implementation of the V-chip (Abelman, 1999), have shown that we do not fear the effects of violent content on ourselves and on our children. Our own experience appears to generate no cause for alarm for the conditions that science and the media keep warning us about. On the other hand, third-person studies (Gunther & Storey, 2003; Hoffner et al.,

2001; Hoffner & Buchanan, 2002; Lo & Niu, 2003) have shown that we do fear its effects on others and on their children. The line of reasoning that connects these dots is pretty straight. Because the conditions are not true for us, they are true somewhere else. It is not true here, so it must be true for people who are different from us. It must be true for "those people."

Minimizing Social Costs Through Deflection

It is the issue of deflection where causationists and contributionists carry the greater social burden for their claim of social importance. The issue here is one of proportion. (Allow us, for a paragraph or two, to let our social science backgrounds shine through.) Two meta-analyses give us the range of possible effect. Hogben (1998) anchors the low end at $r = .11$ and Paik and Comstock (1994) the high end at $r = .31$ (see also Bushman & Anderson, 2001). So let us follow Cantor (2000) and take the middle value of .20. Using the traditional explanation of correlation, the value means that 4% (in a range of 1% to 9%) of the variability in aggression is accounted for by differences in viewing values. Putting all the issues of causation aside, the simple question is whether removing viewing practices from the equation would change the outcome in aggression. Or would what Bloom (2002) calls the "hard to face causes, such as family structure, poverty, abuse, evolution, and even the motivations and predilections of those individuals who choose to engage [agency] in violent behavior" (p. 447) simply pick up the slack as it were? Along these lines, even the most ardent of causationists have argued for other more powerful causes. Anderson has studied both environmental (C. Anderson, Bushman, & Groom, 1997) and personality trait correlates of aggression (K. Anderson, Anderson, Dill, & Deuser, 1998), and Huesmann has argued both for parental disciplining practices (Lefkowitz, Eron, & Huesmann, 1978) and for the transgenerational transmission of aggression (Dubow, Huesmann, & Boxer, 2003), the latter showing correlations with parenting practices of more than twice that of media ($r = .47$). The upshot of what we are arguing here is this: Most everyone—causationists and contributionists alike—acknowledge that the media may be the lesser explanation for the level of social aggression, among a hierarchy of explanations, in society. But causationists and contributionists still argue that the media play "a socially significant . . . part" (to quote Strasburger, 1995) as an explanation of the presence of social aggression. What, *exactly*, does that mean? The media can't both be a lesser explanation and, at the same time, play a socially significant part in the high level of social aggression in society. What, exactly, the causations and contributionists mean, for us at least, remains a conundrum.

Finally, Fergusson and Horwood (1999), writing on deviance, were quite explicit in their conclusions, holding that children most at risk were those from socially disadvantaged backgrounds and dysfunctional families that had a history of parental conflict, mother-child interactional conflict, childhood sexual abuse, parental alcoholism, parental criminal offending, parental illicit drug use, parental smoking as well as early conduct problems, early anxiety/withdrawal, and early smoking experimentation with the child. So there's The List most social scientists have agreed to: the environment, family structure, cross-generational parenting practices, poverty, child sexual abuse, alcoholism and drug use, social disadvantage (read race and ethnicity), community collapse, personality traits, and, of course, media. But choosing media from the list and elevating them to the level of social significance diverts resources from the other items in the list. Its cultural effect is to enhance media as a social issue, rising to the level of poverty and child sexual abuse. And in reflection, it reduces the issues of poverty, child sexual abuse, and the rest to what we, as a culture, clearly see as acceptable.

The suggestion that media scholars, particularly causationists, are foot soldiers in the White, middle-class agenda of privilege is difficult to make. But the unintended consequences of the deflection of attention from material practices of oppression are clear. Every call for regulation of broadcast media or of the open distribution of content is a restriction that strikes first at the poor. The privileged will always find the sources for what they want. Technology has long since rendered impossible any honorable call for regulation in which we will all suffer our losses equally.[4] The result is that media effects research can be viewed as a class of content that is intended to make the world safer for us—we, the privileged—without reducing the perks we enjoy. Media scholars will continue to be vulnerable to this claim as long as they fail to address these issues in their research.

And the charge is significant. We could reduce aggression in our neighborhoods, schoolyards, and homes by having greater equity in social distribution, funding genuine educational reform, and providing substantially more resources to families increasingly forced to use unlicensed or substandard care facilities for their children. But all of those involve costs that we are apparently unwilling to pay. That stated, it seems sensible and prudent to support "urging the [National Science Foundation] to increase efforts to fund research on the impact of emerging media on children's cognitive, social, and emotional development" (Kobar, 2000, p. 6). We are not arguing that social science ignore the social fallout of the mass media. Rather, we are arguing that social science apply some perspective to the relative social risk of the media as compared to the other social influences on behavioral aggression.

Conclusions

This chapter is built on the foundation of a bibliographic archive of more than 1,000 entries (J. Anderson, 2006) that stretch from the 1920s to the present. The works are nearly all by U.S. scholars in U.S. publications. Part of that archival homogeneity is in the method of its construction, but more of it is in the luxury of an academy safe from the destruction of two world wars and uniquely marked by a particular theoretical ideology. The story of the unique confluence of positivism, cognitivism, and individualism in the U.S. fields of psychological study is just beginning to be told as alternate positions work to provide the stage of its telling (see Prilleltensky, 1994; Sampson, 1981; Tierney & Smith, 1997).

The point of this latter marking is that the archive and its contents have to be addressed as a cultural object rather than a monument of veridicality. Its larger part is formed by scholars who appear but once, but there are a hundred or so who have made no small part of their career out of their contributions. About 20 of this number—most often the funded ones—are also advocates, regularly appearing before congressional regulatory committees and a smaller number within them who are also entrepreneurs, selling interventions to parents (J. Anderson, in press).

At its worst, the body of work can be characterized as deeply and fatally flawed. At its most commonplace, it is theoretically undisciplined, opportunistically reasoned, and empirically impoverished, disconnected from the technological and social reality in which it appears, bereft of historical and cultural perspective, and steadfastly advancing a quixotic social agenda from a class-based location. Its findings are banal (is that so . . . people can *learn* and be *influenced* by the media?), a scientizing of the obvious. Its primary effect has been to advance disciplinary interests and individual careers. Its unintended consequence has been to deflect attention from the hard issues of social reform by promising a quick regulatory fix. At its best, it is a considered analysis of the interaction among audience and medium, technology and patterns of use, the modes and modalities of production, and interpretation with a sociocultural ecology of action. It is neither elitist nor fearmongering but recognizes that we all—researcher and respondent alike—live in a world full of mediated resources that can be put to good or ill use.

Nothing of the critique in this chapter, or of the ones that precede and follow, should give any comfort to the media practitioner or deter any media scholar from the critical analysis of content. Content has consequences in the way we put it to work. Media practitioner, scholar, and audience member can use it for good or not.

Eighty years of the commonplace calls of danger have spectacularly failed to motivate either a coherent social policy or a consistent educational initiative. Our answer to the obvious question is that we, the public who provide the political will to sustain social policy and educational initiatives, simply find these calls unbelievable.[5] Furthermore, we believe the risks the media pose are easily mitigated. In a letter to the editor of *The Salt Lake Tribune,* Melody Guerrero of Salt Lake City puts it directly:

> I am going to say it: raise your own kids! I do not want to [raise your children for you]. It was a choice I made long ago [not to have children]. Do not let them run pell-mell down the aisles of the grocery store. Do not let them scream uncontrollably at a restaurant. And if you don't want them to watch something on TV, turn it off! I shouldn't have to do without because you don't want to spend time raising your children. (December 16, 2005, p. A16)

The question for the policy maker is whether Ms. Guerrero's insight is true. Does the cognitive science of effects know better? Are our media the fabled lead pots of Rome, subtlety poisoning our culture? These issues and more appear in what follows. Stay tuned.

Notes

1. This definition was used only for fictional material. A separate definition was developed to investigate the factual content of news and documentaries.

2. This claim is obvious on the face of it. We each know far more individuals (perhaps including ourselves) who watch/interact with violent content with no apparent ill effects.

3. Working at this level of analysis, particular authorship recedes, and the cultural voice moves to the front. These authors write what would be readily recognized as appropriate. This is not a critique of personal probity but a "sociology of science" analysis of "how it works." One can find similar connections throughout the archive (e.g., Dorr, 1981; Haefner & Wartella, 1987). Anderson (of this volume) also notes that he was on the editorial board that approved this publication.

4. Even ones as technologically inept as your authors can create viable content of any sort and distribute it worldwide to those with the capacity to receive it.

5. This circumstance of disbelief is itself blamed on the media by media violence/aggression advocates (Bushman & Anderson, 2001) for their failure to properly publicize the danger.

5

Is It Just Science?

James A. Anderson
Janet W. Colvin

Perhaps you were the generation of the 1920s reading lurid newspaper crime reports or of the one clandestinely listening to radio crime dramas under the protective cover of blankets or you spent every Saturday at the local movie theater watching the latest western shoot 'em up or you rushed down to corner drugstore to buy the new edition of EC comics. Perhaps you can remember when your parents finally bought that television set or you still have your first Atari or Nintendo. Maybe you can mark the date when that high-speed Internet connection finally reached your house or you are now in the middle of your college career. If you fit any of these descriptions, you have been the subject of grave concern by the men and women of science. In each generation, the social sciences of the time have taken up the question of media, using the methodologies currently in vogue. And in each generation, they have found children to be at risk from the media and society to be at risk from the children.

Consider these quotations written across a hundred-year span. Commenting on the harmful character of the press at the turn of the last century, Austrian psychiatrist Gustav Aschaffenburg (1903/1913) wrote,

> Juveniles may easily fall victims to their desire for notoriety, and feel themselves flattered if their heroic [outlaw] deeds are described in the paper, possibly even their picture printed in the so called "police journals." (p. 267)

Author's Note: Janet W. Colvin is an assistant professor at Utah Valley State College. She received her doctorate from the University of Utah in 2005. Her interests include communication theory and instructional communication.

Mary Preston (1941), a pediatrician who was the Victor Strasburger of her day, indicted the motion picture and radio crime drama by writing,

> Of the addicts [children who regularly go to the movies and listen to radio crime drama], 85 per cent admitted listening to radio before going to bed and continuing to think of it on going to sleep. Not only that, but the next step turned out to be that of thinking of the self as the crook committing the crime, and finally progressing to the plane of planning the crime, acting it out, studying the faults of the plan, and rectifying them in the next plan made—in short, a long-continued study in being a criminal. One of these boys, 11 years old, had already acquired three real guns—a pistol, a repeater, and a six-shooter. That movies can have a similar effect was brought to mind when the writer inadvertently had to sit though a cowboy scene with much shooting in it. Not only was the audience largely composed of children from 3 years old and up, a goodly number were armed with toy guns and every time a man was shot, whether cop, crook, or cowboy, each child's gun was aimed at the man on the screen, with a tense expression, each shooter said, "Bang," and then looked satisfied and proud if the man fell. If this is not training to kill, what is it? (p. 157)

And Victor Strasburger (1989) himself in an unsigned editorial tells his fellow pediatricians that they "need to avoid the intellectual trap of minimizing the importance of television's effect on child and adolescent behavior simply because the literature does not contain straightforward, statistically validated research" (p. 446). It clearly is not just the science for him. Finally, at the start of this century, crusading American psychologists Craig Anderson and Brad Bushman (2001) now find the danger in video games:

> Three towns recently experienced similar multiple school shootings. The shooters were students who habitually played violent video games. Eric Harris and Dylan Klebold, the Columbine High School students who murdered 13 people and wounded 23 in Littleton, before killing themselves, enjoyed playing the bloody video game Doom. (p. 353)

The premise of this chapter is that what makes media violence and aggression research most interesting is not its findings but its reproduction. Social science is a product of the cultural milieu in which it appears. It is society that establishes the priorities, provides the funding, and creates the celebrity of congressional hearings and popular reporting. Society drives what is written about. It is one's cultural position, however, that provides the resources for how the writing gets done. Media effects researchers are members of an educated elite; they are nearly universally White, are predominately male, and occupy the middle to upper reaches of socioeconomic class. Although their training and, more important, the editorial practices of publication are intended to suppress cultural leakage in the rhetoric of science, it nonetheless comes through particularly in the introduction, implications, and conclusion sections of the writing. It is there that the cultural work of this research—work that we apparently need performed again and again—gets done.

Consequently, this chapter is a cultural analysis of the media violence/aggression research. It proceeds from a close reading and coding of 302 journal articles selected under the governances of grounded theory from a database of 1,136 articles connected to the media violence/aggression issue. The articles in the database include surveys, experimental work, meta-analyses, critiques, essays, comment and reply, journal editorials, and popular restatements. The media targets of the articles include newspapers (and other periodicals), motion pictures, radio drama, television, video games, music/music videos, and "the Internet." The earliest work appears in the "19 aughts" and the latest in "20 aughts" (1903–2006). An earlier analysis of the database appears in J. Anderson (in press). The sample includes work from each decade, each medium, each content type, and each major player of each publication era (as identified in J. Anderson, in press).

What this chapter is not is an indictment of the authors whose textual fragments appear as elements in the various coding sets. One cannot *not* write from some cultural stance. Objectivity is a simple modernist conceit that serves mainly to close off valuable lines of inquiry. We may indeed gasp at a quotation from the early 1900s: "[Newspapers] excite the morbid appetite and still more morbid curiosity of the lower social classes," but the cultural work that gets done is the same as this quotation from the 1972 Surgeon General's report: "Teenagers from low-income families believe that people behave in the real world the way they do in the fictional world of television."

In both of these cases, science is engaged in the cultural work of class distinction. Note that the truth of the original claim—or better, the quality of the evidence that can be marshaled to support the claim—does not matter in a cultural analysis. The fact that class was chosen as a variable of interest (out of a very large number of possible variables) and that the finding (out of a very large number of findings) was reported is all that counts. These are choices made by a cultural agent who may also be enacting good science, itself a cultural practice. When class-based statements that pose the "lower class" (even the name is telling) as less capable appear across decades of work, one feels confident that the language also serves to reinforce a cultural belief. It's there because we expected it to be there all along.

In the end, the question is, "Why is science interested in that particular variable—the variable of social class?" not "Why did that author write that sentence?" The author wrote the sentence because it was justified by the data, which in turn were made sensible in the cultural practices in which they appeared. What this chapter attempts to do is to illuminate the apparently persistent cultural frame that has supported the reproduction of the media violence/aggression story for more than 100 years. It is quite possible that the science of this issue has long since been put to rest. Perhaps, we do get it: Media content of any sort can have consequences of which we disapprove (its own cultural issue). So if the science is dead, what keeps the story alive? We hope to tell you.

The "we" in this case is not Grimes, Anderson, and Bergen, the authors of this book, but Anderson and Colvin, who are solely responsible for its content. This is a technical chapter in that it relies on analytic procedures and textual evidence to create its argument rather than the more narrative line that the other "we" have been following in the previous chapters. It could easily appear as an appendix, but Grimes, Anderson, and Bergen put it here because it reveals some of the foundation for the narrative line they have been following.

Introduction to the Study[1]

The question of effects is an emblematic issue for the community of media researchers, as we have seen. There are many who are passionate in their support and, perhaps, an equal number who simply dismiss the whole line of reasoning. That dismissal turns on a number of arguments: that the effects model itself is unreasonable; that the research methodologies used in support are artificial, self-fulfilling, and unfalsifiable; that the research is ideologically biased; that the effects concept is employed in race- and class-based cultural work; and that effects research is driven by disciplinary rather than epistemological ends.

This study is a cultural analysis that seeks to develop an understanding of the cultural framework that supports this debate that has continued for more than 100 years. As a cultural study, it is not interested in the results of any study or in the relative truth value of any side in the debate. It is interested in the cultural work that gets accomplished to maintain the proper order of things in society.

The study uses critical analysis to uncover that cultural work. Critical analysis (Fairclough, 2003) is a qualitative approach that attempts to reveal the underlying understandings and motives that make a field of study sensible, relevant, important, resonant, and so on. The study takes a grounded approach that develops its focus and research questions out of the texts themselves, but issues about definitions of content, effects, social consequences, cultural definitions of violence, aggression, gender, race, and the child were certainly predicted to appear.

Methodology

This report is part of a longitudinal study of the media effects literature. We expect that media effects has the cultural legs, if not the scientific ones, to continue as long as technology and content provide new contexts to ask the same questions. The archive will continue to build on both ends of the timeline as we add more historical examples and as scholars and scientists create new publications. At this point in the study, we have a list of 1,136 confirmed journal articles up from the 966 reported by Anderson (in press).

Sampling

In a cultural study of this type, the unit of analysis is the argument not the article, although the article is the only way to access the argument. J. Anderson's (in press) study revealed that the most common authorship was the single appearing author. As he notes, "82 percent of the authors appear as first author only once in the archive, representing 56 percent of all publications." The flip side of those values is that 18% of the authors produce 44% of the publications. Given those characteristics, a random sample of articles was unlikely to produce a representative sample of arguments. Therefore, we used a strategic sample (Hunt, 1970) that focused on the principal traits of the archive.

The most important of these traits for the sample were major publication venues and most active authors for the decades represented in the archive (1940–2000). Those venues and authors were selected for inclusion in the sample and were the majority of items. The years between 2000 and present have been active years both in the explosion of new journals and in the scholarship of effects. We used snowball sampling from online databases to fill those years, and we followed the bibliographic references of the oldest entries to retrieve even earlier works. We then leavened in critical reviews, policy statements, congressional testimony, legal analyses of constitutional and case law, and federal regulation in an attempt to get as broad a sweep of the language in use. The resulting sample was heavily social science—clinical in the earlier years, then experimental and surveys in the later years. It has good depth in this area, but it also reaches out to the margins to include the popular and even occasional fringe argument.

Preparation of the Texts

The study is made possible by the convergence of digital technologies for the archiving of textual materials, for the handling of text as addressable, and for the analysis of digitized textual materials. The steps in this research required producing a clean, flat copy of each textual unit,[2] which was then processed through optical character recognition software to produce an addressable, searchable text file. Once that file is produced, the text can be machine analyzed by word, by sentence, and/or by paragraph. Sections can be marked off for extraction into a common file of all such sections, and lines of argument can be similarly demarcated to produce a unique database of argument types.

The first step in this process is the acquisition of a copy that can be processed. Clearly, the most significant advance in archival work has been the digitization and online distribution of the archive. When this study was first budgeted, some 3 years before this writing, it contained a substantial amount of money for travel to other libraries to track down pristine originals that could be transformed into addressable texts. With full-text copies of most communication journals and many psychology journals coming online in the intervening years, that travel proved unnecessary, although the money was spent on upgrading hardware and specialized software.

Nonetheless, there was still a good deal of effort necessary to obtain copies of work prior to the 1960s, which is the general marker for the modern era of psychological research. In that regard, the digital camera was most helpful as it could produce digital files on location, in ambient (typical library) lighting with appropriate adjustments for the parallax introduced by the binding.

Once the articles were converted to PDF or JPEG files, they were run through optical character recognition (OCR) routines. These routines return a file in Rich Text Format (RTF) that includes both text and graphics for computer-based analysis. OCR routines have error rates that are directly related to the quality of the copy and the font in use for the article. These error rates can be quite high—above 50% in some cases, mostly due to defaced originals. At some point, they become uncorrectable, which meant that a new copy would have to be prepared or the article discarded from the sample. Eight of the original articles selected were lost in that manner. Substitutes that matched by author, topic, and era as closely as possible were selected for inclusion. Error rates, important in machine analysis, are much less important in human coding as we can identify the error and correct it in context or by simply comparing the OCR text with the unprocessed copy.

Coding

Once the RTF files were produced for each document, they were entered into a QSR NVivo project. This software allows an unlimited number of sources of unlimited length to be analyzed by an unlimited number of codes. Coding is done by highlighting text, which can then be extracted into a common file of all text fragments coded under a given code with the connection to the source preserved. That file, in turn, can be subsequently coded. For this study, we used our coding of two article sections, the "Statement of the Problem" (SOP) and the "Implications and Conclusions" (I&C), and two concepts, "violence" and "aggression," to identify what arguments were used to justify the study, what professional or social utilities were claimed for it, and to trace the cultural understandings that were inherent in the conceptualization of violence and aggression.

This type of coding is reductive coding that intends to heighten the likelihood of finding the arguments that are our interest. There is no ontological claim involved. For SOP coding, the first few paragraphs following the abstract up to the start of a description of method were used. For I&C coding, the paragraphs following "Results" were used. Some of the leavening documents were all SOP arguments or all I&C arguments that were coded in a single code with no reduction. For violence and aggression, the documents were simply searched for those terms, and the descriptive text associated with the terms was extracted.

The result of this reductive coding was four files. The SOP file was 252 single-spaced pages with 2,397 paragraphs and 89,017 words that referenced 292 of the 302 sources. The I&C file was 303 single-spaced pages with 2,884 paragraphs and 114,415 words that referenced 294 sources. As can be seen, most but not every document had an introductory or concluding section. The aggression file was 921 single-spaced pages with 12,680 paragraphs and 465,777 words that referenced 243 of the 302 sources. The violence file was 869 single-spaced pages with 12,850 paragraphs and 435,942 words that referenced 233 sources. The apparent discrepancy in sources occurs because some sources use violence or aggression exclusively, and some, such as the meta-analyses or law reviews, merely mention the terms without engaging them.

The arguments in each of these files were coded using the "next unique" method of grounded theory. This is a close reading method that depends on the intimate relationship between the coder and the text rather than a set of rules for classification. These codes were further collapsed according to the observed commonalities within the coded textual fragments (identified by the slash mark in the code name). Codes with five or fewer instances that could not be combined were not included in this analysis as the small number could be just a function of those particular authors. The frequency associated with codes, then, is a measure of our ability to get to the cultural complexities of the argument type, not a representation of the rate of that argument type in the literature.

Nine compiled codes were extracted from the SOP file: theory/previous research, consequences for society, consequences for the child, legislation/policy/regulation, descriptive, critique, historical understanding, cognitive processes, and class/race. These arguments provided the justification for the publication and reading of the article. Eight compiled codes appeared with the I&C data: consequences for society, call for some action, contrarian/disconfirming, advocacy/confirming, interventions, critique, conditions of the effect, and advice. These arguments related the justification of the work in relation to some larger social practice.

Violence and aggression were often used interchangeably in the literature. What might be listed as aggression in the body of the text could become violence in the conclusion. There is little discipline evidenced in the use of these terms. Consequently, a common set of five compiled codes was used for both the violence and aggression files. They were definitions, character, measurement, representation, and performance.

Results

In presenting these results, we shift from a focus on the articles as the unit to a focus on the argument. In the tidy world of rhetorical scholarship, an argument is a claim of what is or ought to be supported by evidence in a logical form. In practice, arguments are much more enthymemic, missing something of premises, evidence, and/or logic. In practice, given the right inflection, "So?" is an effective argument.

Our coding of arguments makes an ontological claim: that the sentences coded (facts of the texts) in the context of the article (local understanding) within this field of discourse (overarching understanding) can be interpreted as argument of the type that would advance claim X, using evidence Y and reasoning Z, even in the absence of any of those elements. For example, if you are considering investing a lot of money in a scheme being promoted by John, and I state, "John lied to his mother about the car," I have in that one sentence created a much larger argument about my trustworthiness, the trustworthiness of John, the severity of his violation (lied to his mother), his character in the matter of the investment, and the risks that are involved in committing funds to his care. The problem for the coder is to recognize that the declarative sentence about John is not an offhand, independent fact but shorthand for an implicit argument.

The codes reported here, then, are interpretations of the text provided by two people who each have spent hundreds of hours in intimate familiarity with this field of discourse, both in the sample and beyond and who together have consulted extensively over the meaning and boundaries of the codes applied. Following Benoit, Pier, and Blaney (1997), we do not report reliability coefficients—they would be meaningless at any rate—but stand on the consensus of the coders on the resonance of the arguments illustrated. In the end, rather than relying on the talisman of a number, the reader will have to evaluate the quality of our claims as presented here. The basis for this requirement is not that we could not have calculated a reliability coefficient and not that it would not have been very high. Any expert in coding knows that we could easily accomplish both. The reason is that we are not interested in the rates of events for which reliability coefficients would be appropriate. Rather, we are interested in evaluating the qualities of common fields of argument.

SOP Codes

Table 5.1 presents the compiled SOP codes and the number of arguments coded for each. The number of arguments exceeds the number of articles as more than one justifying argument could be present in the statement of the problem. Sources coded are listed by reference number. Full entries are provided in the appendix.

Theory/Previous Research

Two codes appeared in far greater frequency that any of the others, *consequences for society* and *theory/previous research*. Theory/previous research is a continuity argument or argument from precedence as it takes some previous finding or theoretical position and connects the present study to it (25):[3]

> The proposition that individuals selectively attend messages that support their predispositions has typically been applied to informational or persuasive content in the mass media. To study whether exposure decisions are based on defensive needs for reinforcement, researchers have compared partisan message selection patterns of Republican vs. Democrat voters, smokers vs. nonsmokers, and Ford vs. Chevrolet owners. This investigation extends the analysis to fictional entertainment content on television, focusing on exposure to violent programming. (p. 5)

This argument type seeks its justification in the advancement of knowledge. This selection is a good example of normal science. Normal science is the Kuhnian notion (Kuhn, 1970) that a field once established moves

Table 5.1   Compiled Codes, Number of Arguments, and Sources Coded for Statement of the Problem

Code	Number of Arguments	Sources Coded
Consequences for society	123	1, 2, 7, 9, 10, 13, 14, 16, 17, 21, 23, 24, 37, 39, 41, 43, 44, 49, 50, 51, 54, 55, 56, 57, 58, 61, 63, 64, 67, 74, 75, 76, 77, 78, 80, 82, 83, 84, 86, 91, 93, 101, 106, 108, 109, 110, 112, 113, 114, 116, 121, 123, 124, 125, 128, 130, 131, 134, 137, 138, 142, 145, 146, 147, 151, 153, 155, 156, 158, 159, 160, 161, 163, 166, 167, 168, 169, 171, 173, 175, 176, 177, 179, 184, 186, 190, 192, 199, 201, 202, 204, 205, 209, 210, 212, 219, 221, 222, 229, 232, 236, 237, 238, 239, 240, 241, 246, 248, 250, 254, 255, 262, 266, 269, 273, 275, 278, 279, 281, 284, 285, 286, 302
Theory/previous research	101	2, 3, 7, 15, 18, 20, 25, 29, 32, 33, 34, 35, 39, 40, 42, 45, 46, 47, 48, 52, 56, 58, 66, 68, 70, 71, 77, 80, 84, 85, 88, 90, 93, 94, 96, 97, 99, 100, 101, 102, 111, 115, 117, 118, 119, 121, 122, 126, 127, 136, 139, 140, 144, 149, 150, 151, 152, 156, 157, 159, 161, 170, 171, 172, 173, 175, 176, 178, 182, 183, 186, 187, 189, 191, 194, 200, 201, 202, 203, 211, 212, 216, 221, 226, 243, 244, 249, 251, 258, 259, 263, 277, 282, 286, 287, 288, 289, 296, 299, 302
Consequences for child	39	5, 24, 57, 59, 60, 62, 65, 75, 80, 82, 95, 103, 113, 126, 135, 179, 195, 197, 209, 210, 215, 217, 218, 220, 226, 227, 231, 233, 234, 242, 260, 264, 267, 268, 275, 284, 293, 294

Code	Number of Arguments	Sources Coded
Historical understanding	37	3, 23, 51, 63, 64, 83, 85, 100, 101, 115, 120, 123, 124, 138, 141, 154, 169, 179, 200, 206, 207, 222, 224, 225, 229, 230, 234, 236, 252, 256, 268, 273, 278, 279, 280, 283, 300
Critique	28	53, 82, 89, 101, 120, 139, 140, 144, 150, 152, 162, 164, 175, 179, 181, 198, 200, 222, 230, 236, 245, 247, 253, 256, 268, 272, 295, 301
Legislation/policy/ regulation	27	4, 22, 27, 77, 82, 84, 116, 129, 132, 134, 141, 142, 165, 166, 180, 185, 188, 190, 192, 208, 211, 253, 257, 270, 283, 300
Descriptive	22	6, 38, 52, 65, 66, 79, 81, 133, 146, 148, 174, 177, 183, 196, 252, 272, 276, 282, 287, 290, 291, 292
Cognitive processes	17	11, 35, 69, 71, 72, 87, 91, 104, 105, 107, 143, 194, 235, 261, 271, 298, 299
Class/race	9	5, 49, 83, 125, 160, 226, 228, 276, 279

forward incrementally, extending the known into the unknown. The last line of the selection clearly makes that connection.

The normal science argument spans the entire time frame of the sample. One of our earliest entries (137) seeks to build on the science of the day:

> In approaching this problem, it will be necessary to determine what certain groups of scientists have had to say in regard to the causation of crime by news of crime, to find out what interested groups have to say, to examine a mass of social facts which have appeared in the newspapers, and then to draw from those facts certain conclusions which shall accord with the scientific development that we are endeavoring to foster. (p. 41)

And nearly 80 years later (284), the news is still the topic, although now the medium is television:

> Traditionally, the public and professional debate about the inappropriateness of media violence for children focuses mainly on the negative effects of violence in entertainment programming. However, since the terrorist attacks on September 11th and the recent coverage of the war in Iraq, the suitability of real-life news violence for children may be doubted more than ever. (p. 1771)

Normal science is analogous to fractal systems in that it becomes a process of self-same reproduction as long as there is energy in the system. The energy in this system is not scientific innovation. As we have seen, the basic argument of effects has been around for more than 100 years, the primary cognitive theory was developed 80 years ago, and the current protocols were well developed 40 to 50 years ago. The energy for this normal science system comes from the innovations in content and technology. As our history demonstrates so well, the newest and most popular technologies will be the current location of media effects research. Old technology disappears from scientific interest as it begins to appear in historical scholarship. In fact, the justifying arguments from history as well as those from description and critique play their part in tandem with normal science to preserve the flow of productivity in this area. As history works to help us understand the present moment of that science, description provides a factual foundation for that science, and as critique analyzes the conduct of that science, scholarship expands in ripples around it. One of the reasons why we are still asking the same questions even though the science may be settled, then, is that we keep constructing new places to ask them.

Consequences for Society

Theory/previous research arguments have clear margins, high recognition, and good face validity. The coder can remain "close to the text," invoking only common warrants of scholarship and science. Consequences for society arguments represent a much more complex set of arguments. These arguments come in three major types: unacceptable levels of violence/aggression in society; unacceptable severity of violence/aggression in society; and the crafting of the perpetrator of violence/aggression.

Levels of Violence. As we have seen, arguments associating media content with juvenile delinquency, crime, and the violence in society begin with the newspapers at the turn of the 20th century and continue as motion pictures and radio reach mass popularity. Looking back at the arrival of television as the predominant medium, writers could comment (82) the following:

Fears that mass media violence is harmful to children and encourages crime and violence can be traced back a century and a half. Each new medium has provided the focus for concerns that there has been a recent and unprecedented rise in juvenile crime and that this has been caused by a new medium which is unprecedented in its glorification of crime and violence. (p. 485)

They become commonplace by the late 1960s following the assassinations of John and Robert Kennedy. Even a bibliography invokes the justification (1):

Recent tragic events in this country have fixed new attention on the prevalence of violence in our society. Intellectuals, politicians, educators and laymen alike have been swift in their indictment of the mass media, particularly television, as a major contributor to the apparent violent tendencies. (p. 101)

By the mid-1980s, the debate over television was fully engaged and yet apparently not sufficiently resolved (204):

Given the pervasiveness of television in U.S. society, it is not surprising that this medium has been, and continues to be, at the center of controversy and public debate. Perhaps the most intense and enduring controversy concerns the consequences of viewing television violence. Critics of the industry have charged that violence on television is a cause of many of the more important social ills of society, while representatives of the industry and a number of social scientists have disputed the scientific basis for such sweeping claims.

   The purpose of this paper is to address an aspect of the television controversy that has received comparatively little attention in the scientific literature but that serves as the basis for many of the calls for some sort of censorship of television content. This is the claim that violence on television is an important cause not simply of "aggression" but of "criminal violence" in society at large. (p. 218)

As the violent crime rates began a precipitous decline from the mid-1990s to the present writing, the arguments took on a temporizing tone (17):

It is doubtful that people are more prone to be violent today than thousands of years ago. In fact, the portion of the world's population who behave violently today is probably lower than in most previous times. Nevertheless, the prevalence of aggressive and violent behavior today is sufficient to make it a social problem worthy of attention around the world. (p. 296)

Intensity of Violence. Intensity of violence is something of a variation on the levels of violence. It is concerned with the character of the aggression/ violence as perpetrated (153):

The question of whether media violence causes people to behave more violently has been a major topic of concern to psychologists, communication scientists, and policy makers for well over 15 years. And it was a topic of concern to at least a few scientists more than 50 years ago when movies first became widely distributed. (p. 125)

Intensity as a justifying issue may have been advanced by the arguments that were developed in the neoassociationist line of research (44):

The greatest number of shocks were sent by the angered men who had witnessed the prize fight and who had been informed that the accomplice's name was Kirk. The latter's name-mediated association with the witnessed aggression had apparently heightened his cue value for aggressive responses causing him to evoke the strongest volume of aggression from the men who were ready to act aggressively. (p. 525)

Intensity was also an issue in excitation transfer research (302):

An individual who is provoked appraises his experience as anger toward his tormentor, and that the intensity of his anger is determined by the degree of physiological arousal he perceives at the time. At later times, his anger is readily reinstated cognitively by again confronting his tormentor, with the intensity of his anger again being determined by prevailing arousal. (p. 287)

Intensity gets transferred out of the laboratory in arguments that link media with the increased willingness of individuals to commit violent acts (12):

Well-supported theory delineates why and when exposure to media violence increases aggression and violence. Media violence produces short-term increases by priming existing aggressive scripts and cognitions, increasing physiological arousal, and triggering an automatic tendency to imitate observed behaviors. (p. 81)

Intensity arguments can be seen as a way of insulating the media effects literature from variations in crime and aggression rates in society. Even if the rates of crime and incivility decline, one can point to some horrific incident with the intimation that the incident would not have occurred without media influence (10):

For many in the general public, the problem of video game violence first emerged with school shootings by avid players of such games at West Paducah, Kentucky (December, 1997); Jonesboro, Arkansas (March, 1998); Springfield, Oregon (May, 1998); and Littleton, Colorado (April, 1999). More recent violent crimes that have been linked to violent video games include a school shooting spree in

Santee, California (March, 2001); a violent crime spree in Oakland, California (January, 2003); five homicides in Long Prairie and Minneapolis, Minnesota (May, 2003); beating deaths in Medina, Ohio (November, 2002) and Wyoming, Michigan (November, 2002); school shootings in Wellsboro, Pennsylvania (June, 2003) and Red Lion, Pennsylvania (April, 2003); and the Washington, DC. "Beltway" sniper shootings (Fall, 2002). (p. 113)

Crafting the Perpetrator. These arguments point to the media's role in creating the aggressor or violent person. In a spectacular example, the two perpetrators of the Columbine High School shootings are specifically singled out (16):

> On April 20, 1999, Eric Harris and Dylan Klebold launched an assault on Columbine High School in Littleton, Colorado, murdering 13 and wounding 23 before turning the guns on themselves. Although it is impossible to know exactly what caused these teens to attack their own classmates and teachers, a number of factors probably were involved. One possible contributing factor is violent video games. Harris and Klebold enjoyed playing the bloody, shoot-'em-up video game Doom, a game licensed by the U.S. military to train soldiers to effectively kill. (p. 772)

The argument, however, usually plays on more generalized fears (94):

> With the increasing prominence of violence in our society, social scientists have been turning their attention to the antecedents of aggressive behavior in children and adults. Television programming with its heavy emphasis on interpersonal violence and acquisitive lawlessness has been assigned a role both in inciting aggression and teaching viewers specific techniques of aggressive behavior. (p. 252)

More than 40 years earlier, the concerns of learning technique from the media were voiced about newspapers (147):

> Other forms of crime [besides swindles] in which the papers give instruction are "hold-up" methods, theft in general and murder. Stories of murder are not merely objectionable because of the instruction given in methods but also because of the suggestion effect that they have on persons faced with a situation that might easily be solved by the elimination of someone else and on persons who are mentally abnormal. (p. 247)

And then again nearly 10 years later, it was the movie photoplay (80):

> The simple facts [are] that boys and young men, when suitably predisposed, sometimes have utilized techniques of crime seen in the movies, have used gangster films to stimulate susceptible ones toward crime, and on occasion in their own criminal actions, have idealized themselves imaginatively as possessing the attractive personality or as engaging in the romantic activities of a gangster screen hero. (p. 517)

An added side bar to this argument is to point to the hidden process of "turning the child" or adolescent or adult (24):

> The impact of TV violence may be immediately evident in the child's behavior or may surface years later, and young people can even be affected when the family atmosphere shows no tendency toward violence.

This policy statement also notes, "Sometimes, watching a single violent program can increase aggressiveness." Given the character of this advice—that a single exposure may damage, that the damage may not appear for years, and that the damage may occur in an otherwise peaceful family life—it is difficult to know what course of action a concerned parent would take other than banning television from the household. In our judgment, such statements are fear-mongering in that they espouse an impossible or very difficult solution.

"Turning the child" arguments turn the reader against the child. The concerns of these arguments are not about the costs to the child (as we shall see immediately below) but about the costs to society as yet another perpetrator is foisted upon the world. They are the costs that accrue to the adult world, the costs to be paid by you and me. If only these children did not watch television, we would be safer. These same sorts of arguments are directed against smokers, drinkers, drug users, thrill seekers, the obese, and other variations from the perfect. Someday, these arguments imply, an extensive media violence user is going to do you harm.

Consequences for the Child

Turning the child arguments show little empathy for the child per se. In such arguments, we do not consider the costs the child so turned has to bear. Experimental, survey, and longitudinal studies that focus on exposure to media violence rarely invoke the child as the location of the effect. When they do, it is typically to describe the cognitive processes of the child (73). It is in child development and in fear research that we begin to find justificatory arguments based on a concern for the exposed child (59):

> Singer has cautioned that exposure of young children to frightening scenes that are beyond their capacity to comprehend may result in long-term emotional disturbances. Other researchers have recently been concerned with children's fears in general, and the necessity to understand and to deal with them so that they do not become excessive or phobic. (p. 431)

Earlier clinical approaches to the problem of media violence also seemed to be more directed toward the child (62):

Every now and then, when tragedy enters into the life of some boy or girl, investigation leads back to the youth's reading of the comic books and their incitement to crime and the community is, for the time being, alerted to the daily menace to our children. Sometimes our cities are moved to take legal action against the publishers and purveyors of this unfit reading matter for children, but at its best such action is necessarily slow and not always immediately effective. In the meantime children continue to buy and read these crime and sex ridden booklets, and the home too often pays little heed until one of its own boys or girls become the victim or perpetrator of a crime. (p. 28)

More recently, child development and child psychologists have focused on the consequences of media in the family (267):

Television may contribute to children's restlessness, dysphoria, fears about daily dangers, and their proneness to aggression. Those parents who are themselves heavy viewers, who lack other interests, and who do not exert efforts to establish rules about television viewing, may provide a home atmosphere that puts their children at risk for a greater dysphoric tendency. Along with modeling their parents' own emotionality, reacting to power-assertive discipline, or forceful prescriptive communications, children's aggressive and emotional styles seem to reflect the heavy dose of frightening and arousing content that makes up television fare. (p. 107)

The shading here seems to clearly appoint the child as victim much in the same way that public service announcements portray children as victims of second-hand smoke. In all of the child arguments, there is empathy for the child that is simply missing in the perpetrator and societal arguments.

Why are so few arguments concerning the costs to the child used to justify the research in this field?[4] The likelihood is that the consequence for the child is seen as a particular event rather than a generalized outcome. It is a clinical concern, not a scientific one. That a child may grow up a social outcast, destined for a life marked by incarceration and heighten risks of violence, is a concern, of course, but not at the level of generalizability as is the rate of violence in society.

The "Not Every Child" Exception

There is a class of arguments that occurs regularly in the literature, both in our sample and outside of it, that was not coded but is worth comment. The argument is the "not every child" exception. This was most famously articulated in the 1972 report to the Surgeon General (*Television,* 1972):

The accumulated evidence, however, does not warrant the conclusion that televised violence has a uniformly adverse effect nor the conclusion that it has an adverse effect on the majority of children. It cannot even be said that the majority of the children in the various studies we have reviewed showed an increase in aggressive behavior in response to the violent fare to which they were exposed. The evidence does indicate the televised violence may lead to increased aggressive behavior in certain subgroups of children who might constitute a small portion or substantial proportion of the total population of young television viewers. (p. 7)

The argument then appears regularly in our sample (variations of the phrasing appear somewhere in 41 sample documents): "operates only on some children" (144, p. 608), "causation of aggression among some children" (210, p. 477), "some children to become more aggressive" (145, p. 1299), "increasing at least some children's . . . antisocial behavior" (153, p. 126), "evident in some children" (85, p. 43), and "not all children who observe a steady diet of violent television go on to display patterns of aggressive behavior" (160, p. 181).

Grimes, Anderson, and Bergen (this volume) answer the question of the some children who might be affected in the chapters that follow. The other side of that question concerning the majority of children who are not affected is perhaps more interesting. Anderson and Meyer (1987) answer that question unequivocally with their claim that the normal (undiagnosed in current therapeutic usage) child has adequate resources and will be unaffected. But a different group of children is suggested by the causationists. One set of researchers (161) offhandedly comment that "true, media violence is not going to turn an otherwise fine child" (p. 218). That comment leads to our questions: Who might be a fine child? What are the conditions necessary that all children might be fine children? What policy and practices will achieve that goal?

Legislation/Policy/Regulation

Unfortunately, we don't find the call for achieving a nation of fine children in this set of arguments. Justificatory arguments in this category follow a number of different lines, including the necessity of governmental action, the limits of action, and the problems associated with taking action. A typical call for action specifies what it wants done (165):

We take the position here that the goals of public policy ought to be twofold: (a) to promote programming that serves the diverse needs of children for information, entertainment, aesthetic appreciation, and knowledge about the world, and (b) to protect children from television content and advertising practices that exploit their special vulnerability. (p. 424)

It is, of course, the government's reluctance and apparent refusal to take any action that would significantly reduce violent content that fuels all of these arguments. There is, then, an insistence to do something (4):

> The basic premise the subcommittee's final report adopted [was] that the government may not regulate directly the content of television programming, no matter how violent, without violating the first amendment. That premise, however, is unfounded. Indeed, several approaches are available for the federal government, acting through its regulatory arm, the Federal Communications Commission (FCC), to take to limit televised violence without infringing upon freedom of speech. (p. 1299)

When the government does take action, however, such as family viewing, the V-chip, and content ratings, the arguments simply appear on the other side (142):

> Much of the public debate surrounding the V-chip, the rating system, and other possible solutions reflects conflicting concerns about protecting the public from adverse effects of violent media while preserving the integrity of the First Amendment. In a recent content analysis of newspaper coverage of the television violence issue during 1994 and 1995, about one quarter of the articles depicted these solutions as censorship or a threat to free speech. (p. 727)

And when government action appears imminent, the calls for alternatives become more pressing (180):

> Though the debate over television violence has raged almost since the first set flickered to life, 1993 witnessed a remarkable shift in the balance of power in favor of would-be regulators. Perhaps because of increased public concern with the rising levels of violence in American society, legislators who were previously willing to rely on industry-initiated measures to deal with the violence problem were now poised to control the nation's video diet with government regulation. In 1993, legislators introduced seven different proposals designed to attack the problem of television violence. If ever there was a time for alternatives that address both the public interest and constitutional concerns, it is now. (p. 1385)

More often than not, it is the scientist who is calling for removal or suppression of violent content. Distrustful of parental action and mindful of the attractions of violence, the scientist, particularly the causationist, sees content control as the best course. It is the commentator, industry advocate, and constitutional scholar who point to the unintended consequences of governmental regulation and the prohibitions of the First Amendment. With but 15% of the population dependent solely on broadcast television and with 100 million home videos reported by *Time* magazine (November 13, 2006) as currently available on www.YouTube.com with 70,000 added daily, this irresolvable debate would appear to be moot. The genie has long left the bottle of opportunity for legislation and regulation, never to return. This departure brings the causationist who believes that "no one is exempt from the deleterious effects of media violence" (11, p. 104) to the difficult game of counterprogramming with "more nourishing fare" (11, p. 106). The scientist joins the social activist in the politics of content.

Class/Race

Relatively few class/race arguments appear in our sample, but that they are not absent from the literature raises its own question. Two of the studies classified here (125, 279) are working the cultural consequences of the portrayal of race and ethnicity. The others are considering the relationship of race and class to media violence and aggression. What are the expectations of how class or race might operate in the media violence/aggression connection? The answer comes pretty quickly (5):

> The present study is concerned with the reactions to, and the uses of, television by parents and children in two different socio-economic statuses. We were interested in the possible differences that such a status difference might make in the role of television, and whether or not parents made an effort to utilize its positive potential and to counteract its poorer features. (p. 145)

The argument comes to its conclusion a few lines later:

> All of our predictions were in the direction of upper-status parents doing less television viewing, being more concerned and aware of their children's viewing, being more restrictive of their children's viewing, suggesting more educational programs to the children, and using television as a means of reward and punishment more often than lower-status parents. (p. 146)

Class and race are closely correlated in the United States, and often one stands for the other. The argument quoted below follows a discussion of "the Negro social condition" (276, pp. 55–56):

> We believe that, in many lower income households, parent-child relations are erratic and inconsistent. Many parents and children see each other on a nonsystematic, disorganized basis. Many lower income husbands often leave the

family unit for one reason or another and, as a result, many women are forced to work. Because of this, they are absent from the home for long periods of time, further emphasizing the fragmented basis of interaction between parent and child. Because of this disruption, we believe the lower income child lacks a source of information which instructs him of his proper role within the family unit. (p. 56)

It then goes on to explicitly reveal race by offering the contrast:

On the other hand, most white, middle-income teen-agers are members of stable family units and relate to their parents on a more systematic basis. In other words, they have models from which to learn behaviors expected of them by society. (p. 56)

The direct identification of class and race as markers of difference in the effects of media violence mostly disappears from the literature by the 1980s. That does not mean that the argument disappeared. A common way to locate our concerns is to introduce terms such as *urban areas, industrial America, inner-city neighborhoods,* and even *ghettos* without mentioning race or class and then to report rates of violent crime and levels of television viewing (160):

In some urban areas of the United States the most common cause of death for young males is now homicide.
    The dramatic increase in interpersonal violence in the past century has occurred at the same time as other dramatic changes in life-styles produced by the great technological revolutions of the 20th century. (p. 154)

The easy conclusion is that, at least, part of the literature is racist. The easy conclusion is wrong. This is an elite authorship acting as the cultural agents of the elite hardly at risk from the elements of popular culture trying to entice an elite readership, equally safe, to stay engaged in the issue. This is the appeal of othering the Other. How happy that *our* young men are not being shot to death; how sad for *them.* How happy that *we* care for our children; how sad for the children of the *absent father.* Let us read more.

Implications of Justification

With an estimated thousands of articles on media violence already published, the problem of how one gets yet another publication in the archive might loom large. What we have seen is that justification comes fairly easily (a) with narratives of normal science that in turn support the symbiotic scholarship, which surrounds that science, as well as (b) the unacceptability of violence in society, whatever the level, (c) by conflating horrific events with the consequences of media exposure, (d) connecting to our fears of the dangerous child or alternatively in presenting the child as victim, (e) participating in the tension between liberation and control, and (f) in othering the Other.

We want to be quick to point out that some justification has to appear for any literature to sustain itself. What appears to be uniquely driving this literature is the unprecedented course of change in technology over the past 100 years; the rise of social science in the same period, with its need for authentication and legitimacy; the irreducible issues of societal violence, social control, and the child; and our continuing need of being Us in an us/them cultural world. Given that the advance of technology and needs of social science continue unabated and that the literature plays into irreducible tensions, it would appear that we are sufficiently justified for another century of work.

I&C Codes

Coding of the I&C (Implications and Conclusions) sections of the articles began by setting aside the conclusions drawn from the evidence, findings, or results. Every competently written article will have such conclusions. Our interest was in implications and conclusions that go beyond the presented evidence. Such arguments can start with phrasing such as the following: "Taken as a whole, the results presented here suggest that. . . ." This is the point where the author begins to enact a role that may go beyond the scientist or scholar to more explicitly reveal his or her cultural agency. For example, if the author is writing an article on an experimental study of an intervention in the association between media violence and aggression, the conclusion that the intervention worked would be a direct conclusion. The conclusion that, therefore, schools, pediatricians, or parents ought to adopt this intervention strategy reaches well beyond the evidence to presume what is in the best interests of schools, pediatricians, or parents. These arguments, nonetheless, represent the payoff for the reader. They are what research texts often refer to as "So what?" arguments. They are the justification provided by the implications of the study.

Table 5.2 presents the compiled I&C codes and the number of arguments coded for each.[5] The number of arguments exceeds the number of articles as more than one justifying argument could be present in the statement of the problem. The reader is reminded that the numbers of

Table 5.2   Compiled Codes, Number of Arguments, and Sources Coded for Implications and Conclusions

Code	Number of Arguments	Sources Coded
Consequences for society	56	4, 11, 13, 14, 18, 34, 38, 40, 49, 50, 67, 77, 80, 87, 102, 120, 124, 142, 146, 148, 160, 163, 164, 168, 170, 177, 179, 181, 182, 184, 189, 190, 191, 196, 205, 207, 208, 217, 218, 221, 222, 225, 229, 236, 238, 240, 246, 250, 252, 253, 254, 257, 266, 268, 273, 278
Call for some action	54	11, 13, 27, 52, 55, 66, 74, 75, 76, 78, 82, 84, 112, 120, 123, 134, 135, 165, 168,169, 180, 182, 200, 206, 207, 210, 219, 225, 231, 234, 241, 246, 247, 248, 253, 258, 262, 264, 266, 268, 272, 275, 282, 283, 284, 287, 290, 291, 292, 294
Advocacy/confirming	52	3, 7, 10, 15, 17, 21, 43, 44, 54, 55, 56, 58, 60, 61, 78, 94, 105, 109, 111, 126, 137, 145, 146, 156, 159, 160, 162, 163, 167, 172, 173, 184, 186, 195, 204, 210, 211, 221, 232, 238, 240, 261, 263, 269, 279, 285, 286, 289
Contrarian/disconfirming	51	2, 20, 28, 30, 35, 39, 41, 45, 57, 59, 62, 80, 84, 97, 101, 103, 105, 106, 108, 126, 128, 140, 150, 164, 172, 179, 187, 193, 200, 204, 206, 213, 215, 219, 228, 229, 234, 235, 239, 243, 244, 249, 259, 281, 288, 293, 295, 301, 302
Interventions	44	11, 14, 17, 24, 41, 56, 69, 60, 65, 72, 76, 82, 83, 91, 113, 136, 138, 153, 155, 156, 161, 185, 186, 213, 214, 215, 219, 231, 233, 237, 238, 240, 247, 248, 249, 253, 254, 262, 264, 265, 291, 292, 294

(Continued)

(Continued)

Code	Number of Arguments	Sources Coded
Critique	41	20, 28, 42, 47, 48, 49, 53, 62, 64, 77, 82, 100, 106, 108, 115, 116, 117, 118, 119, 120, 121, 128, 129, 139, 140, 147, 149, 152, 154, 162, 164, 175, 193, 206, 217, 219, 245, 256, 277, 296, 299
Advice	30	9, 11, 16, 21, 24, 25, 39, 57, 58, 74, 75, 76, 95, 107, 113, 135, 161, 213, 227, 231, 254, 262, 263, 274, 284, 290, 291, 292, 299

arguments are a representation of our ability to get to the complexity of the argument type. We make no claim that the numbers reliably represent the rates of appearance of such arguments in the literature, although they may indeed do so.

Consequences for Society

Authors dream big when considering the implications of their studies for society. Often, the medium of choice is seen as an agent of major social change (49):

> The cinema, despite its lack of culture, may be operating unwittingly to help prepare an order of life in a free and secular society. This idea is purely speculative. But one might interpret the shifting play of motion pictures in response to the selective acts of the mass, as unconscious experiments in feeling out the developing tastes and aspirations of the people and helping to mold them into a consistent pattern of life. (p. 127)

For some, one does not even have to be exposed to any medium (164):

> Television in American society may be related to the diffusion of culture and to alterations in social structure, both of which affect the behavior of virtually all persons in the society regardless of how much television they watch. (pp. 300–301)

But it is the effect of violent content that remains in focus across the span of our sample (146, p. 59):

> The reader who doubts that men can be led to kill by suggestion, and many of those men of the highest moral type, is reminded of the potency of wartime propaganda carried on in no small part through the agency of the press.

Media violence affects a larger group of people than previously believed and interventions for adolescents might be beneficial. Such approaches are needed because a heavy diet of media violence contributes to a societal violence rate that is excessive. (14, p. 2377)

It is hardly surprising that the authors of this sample would find media the agent of significant social consequences or that content can instigate violence or aggression. There were a few other forms of the *consequence for society* argument, such as concern for the threat this line of research posed to the First Amendment (Hoffner et al., 1999), but they were taken by only a few or a single author.

An additional comment appears in order: The word *cancer* appears in 23 and smoking in 35 of the 302 documents. In 13 of those documents[6], some analogy is made between media violence/aggression and the relationship between smoking and cancer. (E. Katz & Foulkes, 1962) had drawn a similar relationship between TV escape and drug use.) The device first appears in our archive in a 1969 article (268, p. 41) that compares the slow pace of recognition of the media violence/aggression problem to the pace that had characterized the acceptance of the smoking and cancer relationship. The device is then absent from our archive until 1999, when the entertainment industry is compared with the tobacco industry in refusing to accept its social responsibility (275). From that point, the argument gets transformed to one that connects media violence/aggression with smoking and lung cancer to make the claim that the media violence/aggression risk is of the same sort. This form of the argument presumably appears so often that M. C. Miller (2001; who rejects the analogy) can use the generic "politicians and researchers" to reference those who use it. The claim itself is well represented in the following quotation (163):

> Perhaps one of the best parallels is the relation between smoking and lung cancer. Not everyone who smokes gets lung cancer, and not everyone who gets lung cancer was a smoker. Smoking is not the only factor that causes lung cancer, but it is an important factor. Similarly, not everyone who watches violent television

becomes aggressive, and not everyone who is aggressive watches violent television. Watching violent TV programs is not the only factor that causes aggression, but it is an important factor. (p. 408)

The strongest use of this device, however, appears in a universal effect claim (161):

But just as every cigarette one smokes increases a little bit the likelihood of a lung tumor someday, the theory supported by this research suggests that every violent TV show increases a little bit the likelihood of a child growing up to behave more aggressively in some situation. (p. 218)

This analogy follows from the universal effect that these authors advance in this study, but it may not fit the facts of either the relationship between smoking and lung cancer or between media violence and aggression. As an editorial in the *Archives of Pediatrics and Adolescent Medicine* points out (108):

Most people who smoke don't get cancer. Most children who watch television do not act violently. My mother is 75 and has been smoking for 60 years. She is healthier than the proverbial horse, but even she acknowledges that smoking is bad for people's health (it just doesn't apply to her). It's about time the television and motion picture industries get on the same wavelength as my mother. (p. 13)

The difference between these two quotations seems quite instructive. The former makes use of a fear appeal (shown by communication researchers to be the least effective approach to encourage individual action); the latter is much more folksy, "C'mon, you know this stuff isn't good for you." In this set of 13, Huesmann, Anderson, and Bushman (e.g., 55) represent the fear appeal group and Garbarino, Miller, and Strasburger the more tempered approach.

By invoking cancer, the fear group seeks to elevate media violence/aggression to the level of social concern that is appropriate to the smoking and cancer link (M. C. Miller, 2001). As M. C. Miller (2001) opines, "By using the analogies of tobacco and firearms, critics of the entertainment industry join two touchstone issues, public health and public safety. The question is whether either analogy is appropriate" (p. 6). That link is without a doubt a significant social concern. The Centers for Disease Control and Prevention estimates that 400,000 deaths from all types of cancer were attributable to smoking; the American Cancer Society estimates that annually, 120,000 people die from smoking-induced lung cancer; and the World Health Organization estimates that more than a billion people will be killed by smoking-related diseases during the 21st century. The question for Miller is whether the "analogy is appropriate" (p. 7). We think it is not. The effort by the fear group to associate a similar concern for the media violence/ aggression link when not a single death, not even a single cross word, can be attributed to media exposure with the certainty of the smoking/ cancer link is clearly ideology and not science.

Call for Some Action

Media reform was the central call for action. In its least complex form, it was a call to reduce violence and become socially responsible. This call was sounded early in the archive (241) and repeated often:

> Bad programs will continue to drive out good programs until producers, sponsors, and advertisers unite in a policy of genuine public service to broadcast programs for children which will contribute to their emotional health and intellectual development and create an understanding and appreciation of American life today. (p. 217)

The promise of the media as a force for social good was longingly recognized in these calls for reform as these quotes spanning 80 years attest (225, p. 339; 13, p. 358):

> If the motion picture is to become the educational force that it is capable of becoming, the censorship must be an internal one. The old notion is outworn that it is necessary "to give the people what they want." It is the function of an educational medium and an entertaining medium also, to give the public what they should have, in order that they may learn to want it. The function of education is to create as well as to satisfy wants. The future of the motion picture is limited only by the foresight of its leaders.

> Finally, we wonder whether exciting video games can be created to teach and reinforce nonviolent solutions to social conflicts. If marketed with the same zeal (and dollars) as the destructive games that currently dominate the market, would they be as profitable? In other words, is it possible to use the profit motive that has for years driven the media-violence machine to turn that machine in a prosocial direction?

But there was also a recognition that researchers have their obligations as well (246):

Somewhere there must be a collaborative meeting ground. Ultimately, researchers must better understand and take into account the social realities of the television industry. Industry officials must accept and be responsive to the social realities of the researchers. Until those two social realities are brought into better conjunction, the viewer will receive less than the best that television has to offer. (p. 824)

One of the critiques of the media violence research is that it is antimedia. Certainly, one could collect phrases and sentences from these calls for reform to make that case. More to the point, however, is that the literature is biased against popular (or "low") culture. Equally important, this negative stance consistently taken in this literature creates a disconnection between the claims of the literature and lives that people live. But in this regard, researchers, rather than acknowledging those social realities, claim to know better (e.g., 30, p. 26; 41, p. 94).

Advocacy/Confirming

Advocacy arguments attempt to extend the scope or the significance of the main findings of the study (240):

Nevertheless, on the basis of the displays presented in this paper, it seems clear that our ability to predict and control antisocial behavior is not at all trivial in practical terms, despite the apparently small r^2s obtained in most studies. For example, there is nothing trivial about being able to reduce rates of aggressive behavior from about 62 to about 38% by means of an experimental intervention, even though the proportion of variance accounted for is less than 6%. (p. 153)

And the argument can also be self-congratulatory (17):

Social-cognitive approaches to understanding human aggression have been developing for over 30 years. Current models converge on a common set of theoretical assumptions, largely because those assumptions have proven useful in organizing the vast research literature and in generating new, testable hypotheses concerning the development, persistence, and change of aggression. (p. 314)

Or sometimes more self-assuring (163):

This review has presented compelling evidence that short-term exposure to media violence stimulates more aggressive and violent behavior in the young viewer immediately and that long-term exposure leads to the acquisition of social cognitions (scripts, world schemas, attitudes, and beliefs) that increase the risk of aggressive and violent behavior in the observers of media violence beyond childhood. The psychological processes through which this happens are well understood by researchers. (pp. 407–408)

But it is in testimony that we find its strongest expression (211):

In summary, the results or our initial, and very limited study, of children's brain activations while viewing entertainment video violence, suggest that the violence is arousing, engaging, and is treated by the brain as a real event that is threatening and worthy of being stored for long-term memory in an area of the brain that makes 'recall' of the events almost instantaneous.

Contrarian/Disconfirming

Contrarian positions develop in response to the perceived critical hysteria directed toward the media (219, 234, 281), to the dominant cognitivist theory (20, 235, 243), to specific tenets of media violence/aggression literature (2, 108, 295), and to the media violence/aggression link itself. We present a few exemplars from this last class of arguments:

This research points to one of the major reasons why many persons may be unaffected by scenes of violence on movie and television screens: Unless they are completely caught up by the story, much of the time as they watch the happenings unfold they are also aware that they are seeing only a fictitious portrayal. This awareness may serve to distance them psychologically from the depicted events, so that the observed occurrences do not activate strong aggressive thoughts, feelings, and action tendencies. (41, p. 104)

However, until future research can elucidate more precisely the mechanisms of action for media reactivity, it may be prudent to reserve judgment concerning endorsing the aggression hypothesis. Nevertheless, we encourage the reader to draw his or her own conclusions regarding these studies and to this end have provided different criteria for evaluating them. (106, p. 403)

There is some evidence that the effects observed in laboratory experiments, and less consistently in field experiments, are due to sponsor effects. The fact that children who are exposed to violence tend to misbehave generally casts doubt on most of the other theoretical explanations of media effects. (97, p. 103)

The data from the study also demonstrate that exposure of urban school-aged children to violence is not a rare event but that many children are exposed to multiple episodes of violent acts. This exposure to violence may provide a constant threat to the safety of children and may influence child-rearing practices. Children in highly violent areas, for example, may be taught to watch television lying prone to avoid being hit by stray bullets through the windows. The walk home from school may become an arena of fear and distress for parents and children. Mothers in violent communities may refrain from bringing their children to playgrounds, denying them the chance to play with other children and explore the environment.

> In our primary care setting, almost all of the urban school-aged children interviewed had been exposed to types of violence that are more direct than media exposure, with a substantial number exposed to multiple episodes of violence. (228, p. 951)

It is interesting to consider that when one adds up the arguments appearing in this code, in the *critique* code (which classifies arguments on protocol or policy) and in the *conditions* code (which classifies arguments on the limits of effects), one gets 125 instances of arguments that temper the universal effect conclusion. Again, the rate is not a reliable indicator of what might be in the literature as a whole, but it does suggest that there has been and still remains a consistent voice of opposition. The question may be, Is anyone listening? We are given scant hope:

> Ultimately, then, Howitt and Cumberbatch base their dismissal of a media violence effect on critiques and misinterpretations of old outmoded theories, an unjustified contempt for and myopic reading of research findings, and a dogged commitment to the unsupported, largely ideological belief in perfectly active audiences. Like their peers Freedman, Fowles, and Jones, they make their argument seem to hold water only through careful inattention and misrepresentation. (162, p. 130)

What seems to be at least one sticking point in getting beyond shouting past one another is the adequacy of simple exposure as the agent of any result. Causationists have gone from modifying exposure with terms such as *heightened exposure* or *excessive exposure* (38 sources can be identified on the term *high levels* alone) to the one conclusion of *any exposure* (161). Yet even in the fairly simple cognitive scripts theory, some active process of learning of the behavior and reinforcement of the enactment has to take place.

If one builds scripts of aggression, then there has to be some "script-building" faculty that is engaged in the process. And if that faculty is engaged, what causes it to be engaged? (There is, of course, an unending regress of causal agents in the cognitive process.) The explanation cannot be located in exposure. It has to be located in script building. Narratives of any sort are certainly resources in that script-building process, but they are not the process, and they are not necessarily narratives of aggression. Such narratives are everywhere, not just in the media. Furthermore, if one enacts aggressive behavior, it has to be deemed successful. What are the conditions in the environment and/or in the person that provide this reinforcement?

The longitudinal studies of Eron and associates that were continued by Huesmann and associates and that provide the strongest case for childhood media being a contributor to adult aggression cannot break into this process. Instead of massaging the same protocol over and over as these longitudinal studies do, it is time to acknowledge that we have taken this protocol as far as it can go. Now it is time to develop new protocols that will address process and performance.

Interventions

The call for interventions takes on something of the character of the great white hope for reclaiming our society from the clutches of media, as this argument in that wonderful language of the 1930s attests:

> Finally, and most important of all, we must equip our citizenry with the understanding, the insight, the discrimination necessary to evaluate critically what they see on the screen, hear on the radio, or read in the press. We have learned in America and elsewhere to make and distribute propaganda faster than we have learned how to resist and evaluate it. (83, p. 42)

But the call for interventions also presents perhaps the clearest case that exposure is an inadequate basis for claiming an effect comes in the nature of the intervention arguments. One such argument (213) points out, "Depending on what they do, parents can socialize children into an orientation toward violent TV that makes them more or less vulnerable to its negative effects" (p. 137). In this conclusion, the author echoes a 58-year prior finding that "elimination of movie horrors and radio crime was found in homes of high standards of child training throughout, regardless of social or of economic standing, or even of intellectual standing in some cases" (227, p. 168).

Given that script building and the reinforcement of enactment have to occur, there is no nonintervention condition in the relationship between exposure and aggressive behavior. What interventions do is raise the likelihood of socially desirable outcomes in the process of development. Unfortunately, what they also do is release us from our larger obligations (254):

> Aggression and violence . . . are multi-determined behaviors stemming from inequities in access to social and economic resources, inequities in the adequacy of medical and educational services, persistent racism and social oppression, and ready access to handguns and firearms. Depictions of violence in the mass media serve to validate and perhaps exacerbate this culture. Decreasing violent content in mass media and the exposure of children and adolescents to such violence, and encouraging parents to monitor and critically discuss media violence are important elements of a multifaceted public health violence prevention effort. (p. 290)

This form of multicausation argument that lists a series of critical social ills and then ends with media content serves to equate the content of the media with, say, pervasive racism and all the others in the list. It also allows the only intervention that is called for—the intervention in content—to appear as most important when it is just the only one we will engage. What interventions are proposed to deal with the inequities, inadequacies, racism, social oppression, and ready access to the means of violence that actually lead the list? And if we don't intervene in those other social ills, will whatever we do with content make any difference?

Advice

Researchers are not shy about giving advice to parents, policy makers, legislators, the general public, and fellow researchers. The most common advice, however, is to the parent. Causationists place a heavy burden on parents:

> Parents need to be as concerned about the beliefs and attitudes that are being conveyed in violent shows as they are about their child mimicking the behaviors shown. The changes in how the child perceives the world from viewing violence and the beliefs about aggression that the child acquires from viewing violence are likely to influence the child's behavior in the long term as much as the specific scripts for aggression that the child learns from viewing violence. (58, p. 350)

In summary, parents need to be on the alert for any video game that encourages or allows the player to harm another creature, human or nonhuman. Such games are very likely teaching the game player subtle but harmful aggression lessons, regardless of how cute the game characters are or how unrealistic the violence appears. (61, p. 14)

And so do child development experts, psychologists, and educationists:

Further, restricting the amount of viewing without substituting socially constructive leisure activities is of questionable value. For example, if normal viewing times are replaced by activities that lead to fighting with siblings or other children, the outcomes of these experiences could be worse than those associated with watching television. (107, p. 58)

Professionals and parents must be aware of all sources of input for their children, not only peers, textbooks, teachers, and relatives but also from the subtle "stranger" in the living room who talks to children daily with complex messages of fear, violence, materialism, and, only infrequently, with messages of sharing, friendship, and concern for others. (263, p. 445)

They should give children guidance and help in learning to listen too and in acquiring discrimination in listening habits [in reference to radio drama]. They should also cooperate with other adult groups in an effort to enrich, extend, and improve educational offerings on TV. There is at present a great opportunity and a great challenge in this endeavor. (290, p. 472)

One wonders what vision of domestic life justifies these far-reaching terms of advice. Estimates run as high as 50% of all children will live in a single-parent household sometime before they are 18 years old and that 31% live in single-parent households at any given time (www.acef.org). Furthermore, the American Academy of Pediatrics estimates that more than 75% of families with children younger than age 5 have both parents working (www.aap.org). These parents will try to do it all and often succeed beyond reasonable expectations, but the fact is that much of the advice is inappropriate and impossible. We simply need a much more reasoned and informed approach to addressing media in contemporary society.

Implications

The implications and conclusion sections of the documents in this sample suggest that vested interests are being aggressively pushed and the social significance of the issue is being hyperextended, that there is more diversity in the literature than one might expect from the reports of those vested in it, that the contrary positions point to an inadequacy of understanding of the processes and performance of aggressive behavior, that the recommended solutions to media violence/aggression seem much more simple than the problem, and that advice often seems disconnected from contemporary family life. It is clear, then, that in this journey of understanding of media effects, we are not only not there yet, but we may have been going round the issues in circles, believing we were making progress.

Aggression and Violence Codes

In our work in coding the statement of problem and implications and conclusion sections of the documents, we were directed by the questions of why this topic has been sustained in research for more than 100 years. In this section of the coding, we were directed by questions concerning the internal consistency of the literature. This question arises because of arguments of consilience or of the preponderance of evidence. In order for convergence to appear or for there to be a preponderance, there has to be a reasonable consistency in the way the topic is understood and addressed in the literature. We proceed to answer this question by examining the claims attached to the terms, their definitions, character, measurement, representation, and performance of violence and aggression as presented in our sample of documents.

Claims

The majority of research in this area suggests a link between media violence and the development of aggressive behavior. The exact nature of this link, however, is open to considerable variation. Some believe the problem to be excessive television of any sort. The key correlation is simply the watching of television in general. "Studies have shown that increased aggressiveness correlates with heavy viewing, regardless of the violence content of programs" (145, p. 1299). Others hold that it is the specific content type that leads to aggressive consequences, as this quotation exemplifies: "Children who are exposed to violent television programming are more likely to be aggressive and to become involved in the juvenile justice system compared with those with less exposure" (65, p. 94).

Still others insist that the relationship is the other way around—aggression is a factor in wanting to view media violence in the first place. An example is the following comment: "Almost all researchers would agree that more aggressive children generally watch more television and prefer more violent television" (153, p. 126). And yet others see something as yet unknown coming into play, influencing both aggression and violence viewing and performance: "a third variable (other than gender, IQ, or age) may cause both aggressive behavior and media violence exposure" (186, p. 214). What consensus develops appears in particular times of the literature and with particular groups of researchers, using particular research protocols. But whenever consensus appears, the alternative voice continues to be heard.

Definitions

The comparison of violence and aggression is so ubiquitous that usually the terms are used interchangeably. This conflation of the two terms, however, has led to a myriad of definitional and measurement problems. In practice, the term *violence* is ordinarily applied to media content. *Aggression,* on the other hand, ordinarily references some consequential action produced by a viewer.

Most articles examined either do not define violence or aggression at all or explain them as overt expressions of physical force with an intent to harm. Some researchers use more specificity in suggesting that violence is a serious or extreme and purposive act done with an intent to inflict harm, pain, injury, or death with or without a weapon and directed at humans. Only one study we reviewed defined violence as an exercise of physical force so as to injure or damage persons *or* property (54).

Aggression is usually more clearly defined than violence but with no more consistency. What forces the clarity is the demands of measurement. What allows the inconsistency is the researchers' definitions of the behaviors to be included in the operational definition. That definition starts with behavioral types. Behavioral types include indirect or direct, intentional affective, and/or instrumental action.

Indirect aggression is behavior that is committed outside the presence of the other party, such as gossiping or stealing. Direct aggression is directed at another person in such ways as shoving, hurling insults, or hitting.

Others, however, disagree with defining aggression along the lines of strict dichotomies. Instead, they suggest that it is more helpful to characterize aggression along dimensions such as "degree of hostile or agitated affect present; automaticity; degree to which the primary or ultimate goal is to harm the victim versus benefit the perpetrator; and degree to which consequences were considered" (17, p. 299).

Although one may think that aggression as a behavior or a type would be a clear and agreed-on definition, this is not the case. Other researchers view aggression as a multifaceted phenomenon that has many determinants, serves diverse purposes, and defies specific definition other than suggesting that intentionality is difficult or impossible to measure and aggression includes physical and verbal acts whose goal-response is injury to an organism. One even operationally defines aggression as "a noxious response to a person or property" (267, p. 110).

Most researchers define aggression as having a necessary proximate goal of intention to harm, but several writers take issue with this and view aggression as a primary human characteristic that is necessary for survival in the struggle for existence, that not all aggression is antisocial. In this stance, aggression may play out in socially acceptable forms of scholastic or athletic events.

In addition, some see *aggression* and *violence* as being interchangeable terms (199), while others view all violence as aggression, but much aggression is not violent (13). For example, car accidents are depicted as being violent without being aggressive (160). A vast number fail to define violence and/or aggression at all, using the terms interchangeably and undefined as though researchers assume the reader understands without clarification what is meant in their use of either term. Variations, then, crop up from researcher to researcher, depending on how they classify the basic meaning of violence and aggression. Without that definitional consistency, and perhaps in addition to it, characterizations vary as well.

Character

Violence seems to be an extremely difficult concept to grasp. Perhaps the best characterization of violence is that its nature is unclear. Consider the following example: "In three different studies of programming, football was ignored by one research team, classified as 'highly violent' by another, and 'nonviolent' by still another" (144, p. 609). So, in general, we're dealing with an ambiguous term. We all talk about violence as if we're talking about the same thing, but that may or may not be the case.

Most view violence as consisting of multiple causal elements ranging from high arousal, neural circuits programmed for violence, priming from aggression, interest in violence, and early learning. One argument (284) suggests that especially in the case of television news content, the notion of violence as characterized by some of such causal elements is too narrow, that it needs to include unintended and structural elements of content and behavior for the nature of violence to be understood. Violence is even seen as being cathartic and possibly beneficial, although this position is strongly attacked (e.g., 40). On the other hand, catharsis was also seen as hampering the war effort by dampening the aggressive spirit, rendering youth incapable of fighting.

The character of aggression is not only unclear and difficult to grasp but also contradictory. For every study that views aggression as being attributable to some sort of internal state such as individual neurophysiological factors, natural tendencies, low imagination, and other biological factors, there is another one that suggests that aggression is externally motivated and developed through priming, different socialization experiences, provocation, scripts, triggers, or learned behaviors. Aggression is seen as a result of unstable or inflated self-esteem, attention-deficit hyperactivity disorder, aversive changes in the conditions of life, expected rewards, hostile schemas, provocation, frustration, and even as a natural outgrowth in children who are accident prone. Little seems to be excluded from the list.

Most of the studies in the past 10 years now adhere to a view that conceptualizes aggression being a combination of these environmental and biological factors and taking place in a multistage process. In this view, the explanation of aggression must explain not only how aggressive patterns are acquired but also how they are "activated and channeled" (30, p. 17). Apropos to this, "a theory [of aggression] must know drive, cue, response, reward, and what's going on inside one's head" (92, p. 441) in order to understand what aggression is and how it can be predicted.

There is, of course, a cultural value in not defining violence. The definition is left to the reader to construct, thereby eliminating any dissent as to the boundaries of what is included. At the same time, not defining violence but defining aggression as, say, the intent to harm allows the two terms to inform one another. Consequently, the egregious violence that appears on the screen (and which nearly all of us who write about media violence/aggression have never experienced) becomes the aggressive behavior that it supposedly causes as opposed to the schoolyard scuffles that may be actually measured.

Measurement

Any time that something like violence or aggression is studied, there is a need for some sort of measurement. Violence has been measured by counting such things as dramatic incident or by participation of particular characters. Researchers have determined violence by levels of exposure to media violence, reflecting, for example, the number of persons viewing television programs, the content of these programs scaled along the dimension of violence, regularity of television viewing, violence of preferred programs, overall television violence viewing, identification with television characters, identification with aggressive television characters, and/or perceived realism of various violent programs.

Questionnaires, self-reports such as the Media Exposure Measure—a semistructured self-report adolescent interview and parent questionnaire measure of the adolescent's television and video game viewing/playing habits, which was developed as a measure of media violence exposure (186)—peer reports, and measurement of responses such as the numbers of shocks given to dolls after exposure to violence have been used as instruments for measuring violence. In addition to these, one frequently used, and often cited, measurement is the Violence Index (117).

The Violence Index defines violence as "the overt expression of physical force against self or other, compelling action against one's will on pain of being hurt or killed, or actually hurting individual's own sense of value and ethics" (qtd. in Kim, 1994, p. 1398). The Violence Index evoked much controversy based on the fact that it was often used to estimate rates of violence when it was never intended to be a statistical finding.

There have also been other debates about the index, particularly in coding cartoon violence, from which there is instant on-screen recovery in the same manner as violence against a human character. Kim (1994) related the Cultural Indicators (CI) team reply: "In response to the controversy over his measurement techniques, Gerbner readily agrees that 'obviously, not all violence is alike,' but that for the purposes of a massive empirical coding study like the Violence Index project, subjective standards are not possible, and the definition currently in use is a reliable and objective one" (p. 1399). Kim argues, however, that if such a technical definition is adopted, then too much counts as violence because it fails to account for the effect of context. The CI team, in response to such attacks, says, "Continued squabbles about technical methodological details of definition and measurement deflect attention from more serious areas of agreement and consensus" (qtd. in Kim, 1994, p. 1399). The response of the CI team to criticism seems to parallel that of the causationists—deny, deflect, and continue on.

Aggression also depends on the means of its measurement—in this case, through self-reports, parental reports, observation, questionnaires, and, in most longitudinal studies, peer reports (most often the Peer Rating Index of Aggression; Walder, Abelson, Eron, Banta, & Laulicht, 1961). Some studies use composite measures of aggressiveness incorporating rumination about violence and values concerning violence as well as aggressive behavior. Some feel that seeing representations of violence will increase accessibility of aggressive thoughts, exacerbate symptoms of emotional disturbance, or lead to copy-cat behaviors at a later date. Others examine heart rate acceleration, blood pressure elevation, and vasoconstriction as indices of excitation. Still others measure such elements as frequency of viewing, counting of (what they perceive as) violent incidents, and identification with aggressive male and female radio, television, film, or video game characters. Again, the issue for us is that all of these measures are surrogates, and each carries its own probability of error. Because there are so many measures of widely different sorts, there would seem to be little consistency in the conceptual understanding of aggression.

Two other major issues with measurement of aggression are, first, although intentionality is a requirement in the conceptual definition of aggression, researchers do not measure the intentionality of the respondent (101). And, second, measures of actual aggressive acts are quite rare as well, and when real-life behavior is the measure, it is typically fantasy or play behavior (254). Critics believe that games, toys, inflated dolls, paper-and-pencil measures of aggression, button-pushing devices, and noise instruments are all, at best, weak simulators of real-life social behavior (122, 289).

Measurement problems link closely with the inability to pin down definitions of both aggression and violence. Until definitions can be clearly delineated, measurement will continue to have problems with consistency. Beyond measurement, an understanding of what it means to represent and perform violence and aggression is inconsistent and varies from study to study.

Representation

Representations of violence in the media have been found in everything from cartoons to prime-time programs, commercials, news broadcasts, feature films, and video games. Given the multiple definitions—or lack thereof—of violence, it is not surprising that every aspect of media has been identified as containing some sort of violence. But not all media violence is equal; some of this violence elicits more outcry than others.

Violence in children's programs has been a particular target. Programs that children view are not only held to contain violence but, as has been argued over the years, to contain even more violence than adult programs (26, 173, 210). For example, it has been claimed that 83.3% of children's programming contains some form of violence (51). And estimates have been given that the average young person will have viewed an estimated

200,000 acts of violence on television alone by the time he or she reaches age 18 (74).

Commercial violence also elicits outcry because of its insertion into every type of program. Advertisements have been reported as containing about three times the number of aggressive acts as prime-time programs (255). The cultural issues in these arguments have to do with the offense taken with the sheer volume of violence presented and vulnerability of the projected audience to the consequences of exposure.

Another aspect of media violence that causes concern is the proportional representation of the age, race, and/or social class of the perpetrator (114). Although there are perpetrators and victims represented in every age, race, and class, the argument here is that there are more lower-class characters presented as perps and victims, thereby reproducing the dominant interests of the social hierarchy, a common argument of critical theory.

Characters who resort to violence do so for a variety of legal or illegal reasons. Legal reasons for violence range from self-defense, protecting family or society, or sanctioned law enforcement, power, or financial gain. Illegal motivations include unsanctioned law enforcement, power, financial gain, or corruption. Interestingly enough, legal reasons are shown much more frequently than violence committed for illegal motives (114). Media portrayals of violent scenes both reinforce and punish consequences for aggressive behavior. Expressing this more succinctly, "the aggressive 'bad guys' are usually punished, and the aggressive 'good guys' usually have a legal right to use force" (27, p. 188).

Similarly, attractive characters almost always reach a happy end regardless of whether there is violence. Both of these representation tendencies seem to be in line with U.S. cultural sensibilities. Perhaps the media do mirror who we are, and that apparently is unsettling. Nonetheless, valuation of depiction depends not only on the context of the representation itself or the context in which the representation takes place but even on how the viewer relates to the representation. Representation of violence and aggression ultimately, as well, depends on the viewpoint of the researcher conducting the research, leading to a vast inconsistency in the way that research is portrayed.

Researchers examining the ostensible effects of media violence have also been concerned about the conditions necessary for those effects. Thirty-five documents record multiple conditions for the effect to occur.[7] Some of these conditions accrue to the content (e.g., justified versus unjustified violence). Others accrue to the aggressor, to the victim, and to the situation. What is rarely addressed is how these other interactions confound the clarity of results of the research or their implications for policy, legislation, regulation, or intervention. So in other words, one cannot say violence, as represented in the media, is the putative agent of subsequent aggression, but rather, "it depends."

Performance

So, if it "depends" whether or not violence is bad or not to watch, the "depends" is actually stipulating whether there is some negative outcome to that viewing. This is actually the real crux of the matter. If viewing violence does not cause any negative outcomes, then there is no reason to prevent it. If, on the other hand, there are serious, negative consequences to such viewing, then it should be curtailed.

Very few studies stipulate what aggressive behavior is in performance. Most studies say something like, "repeated violent television exposure is linked to later aggressive behavior" or, more specifically (in reference to watching movies), "when a villain is defeated aggressively—the consequence may be a weakening of restraints against hostility in angered audience members; they may be more likely to believe it is permissible to attack the 'villains' in their own lives, at least during the time immediately following the movie" (43, p. 229). There is still a plethora, however, of unspecified "violent behavior" following violent media viewing episodes.

Where the violent behavior is stipulated, it focuses on records of violent physical behavior, including physical abuse, moving traffic violations, punching, homicides, and criminal convictions. Studies spotlighting children use fantasy violence toward dolls, toy animals, toy cars, and assaultive behaviors toward objects.

The variations across measures of violent behavior are perhaps less of a problem than the fact that media violence shows a low to absent relationship with violent behavior (128, 204). Thus, we have the problem of research not only describing a wide array of behaviors, all described as being aggressive or violent, but also a seemingly sliding scale of relationship depending on the extremity of the initial depiction as well as the behavioral outcome.

Implications of Violence and Aggression Codes

Violence and aggression are chameleon-like variables seen as the same thing by some and different by others. This has led to measurement problems. Most studies have found some correlation between violence viewing and aggression but little with violent behavior. Nonetheless, careful distinctions are rarely made. Instead, there has been a tendency to make the most of what ambiguity allows.

No one yet knows exactly what triggers violent behavior, internal or external factors, or multiples of these, or how they function to provide scripts for such behavior. What can be asserted is that more research, more *consistent* research, is needed.

Some Concluding Thoughts

The close reading of this literature at first presents the famous booming, buzzing confusion of the newborn, but as familiarity grows, it is quite clear that clusters of arguments are being advanced by different authors. The arguments can be laid out across three axes: The first axis would have consequences for society (COS) and consequences for the child (COC) as its poles. The second would have conditional effect (CE) and universal effect (UE), and the third would have exposure (E), where content is seen as unproblematic in its role as an agent, and interpretation (I), where content has to be activated for an effect to occur. What seems to be apparent in the literature is that communities of practice develop along these axes.

There are several communities represented, the largest of which are the COSUEE, COSCEE, and the COCUEE communities.[8] If we locate the more or less contemporary players (plus/minus 30 years), Eron, Huesmann, C. Anderson, Bushman, and often Strasburger would be the emblematic members of the COSUEE (ko sue e) communities. They act as community members working together, publishing together; they speak a common language and make use of the same sorts of arguments. COSCEE (ko shee) members would include Bandura (later), Berkowitz, D. Anderson, and Zillmann (earlier). The COCUEE (ko ku e) community would include Nathanson, Comstock, Murray, Wartella, Collins, and Cantor. The COC-CEE (ko kee) community would locate Ball-Rokeach, D. Singer, J. Singer, Sprafkin, Gadow, Friedrich, and Huston.

Of the elements that make up these communities, exposure seems to be the unifying condition for when one moves out toward the interpretive pole, one loses the clarity of focus on the other issues. The arguments vibrate between the cultural and the individual, the possible and the inevitable, and between an effect and an enactment. The I (eh) community houses a diverse group, even some adversaries: J. Anderson, Dorr (later), Cumberbatch, Gerbner, Gunter, Howitt, Katz, Rubin, the very recent Potter, Wober, and the later Zillmann. Oftentimes, membership is a result that no other ideational location would serve better.

The appearance of these communities reminds us that we are looking at the traces of organized human practice that, in itself, depends on a set of extended and often collegial relationships and not some disembodied, disconnected practice. As Anderson et al. (2003a) note, R. L. Huesmann calls the people he knows to the table—Berkowitz, Comstock, Donnerstein, Linz, Malamuth, and Wartella—as in an earlier era, and George routinely called on Larry, Michele, Sandra, and Nancy. When we understand the practice of this literature as appearing in extended communities, we realize that the rules of communities apply. In some way, we achieve membership, are recognized as a member, and are separated from other communities; in addition, boundaries are policed, rights extended, and privileges maintained.

Far from being a common literature, the archive contains a diversity of ideological, political, and cultural positions that define the communities that sustain them and establish for members what is appropriate scientific and scholarly practice, as well as what are the warrants for claim, the permissible claims, and the taboo arguments. As we look across the history of COSUEE, we see the community developing increasingly definitive claims about the strength and universality of the effect. The practice of the community has clearly been to achieve that goal as we look at the progressive refinement of arguments toward that end. Choices were made, and when the evidence appeared, a press release was issued.

The literature demonstrates that some communities have been very successful in sustaining themselves, and others have formed, fallen apart, and sometimes reformed. Drawing out comparisons with the OWI (Office of War Information) club during World War II, the COSUEE community has had an unique continuity of leadership for nearly 50 years, successful programs of funding, and access to political power. The I community has had successful centers and strong leaders, but it has lacked that unity of purpose that brings it all together.

In our search for why the media violence/aggression literature continues to grow unabated, we have pointed to a variety of reasons: the ongoing work of normal science, the intractable conditions of and the inevitability of violence and aggression in society, the instability of the universal effect claim, our fears of and for our children, the force of class distinction with a rejection of lower pleasures, the tension between the desire for liberations and the need for control, the deep attraction of a productive protocol, that the literature in its ambiguity and inconsistency produces its own motivation for more to be said, and that media technologies and content do not stand still and thereby give ample motivation for yet another effects study. And now we see one more engine perhaps more powerful than the rest. It is that the work is sustained by the communities in which it appears and is not dependent on conditions beyond the success of the community itself. The work is *symbolic science*—self-authenticating and self-legitimizing. Its pretense is to provide yet another definitive yet irrelevant answer to questions whose terms change in the asking. It is a repetitive effort to stop the flow of human action. And apparently it is all to be continued.

Appendix

Sample Documents

1. Abel, J. D. (1968–1969). Television and children: A selective bibliography of use and effects. *Journal of Broadcasting, 13*(1), 101–105.
2. Abel, J. D., & Beninson, M. E. (1976). Perceptions of TV program violence by children and mothers. *Journal of Broadcasting, 20*(3), 355–363.
3. Adorno, T. W. (1954). How to look at television. *The Quarterly of Film, Radio, and Television, 8*(3), 213–235.
4. Albert, J. A. (1978). Constitutional regulation of televised violence. *Virginia Law Review, 64*(8), 1299–1345.
5. Albert, R. S., & Meline, H. G. (1958). The influence of social status on the uses of television. *Public Opinion Quarterly, 22*(2), 145–151.
6. Albig, W. (1938). The content of radio programs, 1925–1935. *Social Forces, 16*(3), 338–349.
7. Allport, G. W., & Faden, J. M. (1940). The psychology of newspapers: Five tentative laws. *Public Opinion Quarterly, 4*(4), 687–703.
8. American Psychological Association. (1998). *APA resolution on television violence and children.* Washington, DC: Author.
9. American Psychological Association. (2003). *Childhood exposure to media violence predicts young adult aggressive behavior, according to a new 15-year study.* Washington, DC: Author.
10. Anderson, C. A. (2004). An update on the effects of playing violent video games. *Journal of Adolescence, 27*, 113–122.
11. Anderson, C. A., Berkowitz, L., Donnerstein, E., Huesmann, L. R., Johnson, J. D., Linz, D., et al. (2003). The influence of media violence on youth. *Psychological Science in the Public Interest, 4*(3), 81–110.
12. Anderson, C. A., Berkowitz, L., Donnerstein, E., Huesmann, L. R., Johnson, J. D., Linz, D., et al. (2003). Authors' note. *Psychological Science in the Public Interest, 4*(3), ix.
13. Anderson, C. A., & Bushman, B. J. (2001). Effects of violent video games on aggressive behavior, aggressive cognition, aggressive affect, physiological arousal, and prosocial behavior: A meta-analytic review of the scientific literature. *Psychological Science, 12*(5), 353–359.
14. Anderson, C. A., & Bushman, B. J. (2002). The effects of media violence on society. *Science, 295*, 2377–2378.
15. Anderson, C. A., & Bushman, B. J. (2002). Media violence and the American public revisited. *American Psychologist, 57*(6/7), 448–450.

16. Anderson, C. A., & Dill, K. E. (2000). Video games and aggressive thoughts, feelings, and behavior in the laboratory and in life. *Journal of Personality and Social Psychology, 78*(4), 772–790.

17. Anderson, C. A., & Huesmann, L. R. (2003). Human aggression: A social-cognitive view. In M. A. Hogg & J. Cooper (Eds.), *The SAGE handbook of social psychology* (pp. 296–322). Thousand Oaks, CA: Sage.

18. Anderson, D. R. (1986). Television at home: Age trends in visual attention and time with TV. *Child Development, 57*(4), 1024–1033.

19. Anderson, D. R., Field, D. E., Collins, P. A., Pugzles Lorch, E., & Nathan, J. G. (1985). Estimates of young children's time with television: A methodological comparison of parent reports with time-lapse video home observation. *Child Development, 56*(5), 1345–1357.

20. Anderson, J. A. (1981). Research on children and television: A critique. *Journal of Broadcasting, 25*(4), 395–400.

21. Andison, F. S. (1977). TV violence and viewer aggression: A cumulation of study results 1956–1976. *Public Opinion Quarterly, 41,* 314–331.

22. Anonymous. (1989, July 24). Doing violence against violence. *New York Times,* p. A16.

23. Anonymous. (1992, July/August). Sons of violence/blurring the image. *Wired,* p. 13.

24. Anonymous. (2002). Children and television violence. *American Academy of Child and Adolescent Psychology, 13.*

25. Atkin, C., Greenberg, B. S., Korzenny, F., & McDermott, S. (1979). Selective exposure to televised violence. *Journal of Broadcasting, 23*(1), 5–13.

26. Atkin, C. K., Murray, J. P., & Nayman, O. B. (1971). The Surgeon General's research program on television and social behavior: A review of empirical findings. *Journal of Broadcasting, 16*(1), 21–35.

27. Ballard, I. M., Jr. (1995). See no evil, hear no evil: Television violence and the First Amendment. *Virginia Law Review, 81*(1), 175–222.

28. Ball-Rokeach, S. J. (2001). The politics of studying media violence: Reflections 30 years after the violence commission. *Mass Communication & Society, 4*(1), 3–18.

29. Bandura, A. (1965). Influence of models' reinforcement contingencies on the acquisition of imitative responses. *Journal of Personality and Social Behavior, 1*(6), 589–595.

30. Bandura, A. (1978). Social learning theory of aggression. *Journal of Communication, 28*(3), 12–29.

31. Bandura, A. (2001). Social cognitive theory of mass communication. *Media Psychology, 3,* 265–299.

32. Bandura, A., Grusec, J. E., & Menlove, F. L. (1966). Observational learning as a function of symbolization and incentive set. *Child Development, 37*(3), 499–506.

33. Bandura, A., Ross, D., & Ross, S. A. (1961). Transmission of aggression through imitation of aggressive models. *Journal of Abnormal and Social Psychology, 63*(3), 575–582.

34. Bandura, A., Ross, D., & Ross, S. A. (1963). Vicarious reinforcement and imitative learning. *Journal of Abnormal and Social Psychology, 67*(6), 601–607.

35. Baran, S. J. (1974). Prosocial and antisocial television content and modeling by high and low self-esteem children. *Journal of Broadcasting, 18*(4), 481–495.

36. Baran, S. J., Chase, L. J., & Courtright, J. A. (1979). Television drama as a facilitator of prosocial behavior: The Waltons. *Journal of Broadcasting, 23*(3), 277–284.

37. Barr, R., & Hayne, H. (1999). Developmental changes in imitation from television during infancy. *Child Development, 70*(5), 1067–1081.

38. Bartlett, K. G. (1941). Trends in radio programs. *Annals of the American Academy of Political and Social Science, 213*, 15–25.

39. Becker, G. (1972). Causal analysis in R-R studies: Television violence and aggression. *American Psychologist, 27*(10), 967–968.

40. Berkowitz, L. (1964). The effects of observing violence. *Scientific American, 210*(2), 35–41.

41. Berkowitz, L. (1986). Situational influences on reactions to observed violence. *Journal of Social Issues, 42*(3), 93–106.

42. Berkowitz, L. (1994). Is something missing? Some observations prompted by the cognitive-neoassociationist view of anger and emotional aggression. In L. R. Huesmann (Ed.), *Aggressive behavior: Current perspectives* (pp. 35–57). New York: Plenum.

43. Berkowitz, L., Corwin, R., & Heironimus, M. (1963). Film violence and subsequent aggressive tendencies. *Public Opinion Quarterly, 27*(2), 217–219.

44. Berkowitz, L., & Geen, R. G. (1966). Film violence and the cue properties of available targets. *Journal of Personality and Social Psychology, 3*(5), 525–530.

45. Berkowitz, L., & Geen, R. G. (1967). Stimulus qualities of the target of aggression: a further study. *Journal of Personality and Social Psychology, 5*(3), 364–368.

46. Berkowitz, L., & Rawlings, E. (1963). Effects of film violence on inhibitions against subsequent aggression. *Journal of Abnormal and Social Psychology, 66*(5), 405–412.

47. Blank, D. M. (1977). The Gerbner violence profile. *Journal of Broadcasting, 21*(3), 273–279.

48. Blank, D. M. (1977). Final comments on the violence profile. *Journal of Broadcasting, 21*(3), 287–296.

49. Blumer, H. (1936). The moulding of mass behavior through the motion picture. *Publications of the American Sociological Society, 29*, 115–127.

50. Blumler, J. G. (1964). British television—the outlines of a research strategy. *British Journal of Sociology, 15*(3), 223–233.

51. Boemer, M. L. (1984). An analysis of the violence content of the radio thriller dramas and some comparisons with television. *Journal of Broadcasting, 28*(3), 341–352.

52. Bogardus, E. S. (1952). A television scale and television index. *American Sociological Review, 17*(2), 220–223.

53. Bogart, L. (1972–1973). Warning: The Surgeon General has determined that TV violence is moderately dangerous to your child's mental health. *Public Opinion Quarterly, 36*(4), 491–521.

54. Browne, K. D., & Hamilton-Giachristsis, C. (2005). The influence of violent media on children and adolescents: A public health approach. *Lancet, 365,* 702–710.

55. Bushman, B. J., & Anderson, C. A. (2001). Media violence and the American public: Scientific facts versus media misinformation. *American Psychologist, 56*(6/7), 477–489.

56. Bushman, B. J., & Anderson, C. A. (2002). Violent video games and hostile expectations: A test of the general aggression model. *Personality and Social Psychology Bulletin, 28*(12), 1679–1686.

57. Bushman, B. J., & Cantor, J. (2003). Media ratings for violence and sex: Implications for policymakers and parents. *American Psychologist, 58*(2), 130–141.

58. Bushman, B. J., & Huesmann, L. R. (2006). Short-term and long-term effects of violent media on aggression in children and adults. *Archives of Pediatrics and Adolescent Medicine, 160,* 348–352.

59. Cantor, J., & Wilson, B. J. (1984). Modifying fear responses to mass media in preschool and elementary school children. *Journal of Broadcasting, 28*(4), 431–443.

60. Cantor, J., Ziemke, D., & Sparks, G. G. (1984). Effect of forewarning on emotional responses to a horror film. *Journal of Broadcasting, 28*(1), 21–31.

61. Carnagey, N. L., & Anderson, C. A. (2004). Violent video game exposure and aggression. *Minerva Psichiatrica, 45*(1), 1–18.

62. Cavanagh, J. R. (1949). The comics war. *Journal of Criminal Law and Criminology, 40*(1), 28–35.

63. Cawelti, J. G. (1975). Myths of violence in American popular culture. *Critical Inquiry, 1*(3), 521–541.

64. Ceci, S. J., & Bjork, R. A. (2003). Editorial: Science, politics, and violence in the media. *Psychological Science in the Public Interest, 4*(3), i–iii.

65. Cheng, T. L., Brenner, R. A., Wright, J. L., Hari, C. S., Moyer, P., & Rao, M. R. (2004). Children's violent television viewing: Are parents monitoring? *Pediatrics, 114*(1), 94–99.

66. Chory-Assad, R. M. (2004). Effects of television sitcom exposure on the accessibility of verbally aggressive thoughts. *Western Journal of Communication, 68*(4), 431–453.

67. Coffin, T. E. (1955). Television's impact on society. *American Psychologist, 10*(9), 630–641.

68. Cohn, F. S. (1962). Fantasy aggression in children as studied by the doll play technique. *Child Development, 33*(1), 235–250.

69. Collins, W. A. (1970). Learning of media content: A developmental study. *Child Development, 41*(4), 1133–1142.

70. Collins, W. A. (1976). Children's social responses following modeled reactions to provocation: Prosocial effects of a television drama. *Journal of Personality, 44*(3), 488–500.

71. Collins, W. A., Berndt, T. J., & Hess, V. L. (1974). Observational learning of motives and consequences for television. *Child Development, 45*(3), 799–802.

72. Collins, W. A., Sobol, B. L., & Westby, S. D. (1981). Effects of adult commentary on children's comprehension and inferences about a televised aggressive portrayal. *Child Development, 52*(1), 158–163.

73. Collins, W. A., Wellman, H., Keniston, A. H., & Westby, S. D. (1978). Age-related aspects of comprehension and inference from a televised dramatic narrative. *Child Development, 49*(2), 389–399.

74. Committee on Communications. (1995). Media violence. *Pediatrics, 95*(6), 949–950.

75. Committee on Public Education. (1999). Media education. *Pediatrics, 104,* 341–343.

76. Committee on Public Education. (2001). Media violence. *Pediatrics, 108*(5), 1222–1226.

77. Comstock, G. A. (1983). The legacy of the past. *Journal of Communication, 33*(3), 42–50.

78. Cook, T. D., Kendzierski, D. A., & Thomas, S. V. (1983). The implicit assumptions of television research: An analysis of the 1982 NIMH report on television and behavior. *Public Opinion Quarterly, 47*(2), 161–201.

79. Crespi, L. P. (1946). Propaganda, communication, and public opinion: A comprehensive reference guide. *Public Opinion Quarterly, 10*(1), 99–102.

80. Cressey, P. G. (1938). The motion picture experience as modified by social background and personality. *American Sociological Review, 3*(4), 516–525.

81. Csikszentmihalyi, M., & Kubey, R. (1981). Television and the rest of life: A systematic comparison of subjective experience. *Public Opinion Quarterly, 45*(3), 317–328.

82. Cumberbatch, G. (1994). Legislating mythology: Video violence and children. *Journal of Mental Health, 3*(4), 485–495.

83. Dale, E. (1938). Motion pictures and human relations: The motion picture and intergroup relationships. *Public Opinion Quarterly, 2*(1), 39–42.

84. deLeon, D. L., & Naon, R. L. (1974). The regulation of televised violence. *Stanford Law Review, 26*(6), 1291–1325.

85. Dennis, P. M. (1998). Chills and thrills: Does radio harm our children? The controversy over program violence during the age of radio. *Journal of the History of the Behavioral Sciences, 34*(1), 33–50.

86. Donohue, T. R. (1976). Perceptions of violent TV newsfilm: An experimental comparison of sex & color factors. *Journal of Broadcasting, 20*(2), 185–195.

87. Dorr, A. (1981). Television and affective development and functioning: Maybe this decade. *Journal of Broadcasting, 25*(4), 335–345.

88. Duck, J. M., & Mullin, B.-A. (1995). The perceived impact of the mass media: Reconsidering the third person effect. *European Journal of Social Psychology, 25,* 77–93.

89. Eastman, F. (1938). The motion picture and its public responsibilities. *Public Opinion Quarterly, 2*(1, Suppl.), 44–46.

90. Eron, L. D. (1982). Parent-child interaction, television violence, and aggression of children. *American Psychologist, 37*(2), 197–211.

91. Eron, L. D. (1986). Interventions to mitigate the psychological effects of media violence on aggressive behavior. *Journal of Social Issues, 42*(3), 155–169.

92. Eron, L. D. (1987). The development of aggressive behavior from the perspective of a developing behaviorism. *American Psychologist, 42*(5), 435–442.

93. Eron, L. D. (1999). Effects of television violence on children. *Committee on Commerce, Science, and Transportation.* Retrieved June 29, 2006 from http://commerce.senate.gov/hearings/0518ero.pdf

94. Eron, L. D., Huesmann, L. R., Lefkowitz, M. M., & Walder, L. (1972). Does television violence cause aggression? *American Psychologist, 27*(4), 252–263.

95. Fabes, R. A., Wilson, P., & Christopher, F. S. (1989). A time to reexamine the role of television in family life. *Family Relations, 38*(3), 337–341.

96. Fehr, L. A. (1979). Media violence and catharsis in college females. *Journal of Social Psychology, 109*, 307–308.

97. Felson, R. B. (1996). Mass media effects on violent behavior. *Annual Review of Sociology, 22*, 103–128.

98. Forer, R. (1955). The impact of a radio program on adolescents. *Public Opinion Quarterly, 19*(2), 184–194.

99. Fouts, G., & Liikanen, P. (1975). The effects of age and developmental level on imitation in children. *Child Development, 46*(2), 555–558.

100. Fowers, B. J., & Richardson, F. C. (1993). Social science, ideology and confusing one's beliefs with facts: A response to Huesmann. *Theory & Psychology, 3*(3), 381–388.

101. Fowers, B. J., & Richardson, F. C. (1993). A hermeneutic analysis of Huesmann and Eron's cognitive theory of aggression. *Theory & Psychology, 3*(3), 351–374.

102. Freidson, E. (1953). Communications research and the concept of the mass. *American Sociological Review, 18*(3), 313–317.

103. Friedrich, L. K., & Stein, A. H. (1973). Aggressive and prosocial television programs and the natural behavior of preschool children. *Monographs of the Society for Research in Child Development, 38*(4), 1–64.

104. Friedrich, L. K., & Stein, A. H. (1975). Prosocial television and young children: The effects of verbal labeling and role playing on learning and behavior. *Child Development, 46*(1), 27–38.

105. Funk, J. B. (2002). Aggression and psychopathology in adolescents with a preference for violent electronic games. *Aggressive Behavior, 28*, 134–144.

106. Gadow, K. D., & Sprafkin, J. N. (1989). Field experiments of television violence with children: Evidence for an environmental hazard? *Pediatrics, 83*(3), 399–405.

107. Gadow, K. D., & Sprafkin, J. N. (1993). Television "violence" and children with emotional and behavioral disorders. *Journal of Emotional & Behavioral Disorders, 1*(1), 54–63.

108. Garbarino, J. (2001). Violent children: Where do we point the finger of blame? *Archives of Pediatrics and Adolescent Medicine, 155*, 13–14.

109. Geen, R. G. & Berkowitz, L. (1966). Name mediated aggressive cue properties. *Journal of Personality, 34*(3), 456–465.

110. Geen, R. G., & Berkowitz, L. (1967). Some conditions facilitating the occurrence of aggression after the observation of violence. *Journal of Personality, 35*(4), 666–676.

111. Geen, R. G., & Thomas, S. L. (1986). The immediate effects of media violence on behavior. *Journal of Social Issues, 42*(3), 7–27.

112. Geiger, J. R. (1923). The effects of the motion picture on the mind and morals of the young *International Journal of Ethics, 34*(1), 69–83.

113. Gentile, D. A., Lynch, P. J., Linder, J. R., & Walsh, D. A. (2004). The effects of violent video game habits on adolescent hostility, aggressive behaviors, and school performance. *Journal of Adolescence, 27,* 5–22.

114. Gerbner, G. (1970). Cultural indicators: The case of violence in television drama. *Annals of the American Academy of Political and Social Science, 388,* 69–81.

115. Gerbner, G. (1984). Studies on sex and violence: Science or ritual dance? A revisionist view of television violence effects research. *Journal of Communication, 34*(3), 164–173.

116. Gerbner, G., Gross, L., Eleey, M. F., Jackson-Beech, M., Jeffries-Fox, S., & Signorielli, N. (1977). "The Gerbner Violence Profile": An analysis of the CBS report. *Journal of Broadcasting, 21*(3), 280–286.

117. Gerbner, G., Gross, L., Jackson-Beech, M., Jeffries-Fox, S., & Signorielli, N. (1977). One more time: An analysis of the CBS "Final Comments on the violence profile." *Journal of Broadcasting, 21*(3), 297–303.

118. Gerbner, G., Gross, L., Jackson-Beech, M., Jeffries-Fox, S., & Signorielli, N. (1979). On Wober's "Televised violence and paranoid perception: The view from Great Britain." *Public Opinion Quarterly, 43,* 123–124.

119. Gerbner, G. A., Gross, L., Morgan, M., & Signorielli, N. (1980). Comment and letters: Some additional comments on cultivation analysis. *Public Opinion Quarterly, 44*(3), 408–410.

120. Gould, J. (1946). Television: Boon or bane? *Public Opinion Quarterly, 10*(3), 314–320.

121. Greenberg, B. S. (1974–1975). British children and televised violence. *Public Opinion Quarterly, 38*(4), 531–547.

122. Greenberg, B. S., & Wotring, C. E. (1974). Television violence and its potential for aggressive driving behavior. *Journal of Broadcasting, 18*(4), 473–495.

123. Gruenberg, S. M. (1935). Radio and the child. *Annals of the American Academy of Political and Social Science, 177,* 123–128.

124. Gruenberg, S. M. (1944). The comics as a social force. *Journal of Educational Sociology, 18*(4), 204–213.

125. Gunter, B. (1998). Ethnicity and involvement in violence on television: Nature and context of on-screen portrayals. *Journal of Black Studies, 28*(6), 683–703.

126. Hall, W. M., & Cairns, R. B. (1984). Aggressive behavior in children: An outcome of modeling or social reciprocity? *Developmental Psychology, 20*(4), 719–743.

127. Hapkiewicz, W. G., & Roden, A. H. (1971). The effect of aggressive cartoons on children's interpersonal play. *Child Development, 42*(5), 1583–1585.

128. Hartnagel, T. F., Teevan, J. J., Jr., & McIntryre, J. J. (1975). Television violence and violent behavior. *Social Forces, 54*(2), 341–351.

129. Harvey, S. E., Sprafkin, J. N., & Rubinstein, E. (1979). Prime time television: A profile of aggressive and prosocial behaviors. *Journal of Broadcasting, 23*(2), 179–189.

130. Hauser, P. M., Cressey, P. G., Dale, E., & Peters, C. C. (1932). How do motion pictures affect the conduct of children? Methods employed in "Movies and conduct" and "Movies, delinquency, and crime." *Sociology, 6*(4), 231–250.

131. Hawkins, R. P. (1981). Using television to construct social reality. *Journal of Broadcasting, 25*(4), 347–364.

132. Haynes, R. B. (1978). Children's perceptions of "comic" and "authentic" cartoon violence. *Journal of Broadcasting, 22*(1), 63–70.

133. Hazard, W. R. (1965). A specification of Eight Television Appeals. *Journal of Broadcasting, 10*, 45–54.

134. Heinz, J. (1983). National leadership for children's television. *American Psychologist, 38*(7), 817–819.

135. Hess, R. D., & Goldman, H. (1962). Parents' views of the effect of television on their children. *Child Development, 33*(2), 411–426.

136. Hicks, D. J. (1968). Effects of co-observer's sanctions and adult presence on imitative aggression. *Child Development, 39*(1), 303–309.

137. Highfill, R. D. (1926). The effects of news of crime and scandal upon public opinion. *Journal of the American Institute of Criminal Law and Criminology, 17*(1), 40–103.

138. Hirsch, P. M. (1977). Public policy toward television: Mass media and education in American society. *The School Review, 85*(4), 481–512.

139. Hirsch, P. M. (1980). On Hughes's contribution: The limits of advocacy research. *Public Opinion Quarterly, 44*(3), 411–413.

140. Hirsch, P. M. (1981). On not learning from one's own mistakes: A reanalysis of Gerbner et al.'s findings on cultivation analysis. *Communication Research, 8*(1), 3–37.

141. Hoerrner, K. L. (1999). Symbolic politics: Congressional interest in television violence from 1950 to 1996. *Journalism and Mass Communication Quarterly, 74*(4), 684–698.

142. Hoffner, C., Buchanan, M., Anderson, J. D., Hubbs, L. A., Kamigaki, S. K., Kowalczyk, L., et al. (1999). Support for censorship of television violence: The role of the third-person effect and news exposure *Communication Research, 26*(6), 726–742.

143. Hoffner, C., & Levine, K. J. (2005). Enjoyment of mediated fright and violence: A meta-analysis. *Media Psychology, 7*, 207–237.

144. Holden, C. (1972). TV violence: Government study yields more evidence, no verdict. *Science, 175*(4022), 608–611.

145. Holden, C. (1982). TV report affirms violence-aggression link. *Science, 216*(4552), 1299.

146. Holmes, J. L. (1929). Crime and the press. *Journal of the American Institute of Criminal Law and Criminology, 20*(1), 6–59.

147. Holmes, J. L. (1929). Crime and the press (concluded). *Journal of the American Institute of Criminal Law and Criminology, 20*(2), 246–293.

148. Holz, J. R., & Wright, C. R. (1979). Sociology of mass communications. *Annual Review of Sociology, 5*, 193–217.

149. Howitt, D. (1972). Television and aggression: A counter argument. *American Psychologist, 27*(10), 969–970.

150. Howitt, D., & Cumberbatch, G. (1974). Audience perceptions of violent television content. *Communication Research, 1*(2), 204–223.

151. Hoyt, J. L. (1970). Effect of media violence "justification" on aggression. *Journal of Broadcasting, 14*(4), 455–464.

152. Huesmann, L. R. (1973). Television violence and aggression: The causal effect remains. *American Psychologist, 28*(7), 617–620.

153. Huesmann, L. R. (1986). Psychological processes promoting the relation between exposure to media violence and aggressive behavior by the viewer. *Journal of Social Issues, 42*(3), 125–139.

154. Huesmann, L. R. (1993). Cognition and aggression: A reply to Fowers and Richardson. *Theory & Psychology, 3*(3), 375–379.

155. Huesmann, L. R., Eron, L. D., & Dubow, E. F. (2002). Childhood predictors of adult criminality: Are all risk factors reflected in childhood aggressiveness? *Criminal Behaviour and Mental Health, 12*, 185–208.

156. Huesmann, L. R., Eron, L. D., Klein, R., Brice, P., & Fischer, P. (1983). Mitigating the imitation of aggressive behaviors by changing children's attitudes about media violence. *Journal of Personality and Social Behavior, 44*(5), 899–910.

157. Huesmann, L. R., Lagerspetz, K., Akademi, A., & Eron, L. D. (1984). Intervening variables in the TV violence-aggression relation: Evidence from two countries. *Developmental Psychology, 20*(5), 746–775.

158. Huesmann, L. R., Lefkowitz, M. M., & Eron, L. D. (1984). Stability of aggression over time and generations. *Developmental Psychology, 20*(6), 1120–1134.

159. Huesmann, L. R., & Malamuth, N. M. (1986). Media violence and antisocial behavior: An overview. *Journal of Social Issues, 42*(3), 1–6.

160. Huesmann, L. R., & Miller, L. S. (1994). Long-term effects of repeated exposure to media violence in childhood. In L. R. Huesmann (Ed.), *Aggressive behavior: Current perspectives* (pp. 153–186). New York: Plenum.

161. Huesmann, L. R., Moise-Titus, J., Podolski, C., & Eron, L. D. (2003). Longitudinal relations between children's exposure to TV violence and their aggressive and violent behavior in young adulthood: 1977–1992. *Developmental Psychology, 39*(2), 201–221.

162. Huesmann, L. R., & Taylor, L. D. (2003). The case against media violence. In D. Gentile (Ed.), *Media violence and children* (pp. 107–130). Westport, CT: Greenwood.

163. Huesmann, L. R., & Taylor, L. D. (2006). The role of media violence in violent behavior. *Annual Review of Public Health, 27,* 393–415.

164. Hughes, M. (1980). The fruits of cultivation analysis: A reexamination of some effects of television watching. *Public Opinion Quarterly, 44*(3), 287–302.

165. Huston, A. C., Watkins, B. A., & Kunkel, D. (1989). Public policy and children's television. *American Psychologist, 44*(2), 424–433.

166. Huston, A. C., & Wright, J. C. (1998). Television and the informational and educational needs of children. *Annals of the American Academy of Political and Social Science, 557,* 9–23.

167. Huston-Stein, A., Fox, S., Greer, D., Watkins, B. A., & Whitaker, J. (1981). The effects of TV action and violence on children's social behavior. *Journal of Genetic Psychology, 138,* 183–191.

168. Hyman, H. H. (1973–1974). Mass communication and socialization. *Public Opinion Quarterly, 37*(4), 524–540.

169. Inglis, R. A. (1938). An objective approach to the relationship between fiction and society. *American Sociological Review, 3*(4), 526–533.

170. Innes, J. M., & Zeitz, H. (1988). The public's view of the impact of the mass media: A test of the 'third person' effect. *European Journal of Social Psychology, 18,* 457–463.

171. Jackson-Beeck, M., & Sobal, J. (1980). The social world of heavy television viewers. *Journal of Broadcasting, 24*(1), 5–11.

172. Jegard, S., & Walters, R. H. (1960). A study of some determinants of aggression in young children. *Child Development, 31*(4), 739–747.

173. Johnson, J. G., Cohen, P., Smailes, E. M., Kasen, S., & Brook, J. S. (2002). Television viewing and aggressive behavior during adolescence and adulthood. *Science, 295,* 2468–2471.

174. Jones, D. B. (1942). Quantitative analysis of motion picture content. *Public Opinion Quarterly, 6*(3), 411–428.

175. Kaplan, R. M. (1972). On television as a cause of aggression. *American Psychologist, 27*(10), 968–969.

176. Katz, E., Blumler, J. G., & Gurevitch, M. (1973–1974). Uses and gratifications research. *Public Opinion Quarterly, 37*(4), 509–523.

177. Katz, E., & Foulkes, D. (1962). On the use of the mass media as "escape": Clarification of a concept. *Public Opinion Quarterly, 26*(3), 377–388.

178. Kay, H. (1972). Weaknesses in the television-causes-aggression analysis by Eron et al. *American Psychologist, 27*(10), 970–973.

179. Keliher, A. V. (1938). The motion picture and problems of youth. *Public Opinion Quarterly, 2*(1, Suppl.), 53–54.

180. Kim, S. J. (1994). Viewer discretion is advised: A structural approach to the issue of television violence. *University of Pennsylvania Law Review, 142*(4), 1383–1441.

181. Klapper, J. T. (1957–1958). What we know about the effects of mass communication: The brink of hope. *Public Opinion Quarterly, 21*(4), 453–474.

182. Klapper, J. T. (1963). Mass communication research: An old road resurveyed. *Public Opinion Quarterly, 27*(4), 515–527.

183. Klapper, J. T., & Lowenthal, L. (1951–1952). The contributions of opinion research to the evaluation of psychological warfare. *Public Opinion Quarterly, 15*(4), 651–662.

184. Klinder, L. J., Hamilton, J. A., & Cantrell, P. J. (2001). Children's perceptions of aggressive and gender-specific content in toy commercials. *Social Behavior and Personality, 29*(1), 11–20.

185. Kolbert, E. (1994, May 9). Television. *New York Times,* p. D7.

186. Kronenberger, W. G., Mathews, V. P., Dunn, D. W., Wang, Y., Wood, E. A., Larsen, J. J., et al. (2005). Media violence exposure in aggressive and control adolescents: Differences in self and parent reported exposure to violence on television and in video games. *Aggressive Behavior, 31,* 201–216.

187. Kuhn, D. Z., Madsen, C. H., Jr., & Becker, W. C. (1967). Effects of exposure to an aggressive model and "frustration" on children's aggressive behavior. *Child Development, 38*(3), 739–745.

188. Kunkel, D., & Murray, J. (1991). Television, children, and social policy: Issues and resources for child advocates. *Journal of Clinical Child Psychology, 20*(1), 88–93.

189. Langley, T., O'Neal, E. C., Craig, K. M., & Yost, E. A. (1992). Aggression-consistent, -inconsistent, and -irrelevant priming effects on selective exposure to media violence. *Aggressive Behavior, 18,* 349–356.

190. Lazarsfeld, P. F. (1955). Why is so little known about the effects of television on children and what can be done? Testimony before the Kefauver committee on juvenile delinquency. *Public Opinion Quarterly, 19,* 243–251.

191. Levinger, G. (1986). The Editor's Page. *Journal of Social Issues, 42*(3), i–ii.

192. Linz, D., Penrod, S., & Donnerstein, E. (1986). Issues bearing on the legal regulation of violent and sexually violent media. *Journal of Social Issues, 42*(3), 171–193.

193. Locke, E. A. (1974). Is violence itself necessarily bad? *American Psychologist, 29*(6), 149.

194. Lorch, E. P., Bellack, D. R., & Augsbach, L. H. (1987). Young children's memory for televised stories: Effects of importance. *Child Development, 58*(2), 453–463.

195. Lovaas, O. I. (1961). Effect of exposure to symbolic aggression on aggressive behavior. *Child Development, 32*(1), 37–44.

196. Maccoby, E. E. (1951). Television: Its impact on school children. *Public Opinion Quarterly, 15*(3), 421–444.

197. Maccoby, E. E. (1954). Why do children watch television? *Public Opinion Quarterly, 18*(3), 239–244.

198. Maggi, L. (1998, June 28). A senator's fight against TV excess. *New York Times,* p. A1.

199. Malamuth, N. M., & Briere, J. (1986). Sexual violence in the media: Indirect effects on aggression against women. *Journal of Social Issues, 42*(3), 75–92.

200. McCormack, T. (1978). Machismo in media research: A critical review of research on violence and pornography. *Social Problems, 25*(5), 544–555.

201. McLeod, D. M., Eveland, J. W. P., & Nathanson, A. I. (1997). Support for censorship of violent and misogynic rap lyrics: An analysis of the third-person effect. *Communication Research, 24*(2), 153–174.

202. McLeod, J., Ward, S., & Tancill, K. (1965–1966). Alienation and uses of the mass media. *Public Opinion Quarterly, 29*(4), 583–594.

203. Merrill, I. R. (1961). Broadcast viewing and listening by children. *Public Opinion Quarterly, 25*(2), 263–276.

204. Messner, S. F. (1986). Television violence and violent crime: An aggregate analysis. *Social Problems, 33*(3), 218–235.

205. Meyer, T. P. (1971). Some effects of real newsfilm violence on the behavior of viewers. *Journal of Broadcasting, 15*(3), 275–285.

206. Miller, M. C. (2001, September). Does violence in the media cause violent behavior? *The Harvard Mental Health Letter,* pp. 5–8.

207. Mishler, A. L. (1955). Seduction of the innocent. *Public Opinion Quarterly, 19*(1), 115–117.

208. Molitor, F. (1994). Children's toleration of real-life aggression after exposure to media violence: A replication the Drabman and Thomas studies. *Child Study Journal, 24*(3), 191–207.

209. Morrisett, L. N. (1973). Television technology and the culture of childhood. *Educational Researcher, 2*(12), 3–5.

210. Murray, J. P. (1973). Television and violence: Implications of the Surgeon General's research program. *American Psychologist, 28*(6), 472–478.

211. Murray, J. P. (2003). Testimony of John P. Murray. *Committee on Commerce, Science, and Transportation.* Retrieved June 29, 2006, from http://commerce.senate.gov/hearings/testimony.cfm?id=706&wit_id=1883

212. Murray, J. P., Nayman, G. B., & Atkin, C. K. (1971–1972). Television and the child: A comprehensive research bibliography. *Journal of Broadcasting, 16*(1), 3–19.

213. Nathanson, A. I. (1999). Identifying and explaining the relationship between parental mediation and children's aggression. *Communication Research, 26*(2), 124–143.

214. Nathanson, A. I. (2001). Parents versus peers: Exploiting the significance of peer mediation of antisocial television. *Communication Research, 28*(3), 251–274.

215. Nathanson, A. I., & Yang, M.-S. (2003). The effects of mediation content and form on children's responses to violent television. *Human Communication Research, 21,* 516–546.

216. Nelson, J. D., Gelfand, D. M., & Hartmann, D. P. (1969). Children's aggression following competition and exposure to an aggressive model. *Child Development, 40*(4), 1085–1097.

217. O'Connor, J. J. (1990, February 20). Insidious elements in television cartoons. *New York Times,* p. C20.

218. Oliver, M. B. (1993). Adolescents' enjoyment of graphic horror: Effects of viewers' attitudes and portrayals of victim. *Communication Research, 20*(1), 30–50.

219. Olson, W. C. (1934). Social significance of the cinema. *The School Review, 42*(6), 466–470.

220. Osborn, D. K., & Endsley, R. C. (1971). Emotional reactions of young children to TV violence. *Child Development, 42*(1), 321–331.

221. Paik, H., & Comstock, G. A. (1994). The effects of television violence on anti-social behavior: A meta analysis. *Communication Research, 21*(4), 516–546.

222. Paley, W. S. (1941). Broadcasting and American society. *Annals of the American Academy of Political and Social Science, 213*, 62–68.

223. Peiser, W., & Peter, J. (2000). Third-person perception of television-viewing behavior. *Journal of Communication, 50*(1), 25–45.

224. Phillips, D. (1937). A unit on the use of radio. *The English Journal, 26*(1), 33–38.

225. Poffenberger, A. T. (1921). Motion pictures and crime. *The Scientific Monthly, 12*(4), 336–339.

226. Potter, W. J., & Tomasello, T. K. (2003). Building upon the experimental design in media violence research: The importance of including receiver interpretations. *Journal of Communication, 53*(2), 315–329.

227. Preston, M. I. (1941). Children's reactions to movie horrors and radio crime. *Journal of Pediatrics, 19*(2), 149–168.

228. Purugganan, O. H., Stein, A. H., Silver, E. J., & Benenson, B. S. (2001). Exposure to violence among urban school-aged children: Is it only on television? *Pediatrics, 106*(4, Suppl.), 949–953.

229. Quigley, M. (1937). Public opinion and the motion picture. *Public Opinion Quarterly, 1*(2), 129–133.

230. Quigley, M. (1938). The function of the motion picture. *Public Opinion Quarterly, 2*(1, Suppl.), 47–49.

231. Rachford, H. F. (1944). Developing discrimination in radio listening. *The English Journal, 33*(6), 315–317.

232. Reid, P., & Finchilescu, G. (1995). The disempowering effects of media violence against women on college women. *Psychology of Women Quarterly, 19*, 397–411.

233. Reid, S. (1940). Hollywood hokum—The English teacher's responsibility. *The English Journal, 29*(3), 211–218.

234. Rhodes, R. (2006). The media violence myth. Accessed June 23, 2006, from http://www.abffe.com/myth2.htm

235. Rice, M., & Wartella, E. (1981). Television as a medium of communication: Implications for how to regard the child viewer. *Journal of Broadcasting, 25*(4), 365–372.

236. Riley, J. W., Cantwell, F. V., & Rittiger, K. F. (1949). Some observations on the social effects of television. *Public Opinion Quarterly, 13*(2), 223–234.

237. Roberto, A. J., Meyer, G., Boster, F. J., & Roberto, H. L. (2003). Adolescents' decisions about verbal and physical aggression: An application of the theory of reasoned action. *Human Communication Research, 29*(1), 135–147.

238. Robinson, T. N., Wilde, M. L., Navracruz, L. C., Haydel, K. F., & Varady, A. (2001). Effects of reducing children's television and video game use on aggressive behavior: A randomized controlled trial. *Archives of Pediatrics and Adolescent Medicine, 155,* 17–23.

239. Roloff, M., & Greenberg, B. S. (1979). Resolving conflict: Methods used by TV characters and teenage viewers. *Journal of Broadcasting, 23*(3), 285–300.

240. Rosenthal, R. (1986). Media violence, antisocial behavior, and the social consequences of small effects. *Journal of Social Issues, 42*(3), 141–154.

241. Rowland, H. (1944). Radio crime dramas. *Educational Research Bulletin, 23*(8), 210–217.

242. Rubin, A. M. (1977). Television usage, attitudes and viewing behaviors of children and adolescents. *Journal of Broadcasting, 21*(3), 355–369.

243. Rubin, A. M. (1981). An examination of television viewing motivations. *Communication Research, 8*(2), 141–165.

244. Rubin, A. M. (1984). Ritualized and instrumental television viewing. *Journal of Communication, 34*(3), 67–77.

245. Rubinstein, E. (1981). Research on children and television: A critique. *Journal of Broadcasting, 25*(4), 389–393.

246. Rubinstein, E. A. (1983). Television and behavior: Research conclusions of the 1982 NIMH report and their policy implications. *American Psychologist, 38*(7), 820–826.

247. Rue, V. M. (1974). Television and the family: The question of control. *The Family Coordinator, 23*(1), 73–81.

248. Rule, B. G., & Ferguson, T. J. (1986). The effects of media violence on attitudes, emotions, and cognitions. *Journal of Social Issues, 42*(3), 29–50.

249. Russell, G. W., & Pigat, L. (1991). Effects of modeled censure/support of media violence and the need for approval on aggression. *Current Psychology, 10*(1/2).

250. Sacco, V. F. (1982). The effects of mass media on perceptions of crime: A reanalysis of the issues. *The Pacific Sociological Review, 25*(4), 475–493.

251. Santrock, J. W., Smith, P. C., & Bourbeau, P. E. (1976). Effects of social comparison on aggression and regression in groups of young children. *Child Development, 47*(3), 831–837.

252. Sarnoff, D. (1941). Possible social effects of television. *Annals of the American Academy of Political and Social Science, 213,* 145–152.

253. Scantlin, R. M., & Jordan, A. B. (2006). Families' experiences with the V-chip: An exploratory study. *Journal of Family Communication, 6*(2), 139–159.

254. Schooler, C., & Flora, J. A. (1996). Pervasive media violence. *Annual Review of Public Health, 17,* 275–298.

255. Schuetz, S., & Sprafkin, J. N. (1979). Portrayal of prosocial and aggressive behaviors in children's TV commercials. *Journal of Broadcasting, 23*(1), 33–40.

256. Seldes, G. (1941). The nature of television programs. *Annals of the American Academy of Political and Social Science, 213,* 138–144.

257. Shah, S. A. (1972). Policy on TV violence. *Science, 177*(4043), 9.

258. Shrum, L. J. (1995). Assessing the social influence of television: A social cognition perspective on cultivation effects. *Communication Research, 22*(4), 402–429.

259. Siegel, A. E. (1956). Film-mediated fantasy aggression and strength of aggressive drive. *Child Development, 27*(3), 365–378.

260. Siegel, A. E. (1958). The influence of violence in the mass media upon children's role expectations. *Child Development, 29*(1), 35–56.

261. Silverman, L. T., & Sprafkin, J. N. (1980). The effects of Sesame Street's prosocial spots on cooperative play between young children. *Journal of Broadcasting, 24*(2), 135–147.

262. Singer, D. G. (1983). A time to reexamine the role of television in our lives. *American Psychologist, 38*(7), 815–816.

263. Singer, D. G. (1989). Children, adolescents, and television—1989: I. Television violence: A critique. *Pediatrics, 83*(3), 445–446.

264. Singer, D. G., & Singer, J. L. (1981). Television and the developing imagination of the child. *Journal of Broadcasting, 25*(4), 373–387.

265. Singer, D. G., & Singer, J. L. (1998). Developing critical viewing skills and media literacy in children. *Annals of the American Academy of Political and Social Science, 557,* 164–179.

266. Singer, J. L., & Singer, D. G. (1983). Psychologists look at television: Cognitive, developmental, personality, and social policy implications. *American Psychologist, 38*(7), 826–834.

267. Singer, J. L., & Singer, D. G. (1986). Family experiences and television viewing as predictors of children's imagination, restlessness, and aggression. *Journal of Social Issues, 42*(3), 107–124.

268. Skornia, H. J. (1969). What TV is doing to America: Some unexpected consequences. *Journal of Aesthetic Education, 3*(3), 29–44.

269. Slater, M. D., Henry, K. L., Swaim, R. C., & Anderson, L. L. (2003). Violent media content and aggressiveness in adolescents: A downward spiral model. *Communication Research, 30*(6), 713–736.

270. Smythe, D. W. (1950). A national policy on television? *Public Opinion Quarterly, 14*(3), 461–474.

271. Sprafkin, J. N., & Rubinstein, E. A. (1979). Children's television viewing habits and prosocial behavior: A field correlational study. *Journal of Broadcasting, 23*(3), 265–276.

272. Sprafkin, J. N., Silverman, L. T., & Rubinstein, E. (1980). Reactions to sex on TV: An exploratory study. *Public Opinion Quarterly, 44*(3), 303–315.

273. Stephens, H. B. (1926). The relation of the motion picture to changing moral standards. *Annals of the American Academy of Political and Social Science, 128,* 151–157.

274. Strasburger, V. (1989). Editorial comment: Children, adolescents, and television: The role of pediatricians. *Pediatrics, 83*(3), 446.

275. Strasburger, V. C., & Donnerstein, E. (1999). Children, adolescents, and the media: Issues and solutions. *Pediatrics, 103*(1), 129–139.

276. Surlin, S. H., & Dominick, J. R. (1970–1971). Television's function as a "third parent" for Black and White teen-agers. *Journal of Broadcasting, 15*(1), 55–64.

277. Swanson, D. L. (1987). Gratification seeking, media exposure, and audience interpretations: Some directions for research. *Journal of Broadcasting & Electronic Media, 31*(3), 237–254.

278. Talbert, E. L. (1931). The modern novel and the response of the reader. *Journal of Abnormal and Social Psychology, 26*(4), 409–414.

279. Taylor, H., & Dozier, C. (1983). Television violence, African-Americans and social control 1950–1976. *Journal of Black Studies, 14*(2), 107–136.

280. Thomson, R., & Holland, J. (2002). Young people, social change and the negotiation of moral authority. *Children & Society, 16*, 103–115.

281. Thrasher, F. M. (1949). The comics and delinquency: Cause or scapegoat. *Journal of Educational Sociology, 23*(4), 195–205.

282. Turner, C. W., Hesse, B. W., & Peterson-Lewis, S. (1986). Naturalistic studies of the long-term effects of television violence. *Journal of Social Issues, 42*(3), 51–73.

283. Turow, J. (1980). Non-fiction on commercial children's television: Trends and policy implications. *Journal of Broadcasting, 24*(4), 437–448.

284. van der Molen, J. H. W. (2004). Violence and suffering in television news: Toward a broader conception of harmful television content for children. *Pediatrics, 113*, 1771–1775.

285. Vidal, M. A., Clemente, M., & Espinosa, P. (2003). Types of media violence and degree of acceptance in under-18s. *Aggressive Behavior, 29*, 381–392.

286. Walters, R. H., & Willows, D. C. (1968). Imitative behavior of disturbed and nondisturbed children following exposure to aggressive and nonaggressive models. *Child Development, 39*(1), 79–89.

287. Wartella, E., & Jennings, N. (2000). Children and computers: New technology, old concerns. *The Future of Children, 10*(2), 31–43.

288. Williams, J. W., & Wotring, C. E. (1976). Mediated violence and victim consequences: A behavioral measure of attention and interest. *Journal of Broadcasting, 20*(3), 365–372.

289. Williams, J. F., Meyerson, L. J., Eron, L. D., & Semler, I. J. (1967). Peer-rated aggression and aggressive responses elicited in an experimental situation. *Child Development, 38*(1), 181–190.

290. Witty, P. (1952). Children's reactions to TV—a third report. *Elementary English, 29*, 469–473.

291. Witty, P. (1953). Children's reactions to TV: A fourth report. *Elementary English, 30*, 444–451.

292. Witty, P. (1955). Children and TV: A sixth report. *Elementary English, 32*, 469–476.

293. Witty, P. A., & Sizemore, R. (1954). Reading the comics: A summary of studies and an evaluation II. *Elementary English, 31*, 43–49.

294. Witty, P. A., & Sizemore, R. (1954). Reading the comics: A summary of studies and an evaluation III. *Elementary English, 31*, 109–114.

295. Wober, J. M. (1978). Televised violence and paranoid perception: The view from Great Britain. *Public Opinion Quarterly, 42*(3), 315–317.

296. Wober, J. M. (1979). Televised violence and viewers perceptions of reality: A reply to criticisms of British research. *Public Opinion Quarterly, 43*(2), 271–273.

297. Wober, J. M. (1991). Light and heavy television viewers: Their pictures in the public mind. *Journal of Educational Television, 17*(2), 101–108.

298. Wolf, T. M., & Cheyne, J. A. (1972). Persistence of effects of live behavioral, televised behavioral, and live verbal models on resistance to deviation. *Child Development, 43*(4), 1429–1436.

299. Wright, J. C., & Huston, A. C. (1983). A matter of form: Potentials of television for young viewers. *American Psychologist, 38*(7), 835–843.

300. Wurtzel, A. (1983). Television policy research and the social science community: An industry perspective. *American Psychologist, 38*(7), 844–848.

301. Young, K. (1935). Children's sleep; The emotional responses of children to the motion picture situation; Motion pictures and standards of morality; Motion pictures and youth: A summary; Motion pictures and youth: Getting ideas from the movies; Motion pictures and the social attitudes of children; The social conduct and attitudes of movie fans; Movies, delinquency, and crime; Movies and conduct; Our movie made children. *American Journal of Sociology, 41*(2), 249–255.

302. Zillmann, D., & Day, K. D. (1974). Strength and duration of the effect of aggressive, violent, and erotic communications on subsequent aggressive behavior. *Communication Research, 1*(3), 286–304.

Notes

1. This study was made possible by a grant from the University of Utah Research Committee. Its support is gratefully acknowledged.

2. The authors have recommended a special place in hell for those whose lack of civic conscience leads them to underline, highlight, or otherwise deface journals intended for all to read in their original condition.

3. We are using a referencing convention here that identifies the source of the quotation but at the same time reminds us that the argument is a cultural product and that the quote in hand is only a particular instantiation. We are not claiming that the author(s) intentionally produced a category of argument, although they may have. When references appear in the standard style, they are being used to support or advance a line of thought rather than as an exemplar.

4. While not to be reported here, we can note that such concerns are often raised in articles, but not as justifying arguments.

5. Four other codes appeared in the coding procedure—conditions for the effect (35 sources), consequences for the child (34 sources), gender (25 sources), and descriptive (25 sources)—and are not reported here as the analytical findings were repetitive.

6. Sources 10, 11, 15, 54, 55, 61, 76, 108, 161, 162, 206, 268, and 275.

7. Sources 11, 19, 30, 34, 40, 41, 44, 46, 63, 80, 86, 90, 97, 102, 107, 109, 111, 121, 122, 135, 145, 150, 151, 153, 155, 157, 158, 159, 160, 161, 171, 199, 202, 216, and 235.

8. COSUEE is a combination of Consequence for Society, Universal Effect, and Exposure; COSCEE is Consequence for Society, Conditional Effect, and Exposure; COCUEE is Consequence for the Child Universal Effect and Exposure. Other communities are named by their appropriate combinations.

6

The World According
to Causationists

Theories can often have consequences outside their narrow domain of interpretation and explanation that are unintended and potentially catastrophic. This is because theories are also *necessarily* connected to the larger fabric of reality, a physical science reality or a social science reality. For instance, the successful quest in cosmology for the cosmological holy grail, the so-called unifying theory, where all constituent theories complement rather than contradict or obstruct one another, would lend a seamlessness to the cosmological sciences that does not now exist. Physicists understand the need for a unifying theory (assuming one is attainable), and to their credit, they keep this in mind as they create constituent theories to account for what they see in the heavens. In other words, to propose a cosmological theory that doesn't comport with extant theories could result in a kind of cosmological chaos, where the universe becomes scrambled because clashing theories create impossible circumstances for galactic or even human survival. Communication theories are not in the same league with cosmological theories, of course. But that doesn't mean that communication theorists shouldn't pay attention to the ontological landscape around them as they draw up explanations for the way the universe of message making works. Indeed, the communication version of a unifying theory may not be practical or even relevant. But communication scholars can at least create social scientific theories that don't interfere with or contradict one another.

Thus the problem at hand: The causationists have proposed theories that predict a causal relationship between exposure to media violence and behavioral aggression. But these theories have consequences for the stability and coherence of other social science theories. We argue that the causal hypothesis has empirically counterfactual implications for other attributes of human behavior and culture, which rob the causal hypothesis of its plausibility, of its face validity. We will explain why this is the case and lay the groundwork for a solution to this problem.

The Ontological Problem

In what sort of world does any given person believe he or she lives? That is, how does that person assess the world in which she or he lives? Is it a dangerous world replete with threats? Or is it a benign world, which is mostly manageable? Perhaps for some, it's a kind world with the occasional threat or problem, but a world that mostly "works out fine." If we're prone to thinking deep thoughts, then those thoughts surely encompass some of these questions. And our answers to those questions then predict how we will behave in whatever world in which we find ourselves.

The causationists' view of the relationship between the consumption of media violence and the behavior they hypothesize that occurs as a result of media violence consumption has serious consequences for ontology. That is, the causal hypothesis creates a kind of "ontological havoc." Indeed, this is something that has received almost no attention in critiques of the hypothesis, although we have touched on this subject previously (Bergen & Grimes, 1999; Grimes & Bergen, 2001). And here is why the issue is so fascinating.

One cannot posit the causal hypothesis without taking into account what it would mean were the hypothesis true. Consider, for example, the fact that Huesmann et al. (2003) rated the Roadrunner cartoon series as "very violent." The Bionic Woman and the Six Million Dollar Man were similarly rated. To equate—even if implicitly—comic slapstick or exaggerated caricature with violence that one might witness in one's home, neighborhood, or school puts causationists in a difficult position. This is what happens when causationists assert their notorious 8,000 murders claim. This is the often-quoted assertion that is seen in a lot of causationists' work: "Researchers have estimated that by the time a child finishes elementary school, he/she will have seen approximately 8,000 murders and over 100,000 other acts of violence on TV" (S. Smith & Donnerstein, 1998). Just consider what elevating mediated violence on the same order of magnitude that violence, witnessed first hand, implies.

To do so would describe a culture that doesn't recognize artistic irony as a device implicit in storytelling. We would live in a dense, literalistic culture whose citizens are unable to differentiate dramatic caricature from serious acts of social chaos. Aesthetics, the nature of the fine arts—all would be refracted and reshaped by the dense literalism of such a culture. The representationalism of the fine arts; their ability to portray society ironically, comedically, or even threateningly; and thus their ability to provide the vicarious pleasure that is part of the enjoyment of art—none of it would be possible. And it doesn't stop there.

Our ability to make our way through life as a species that can accurately assess real from imagined external threats would be devastatingly compromised. Therefore, a dramatic decrement in threat assessment skills, which most of the clinical sciences currently ascribe to people with psychopathological ailments, would have to apply to psychologically well people. The social psychological development of the species would have to be reconsidered if what is a clear and present danger, and what isn't, are blurred to the point of indistinguishability, not by disease but simply by the way we as a species are built. The point is that you can't rearrange social normatives to make the causal hypothesis work without also accounting for the ontological upheavals that would have to occur elsewhere in the social fabric. To put it another way, one can't, in the same culture, celebrate the artistic genius of Shakespeare and then seriously posit the literalism of the advocates of the causal hypothesis. We should be able to weep at the conclusion of movie director Douglas Sirk's 1959 classic tear-jerker *Imitation of Life* and simultaneously understand that it's just a movie, that the characters portrayed in the movie aren't real, no one died, yet the travails through which the fictional characters suffered can also provoke honest emotions in most moviegoers.

The psychiatrist and novelist Jonathan Kellerman (1999) recounts how his otherwise benign, sweet-natured daughter enjoyed slasher movies as a child. His interpretation of his daughter's enjoyment was that she had engaged in an act of meaning making that rendered the horrific violence she was watching as entertainment—as did Shakespeare's audiences, as do the Roadrunner cartoons' young viewers, as do we when we watch actress Juanita Moore "die" as the character Annie Johnson in *Imitation of Life*. In other words, the dramatic portrayals are taken for what they are by most audiences, not as demonstrations of the present and immediate breakdown of civil society—or as a threat to one's safety. What Kellerman's daughter does with what she watches is what all psychologically well people do. But the causationists have confused all of this by (inadvertently, we presume) describing a population that is neither here nor there, not psychopathological but possibly afflicted by "other factors" (Comstock, 2006) that are similar to psychopathology: not quite psychopathological but not quite "normal" either. This might help explain why, in their opinion, media violence is such a destructive social force. Society, for the causationists, it seems, is an indistinguishable amalgam undifferentiated by illness, susceptibility (except, perhaps, for the very youngest viewers), or even psychological wellness. So the question of who—precisely, particularly, explicitly—*is* harmed by media violence is never definitively answered by the causationists. To take a rather crude example, if life expectancy were 35 years or thereabouts, this would change reality for the world in which each of us lives. Indeed, it would change our world, period. Thus, getting a handle on just what life expectancy is for most of us helps shape the reality—the ontology—that describes our existence, our being, not to mention government policy, the nature of the economy, and a host of other tangential matters associated with human longevity. It is not unreasonable, then, to expect an answer to the question, Who exactly, precisely, particularly is putatively harmed by media violence? The answer to that question has repercussions for a multitude of human dimensions, not just on the media violence dimension.

But because media violence and genuine violence appear to be isomorphic under the causationists' conceptualization—certainly the 8,000 murders characterization illustrates that—this suggests (at least to us) that the causationists are approaching the media violence study question through the prism of ideology, a disdain of popular culture, a hyperbolic sense of the power of the media to activate antisocial behaviors. The causationists' likely unwillingness to apply the ontological consequences to the rest of the world, necessitated by the rearrangement of those consequences that occurs when they make the causal argument, suggests a peculiar view of media influenced by something other than life's experiences. Perhaps decades of laboratory and some field experiments, in which variables have been defined that enhance the probability of a causal outcome, which results in aggression, have distorted causationists' view of the study question. That is, the way in which they operationalize the variables they use, as well as the manner in which they manipulate them, gives those investigators an unwarranted confidence in their conclusions that have led to the problems, the confusion, and the misunderstanding that characterizes much of their work.

We might weep at the end of *Imitation of Life;* recoil at the relentless, grinding violence of Quentin Tarantino's 1992 movie *Reservoir Dogs;* or otherwise be emotionally and intellectually affected by the many media images that we see every day. But, like Kellerman's daughter, there's something about the violence and the sadness of the work of Tarantino, Sirk, or Shakespeare that is quite simply *different* than nondramatic violence experienced in the first person. Otherwise, there would be more John Hinckleys, who are unable to distinguish between the vicariousness that constitutes the aesthetic of dramatic portrayal, and real, experienced, lived life. It was Hinckley's inability to distinguish between Jodi Foster's character, Iris Steensma, in Martin Scorsese's 1976 movie *Taxi Driver,* as well as Hinckley's attempt to murder the president of the United States in 1981 to impress the prostitute Steensma (or the actress Jodi Foster), that suggests what the world would be like if it interpreted media violence as literally as the causationists suggest is the case.

Why does the well personality recoil at *Reservoir Dogs* yet is not provoked to behave aggressively after watching the movie? Put another way, why is the unwell personality provoked by a violent movie *and then* egged on to behave aggressively, similarly to what we (Grimes et al., 2004) saw when we exposed children with a diagnosed cluster of psychopathologies to media violence? Perhaps two Stanford professors provide part of the answer.

The Ontological Problem—Solved

Byron Reeves and Clifford Nass, two communication professors at Stanford University, wrote a fascinating book about humans' response to mediated messages based on the assumption that those messages are viewed as if they were genuine, lived, first-person experiences (Reeves & Nass, 1996). The reason for this response, they argue, is that the human brain's architecture is not configured to distinguish between first-person experiences and mediated experiences. Mediated experiences evoke the same emotions, concerns, and fears that first-person experiences evoke. The reason, Reeves and Nass (1996) argue, is that mediated experiences have come into the realm of human perception so late in the evolutionary development of our brains that we don't have a neural mechanism to differentiate between what is real and what is mediated. With respect to emotions, concerns, fears, and other associated reactions, media users view mediated experiences, as well as first-person experiences, similarly. Reeves and Nass write,

> [It has been claimed] that people can intentionally forget about the fact that media are artificial and produced elsewhere and can *pretend* that what's in front of them is real. People supposedly suspend disbelief because it's enjoyable to pretend. Our studies, however, question how willing this suspension really is. . . . The burden of adding thoughts about a distant source to thoughts about the ones in front of you will burn mental energy. . . . Accepting what is present—that mediated life is real life—is not work at all. (p. 187)

That is, the authors are arguing that it is easier, and thus less mental work and a more efficient use of cognitive resources, to embrace the mediated dramatic messages we see just as we embrace events and social situations before us that are nonmediated. So, we accept mediated messages as genuine experiences—for example, Annie's death, which causes us to weep—rather than remain circumspect, knowing that the actress Juanita Moore, who plays Annie, is only acting and didn't actually die. According to Reeves and Nass's (1996) reasoning, to maintain that circumspect knowledge in working memory as we watch the death scene would require too much mental work. So we automatically, as a matter of reflex, "forget" the underlying fictive portrayal of what we see and accept it as real. This, then, explains the sadness and regret we feel upon the death of poor Annie Johnson.

We believe Reeves and Nass's (1996) explanation does, indeed, account for why we weep at heartrending fictional tales and why we're horrified, for example, by the grizzly murder of a person at the hands of a killer in Tobe Hooper's 1974 blood-and-guts thriller *The Texas Chain Saw Massacre*. It suggests a model by which the neural/cognitive mechanics underlying the commonly used phrase "suspension of belief" operate. Those points stipulated, nowhere in the Reeves and Nass exposition, or in the ecology of media literature in general, does anyone plausibly argue that psychologically well human beings *cannot* differentiate between fiction and first-person experience. That is, suspension of belief (what we have been calling "vicarious experience") is a fixed, time-limited, sharply defined cognitive phenomenon that, among psychologically well people, does not inhibit their ability to behave appropriately in the nonmediated world. Suspension of belief does not equate with suspension of common sense, or a suspension of one's sanity, or a suspension of the ability to discriminate, *when it counts*, between what's experienced in the first person and what's experienced as dramatic portrayal. Any psychologically well person seeing Mark Robson's 1974 movie *Earthquake* would not be likely to place a panicked call to relatives in Los Angeles to check on their safety, to hurriedly place sell orders on investments in California companies, or to otherwise engage in behavior that would suggest that an actual earthquake had taken place.

We saw the sharply drawn difference between vicarious experience, as well as first-person experience, in our work with psychopathologically afflicted children at the Menninger Clinic as compared to the psychologically well children we tested as well (e.g., Grimes et al., 2004). Psychologically well 12- to 15-year-old children can functionally differentiate between make-believe and reality, as can well adults. To argue otherwise defies common sense, not to mention decades of psychological and psychiatric evidence that demonstrates perceptual characteristics of people afflicted with psychopathology and those who are not so afflicted.

Thus, the melding of firsthand with secondhand experience is the key to understanding how causationists have gotten matters so muddled:

Consumers of dramatic portrayal enjoy the experience of sadness or fright but do not confront the real-world consequences of either sadness or fright. Those who suffer from certain categories of psychopathology (categories we will examine later) live in a world where the sharp separation between first-person experience and vicarious experience is blurred. To presume that blurring the two is "normal" is to summarily and inadvertently redefine psychological wellness, as well as psychopathology. We don't think causationists intend to do that. (And, by the way, we don't think Reeves and Nass [1996] intend to do that.) But the causationists do it nonetheless. And the causationists must accept the consequences for doing so.

The Axiological Problem

Let's move from the ontological to the axiological—those questions of value that are implied by theories. What is it we know about media violence and its relationship to aggression in society? With some exceptions, most of the work performed in this study area claims to be scientific, objective, dispassionate, the subject of distanced inquiry that poses hypotheses (J. Anderson, 2006). That is, values are not claimed by causationists to be part of their analysis of the media violence/behavioral aggression issue. The problem with this assumption as it is made by the causationists—that all knowledge of the media violence issue is obtained through dispassionate analysis—is that it ignores the strong biases, predilections, and predispositions the scientists bring to the study area as well as the cultural values they bring to the study area. That is, they appear to ignore the strong cultural influence that factors into what we consider "violent," "aggressive," and the like.

Whether violent media content causes or is a partial cause of aggression later in life is not just a communication question. It has value-laden implications for the rest of society if what the causationists claim is true. A well-known nonmedia violence example of the axiological problem, which may help illustrate this issue, is found in the furious debate between advocates of evolution and advocates of creationism and/or intelligent design. Part of the reason the fires have been stoked on this debate is because of the consequences for all of science that would obtain were creationism or intelligent design to become the principal scientific explanations of the origin of life. In other words, one cannot simply contain the implications of the debate to the selection of public school biology textbooks. The implications for what we know and how we know it (that is, our epistemology), were intelligent design or creationism true, would be important in ways that go far beyond the study of science (the axiology of the choice between the two explanations). And, indeed, the implications that intelligent design and creationism have in that respect are what most concern many of America's university presidents. That is, one clear implication of the belief that creationism or intelligent design shaped the origin of life is that an advocate is unlikely to approach biological research from a position that would make sense to most biologists. Rather, the adoption of creationism or intelligent design would render the scientifically dispassionate study of life irrelevant. After all, under the rubric of creationism or intelligent design, we're talking about the creation of the universe by the creator! The mechanics of how that creation took place, although interesting, is the work of scientific accountants. Religious potentates would take center stage with regard to this question.

General scientific acceptance of creationism or intelligent design would mean, for instance, that spiritualism and science travel together. Knowing where the hand of the creator has imposed a biological design on a living organism, as well as where nontheological causes and processes intersect, would have to be calculated.

Certainly, millions of Americans have made their accommodations with creationism or intelligent design by buying into one or both concepts (National Science Board, http://www.nsf.gov/nsb). They have done so on the basis of value—that it is the right thing to believe regardless of scientific opposition to its truth. Yet the consequences for those who have bought into that reality don't have many practical implications for them. The new car business, the shoe sales business, and the construction business can pretty much remain the same—that is, the way a building is built doesn't change—whether creationism or natural selection is at work. But for bench scientists, chemists, physicists, anthropologists, and geologists, even poets and philosophers, the adoption of creationism or intelligent design has the most profound consequences. This is because all of what they know about the way the world works would have to be squared against the theological factor. So the many implications such a reality would have for the natural, medical, and biological sciences and the humanities would precipitate the most profound, earth-shaking reassessment of what humanity both knows about itself and what its values are.

The causationists ask us to make a similar reassessment about the world of media. Just consider the 8,000 murders assertion ("Researchers have estimated that by the time a child finishes elementary school, he/she will have seen approximately 8,000 murders and over 100,000 other acts of violence on TV."). Then consider this one: The Legislative and Federal Affairs officer for the American Psychological Association, Jeffrey McIntyre, stated in 1999 that "the evidence [that media violence is a cause for increased social aggression in society] is overwhelming. To argue against it is like arguing against gravity" (Mifflin, 1999). And then there is the stunning claim by Huesmann that he has all this figured out such that he can calculate a kind of metric one can apply to media violence exposure: "Just as every cigarette increases the chance that someday you will get lung cancer, every exposure to [media] violence increases the chances that someday a child will behave more violently than they otherwise would"[1] (Mifflin, 1999). And finally, you can't get more authoritative endorsements of the causal hypothesis (as it pertains to media violence) than from the American Psychological Association—and the American Medical Association, the American Academy of Pediatrics, the American Academy of Child and Adolescent Psychology, and the National Institute of Health (Mifflin, 1999). All claim that consumption of media violence promotes/contributes to/increases the likelihood of a person's resort to aggressive behavior as a social manipulation tool. For the causationist, the data are in. The problem has been identified and the time has come to find a solution to the societal problem posed by media violence.

The problem, of course, is that the trend that began in the late 1970s to banish conditionals and to adopt hard-line causation didn't occur because of the science that undergirds this research area. Prior to the 1970s, media sociologists viewed audiences as differentially affected—or *not* affected—by media violence. Sociological theory had a strong bias toward individual differences, away from homogeneity and toward heterogeneity, which made mass suggestion/influence/homogeneous mass response unlikely (Blumer, 1946). Freidson (1953) argued that, with respect to *media audiences* (as opposed to the undifferentiated "mass"), they do tend to behave homogeneously, but

> the behavior of members of the audience . . . does not seem to conform to criteria of collective behavior in general; rather, it seems to be distinctly social.

That is, group behavior is not mass, lock-step societal behavior. With respect to reactions toward the mass media, the mass as such does not react as a mass, as society at large. Rather, the mass subdivides into social groups, which react to media based on the social characteristics of those groups. Thus, the clean-living people of Function Junction, USA, may demand that the local movie theater delete a particularly offensive movie from its offerings, a movie that plays well in larger cities around the country. The point we're making is not that Blumer, Freidson, or any other mid-20th-century sociologist is correct in his or her characterization of society. The point is that these media sociologists didn't view the mass (the "mass" to whom mass communication is directed) as homogeneously vulnerable to media products. Quite the contrary. These social subgroups were not so much "vulnerable" to the mass media as they were receptive to its appealing cultural messages. As conceptualized by these sociologists, this was a cultural—not a pathological—appeal. As we read these mid-century sociologists and media researchers, a cultural appeal might present social problems to be sure. But these sociologists didn't pathologize any of this. The pathological version of latter-day group vulnerability appears to be an invention of the mid to late 1970s. Therefore, this shift to the absolutist, generalized effect argument was not motivated by new discoveries or better methodologies in the study of media violence. That is, the evidence for a connection between the consumption of media violence and social aggression has not changed from its earliest representation, and the methodology is essentially that which was developed in the 1920s. What has occurred are changes in the cultural and political realms.

What we think has happened in media violence research is that a confluence of scientific and political interests developed, in the late 1970s, as television reached its near 100% penetration throughout U.S. society. Television increasingly challenged various community, religious, or other principled standards and, in so doing, was "sliming" the culture with a sociopathy, a pathology that could, among other evils, increase levels of social aggression. We contend that these cultural concerns precipitated an initial wave of studies, beginning in the 1970s, which were sustained by private and public grants awarded through the 1990s, as we outlined in Chapter 3. And then this is what happened: Although it may not have been the causationists' explicit intention, the outcome was the same. "If we repeat the same basic study often enough, it will become true." Clearly, the convergence argument demonstrates this implicit claim (e.g., Glymour, Glymour, & Glymour, 2006). This is the argument that, because so many studies point to the same outcome, those studies "converge" to strongly suggest a causal relationship between violent media exposure and behavioral aggression.

The absolutist statements of causationists and professional associations, such as the American Psychological Association, do damage to scientific progress because they come dangerously close to suggesting that inquiry into the validity of the causal hypothesis is a waste of time. If the American Psychological Association's Jeffrey McIntyre is correct, that the causal hypothesis is as indisputable as the theory of gravity, what time-wasting fool would wish to dispute either? The result is an adoption of an "of course it's true" attitude that prevents the careful investigation of alternatives. Consider the work that Reynolds (1999a, 1999b) has conducted with regard to maternal prenatal smoking as it relates to low birth weight in children. He asserts that the assumption that smoking is deadly is so culturally pervasive and thus so widely held—even among experimentalists—that it is easy to see causality in what otherwise would be understood to be a garden-variety correlational relationship. Thus, the conventional wisdom that smoking is an across-the-board health hazard has seeped into the interpretation of data that don't show a conclusive causal relationship. He points to the Surgeon General's criteria for inferring causality from correlational data (U.S. Public Health Service, 1964). (Such criteria must be promulgated because there are some experiments that, for ethical reasons, can't be made causal, only correlational.) It is just this special circumstance, where causal experiments can't be performed (you can't intentionally make a pregnant woman smoke to see if her baby is born with a defect), that are especially vulnerable to the tendency to see what one wants to see in the data.

Reynolds's (1999a, 1999b) concern has been focused on the idea that smoking among pregnant mothers results in low birth weight. What Reynolds and colleagues (Kamel, Gardner, & Freedland, 1996; Larroque, Kaminski, Lelong, Subtil, & Dehaene, 1993) have suggested is that, among all the bad things smoking can and should be attributed to, low birth weight is not among them. The empirical evidence does not definitively support the smoking-causes-low-birth-weight conclusion because there is convincing evidence otherwise. Indeed, as Reynolds (1999b) points out, smoking, ironically, may *promote* normal birth weight, which, as Reynolds would hasten to point out, does not make the case that one ought to smoke. Yet, the presumption that smoking is a universally harmful behavior may have led researchers to assume that it must be responsible for low birth weight and thus read the data that way. The notion that smoking is universally harmful, that it does not have isolated null or even salutary health effects, has surely inhibited research into other causes for illnesses that are automatically attributed to smoking.

And so, as Reynolds (1999b) notes, important clues pointing to other causes such as caffeine consumption, or methodological problems that make it difficult to attribute smoking to low birth weight, may not be noticed or may be ignored. In other words, repeated studies, in which low birth weight and smoking are correlated, plus the general assumption that smoking must be causally related to low birth weight (because smoking is always bad for you), lead to the conclusion that maternal prenatal smoking causes low birth weight.

In much the same way that smoking is ipso facto presumed to universally be responsible for bad consequences, watching media violence is likely presumed to have universally inherently bad consequences by causationists. And here is where the worm may have turned toward the end of the last century with respect to broad brushing the putative harmful effects of media violence to the population at large. Look at the age and socioeconomic status of the cohort that does this type of media research. Most are White, upper income, and exceptionally well educated. Now pair that demographic with the likes of the Comedy Channel's *South Park*, *Beavis and Butt-Head,* or *Jackass.* Would that programming appeal to that cohort? For people with similar cultural, economic, and educational backgrounds, cable and broadcast fare are probably alien to both what they grew up with when *they* watched television as children and counter to the shared culture and aesthetic they identify with.

We should indemnify ourselves and concede that it's for the causationists to say whether broadcast and cable television's programming decisions over the past 25-year period in which causationist arguments have reached their own certainty keeps them focused on their hypothesis. But reaction to the contemporary mass media by voters in the 2004 presidential election suggests that there's a strong social concern about the way in which the mass media have affected the culture (Kohut, 2005). It seems likely, at least to us, that the 25-year focus on the putative society-wide damage that violent media inflict would have a natural constituency among ordinary Americans as well as their political leadership.

There was also a shift to the political right at just about the same period in which the causal hypothesis was coming into its own as an accepted premise of how media violence harms society. That the Congress began, in the 1980s, to hold hearings about the "national epidemic" called media violence (Bergen & Grimes, 1999; Schorr, 1981) *and* the emergence of the causal hypothesis may warrant its own cause-and-effect conclusions. In any event, if we're correct, the cultural and political context from which this concern arose may lead researchers to expect to see certain outcomes in otherwise ambiguous or even benign data sets, especially when the stimulus material is so offensive, on its face, to older Americans. That can motivate research questions that have a strong presumptive orientation before one enters the laboratory or conducts a field experiment.

One colleague once compared this phenomenon to that of an Ouija board piece that seems to head, all its own, toward a yes or no answer to a question asked of the swami. And just as the Ouija piece seems to lead to a conclusion that's independent of the will of the Ouija board players, the predisposition one brings to a study area—such as media violence, the epidemiology of smoking, the origins of humanity—can also appear to drive conclusions independently of an investigator's predispositions.

This Ouija board phenomenon comes through quite clearly in a passage of research we cited in earlier work (Grimes & Bergen, 2001, in press). Victor Strasburger, the pediatrician and media violence foe, once acknowledged that trying to establish a connection between watching media violence and aggression later in life is a "mission impossible" (Strasburger, 1995). This is because television is everywhere. If there were ever a single variable that is an inextricable part of the background noise of American life, television is certainly a candidate. As Strasburger (1995) noted, "[Both field and laboratory research] still cannot assess the most crucial linkage: the cumulative effects of TV viewing over an extended period of time." But then he cites six studies (Huesmann & Eron, 1986; Huesmann, Eron, Lefkowitz, & Walder, 1984; Lefkowitz, Eron, Walder, & Huesmann, 1972; Milavsky, Kessler, Stipp, & Rubens, 1982; Singer & Singer, 1981; Singer, Singer, & Rapaczynski, 1984) that "point toward a strong connection between TV violence and aggressive behavior." Then he refers to a "remarkable 10-year longitudinal study" by Liebert and Sprakfin (1988) that plots participants' exposure to media violence early in life and later adult aggressive behavior. Strasburger concludes, "Although the data do not point to media violence as the major cause of violence in society, it is certainly a socially significant one." The Ouija piece seems, yet again, to be moving under its own power.

When, several years ago, we suggested that media violence research is partially determined as much by one's own predilections and biases as much as it's determined by traditional social science research methods, we got a fierce rebuke. As John P. Murray and Ellen Wartella—two of the most distinguished and prolific causal advocates in media violence research—made clear, they are scientists whose personal predilections, prejudices, and preferences most certainly *do not* intersect with their interpretation of data. To them, this is strictly an empirically based research area. The idea that anything as unscientific as preferences and prejudices would intrude on the research question insulted them (Murray & Wartella, 1999). And why wouldn't it? To argue otherwise is like "[arguing] against gravity" (Mifflin, 1999).

Before we appeared on the scene with our anticausationist arguments, Berkowitz (1986, p. 94) had developed a response to the anticausationists who've preceded us. And the argument goes like this: Anticausationists are committing a "fundamental attribution error." That is, they overemphasize the contribution that personal "characteristics and dispositions" play in determining a person's behavior. Berkowitz suggests that the correct way to view the problem is to consider more carefully the role environmental factors play in determining behavior. Berkowitz also suggests that most people are not aware of the influence environmental factors can have on our behavior. He makes the argument this way: "In most instances the effects of observed violence are probably too weak to be noticed by the audience. This does not mean, of course, that society can safely disregard the widespread portrayal of aggression in the mass media." What Berkowitz does not do, or is unable to do, is explain the mechanical/clinical/cognitive theory base that would drive this attributional process. In other words, Berkowitz's explanation is, indeed, an explanation. But that explanation doesn't *explain* much.

Huesmann and Malamuth (1986) also speculated as to why the causationist position isn't readily embraced by everyone—and thus why the anticausationist position ought to be disregarded. First, they believe critics atomize the body of work in this area, which means critics nitpick individual studies, which have flaws that are easy to exploit. Huesmann and Malamuth suggest that the body of work should not be picked apart. That is, the mosaic of evidence, created by many scholars over many years, leads to a better understanding of the phenomenon under study. That's what has been called the "convergence argument," something we will study in greater detail in this chapter.

Second, Huesmann and Malamuth (1986, p. 2) argue that critics of causation inappropriately disregard laboratory research, which they argue provides the crucial evidentiary base for causality. Those critics—Jonathan Freedman (1984), for instance—point out that the lab research that constitutes the "well-controlled" causal evidence to which Huesmann and Malamuth refer (p. 2) does not actually measure aggression but only surrogates to aggression (e.g., a person's striking a doll in a lab). Second, Freedman asserts that media violence lab studies suffer from strong experimenter demand effects. That is, because the experimenter chooses the movies and TV programs that are shown in the lab, Freedman argues that lab subjects would be likely to approve of the aggression shown to them because they believe the experimenter approved of it by virtue of having chosen it to show it to them. Finally, Freedman argues that the aggressive material that's been shown to lab subjects constitutes so little of what's actually in the movies and on TV that it bears little relationship to what's actually in the commercial marketplace.

In any event, that pesky assertion—the 8,000 murders assertion—describes a media environment whose harm is sui generis: an entertainment product that naturally interacts with a society that is dispositionally prone to aggression. The 8,000 murders assertion reveals a distinct way of viewing the world. Causationists view violent media as inherently pernicious and people who consume them as inherently susceptible to those pernicious media. Of course, this inexorably creates a toxic mix in the causationists' view.

Our view is that "media violence" and "behavioral aggression" cannot be taken for granted; that is, they cannot be manipulated as variables as if they were inert, stable, culturally immutable concepts. (This is a bit of what Freedman was arguing.) Media violence and behavioral aggression are culturally mutable, a mutability that is intimately connected to particular times and places in American social history. That, of course, doesn't mean that they're so ephemeral that they can't be studied or otherwise examined. Rather, it means that their cultural dependency *must* be taken into account first before they can be used to make valid inferences about how, or whether, they interact with one another.

This notion of the cultural dependency of normative values is not new. It's been a theme across a number of subspecialties in communication research, especially with respect to the history of literacy (Nord, 1995). In much the same way that early 20th-century newspaper readers read the text to support their political and social biases (thus leading to letters to the editor that the *editor* was imbuing news stories with bias), we believe researchers who see psychological ruin in violent media messages are falling victim to the same tendency. If this is true, these media researchers are in good company.

The Spanish philosopher George Santayana (1952) argued that the British philosopher Bertrand Russell was wrong to view ethical principles as stand-alone immutables, unperturbed by temporal or cultural influence. In that same way, we view "media violence," "sociopathic aggression," and "harm" as culturally and temporally contingent as well. In other words, what's right, correct, and proper changes with time and with the evolution of culture and civilization. Michel Foucault, the French existentialist, went so far as to define mental illness as behavior that society, at any given time in its evolution, will not tolerate (Foucault, 1961). Foucault's point is that psychological abnormality is not inert but something that is interpreted against social mores at a given moment in social history. Indeed, Georges Canguilhem's book, titled *The Normal and the Pathological* (Canguilhem, 1989), explores the origins of society's definition of pathological behavior, a definition that has a strong cultural contingency. For instance, that which is "aggression" may undergo a redefinition between one's childhood and one's commission of an aggressive act as an adult.

Consider two of several dependent variables that Huesmann and his colleagues (Huesmann et al., 2003) define as aggression: "trying to get others to dislike [a] person," "calling [a] person names," and "belittling a person's physical looks or abilities." In a latter-day culture, especially sensitive to the supremacy of the individual as well as the rights of the individual, civil and otherwise, "trying to get others to dislike a person" might be considered aggressive. On the other hand, for our junior high school counselor friends, this is part of the social maturation process in this age group. Something that the costs and benefits of which have to be learned. Rather than an instance of aggression, it may be a necessary developmental stage in becoming a functional adult.

The current political climate makes relativism, especially in morals and ethics, problematic. Current political thinking asserts that it's bad to be relativistic; there are enduring values that stand apart from contemporary changes in mores and preference. Yet, we view relativism, as illustrated by Santayana, Foucault, Canguilhem, and Nord, to be a valid way of knowing, a valid epistemological tool. Relativism, then, is a worldview that can help explain, in any given epoch, what it means to be good, bad, evil—and what is considered by society to be "violent," to be "aggressive." It is the absence of relativism, used as an analytical tool, that helps create the brittleness and the resultant logical difficulties of the causal hypothetical position.

Then there's a peculiarly American problem: the bourgeois nature of media research in this country. As Chast's cartoon neatly illustrates, we Americans are so fortunate, with so many of life's comforts, that we tend to worry about what, to the rest of the world, may seem trivial. As Buckingham (1998) noted, a society that can afford to worry about media violence is a society very well off indeed . . . a bit bourgeois, in fact. Our causationist colleagues seriously entertain the idea that Roadrunner cartoons and other silly displays of aggression could actually constitute harm.

These, then, are some epistemological issues that refract and bend the way causationists view the world in which the media operate. Media violence and behavioral aggression are contingent on the social context within which they appear. They vary in definition depending on the cultural surroundings within which they manifest themselves. In addition, the strained, literalistic rendering of dramatic portrayals of acts of violence by causationists is problematic. The equation of media violence to acts of societal-level murder and mayhem challenge credulity.

Two attributes of the causal literature are especially worrisome to us. Two attributes that we don't think have received enough attention. The first, as promised earlier in this chapter, is an examination of the peculiar notion of "convergence." The second is the even more peculiar notion of what the causationists mean by "behavioral aggression." First, convergence.

The Notion of "Convergence"

Convergence is a kind of software patch that media violence causationists use to compensate for the fact that there is no definitive causal connection between consumption of media violence and aggression later in life. Here is the first explication of convergence that we have been able to find in the literature. It was written in 1982 by Eli Rubenstein, a researcher who, along with other researchers, issued a 10-year assessment of the putative effect of media violence on society for the National Institute of Mental Health. Rubenstein wrote,

> Most television researchers look at the totality of the evidence and conclude . . . that the *convergence* [emphasis added] of most of the findings about televised violence and later aggressive behavior by the viewer supports the positive conclusion of a causal relationship.

However, he added,

> A few researchers, looking at each piece of research individually and finding flaws in design and/or methodology, conclude that the case has not been made for a causal relationship.

Can you see the "software patch" function that convergence serves? Even though individual studies may not make the definitive causal argument, the whole lot of them "converge" to point toward causality. "Supports a positive conclusion of a causal relationship"; what does *supports* mean? It should be clear how ill defined, indistinct, and otherwise unclear convergence is, at least as it's explicated by Rubenstein.

If you think we are leaning too heavily on Rubenstein, consider the fact that convergence is perhaps *the* single most important assumption that causationists rely on to make their case. References to convergence, or similar terms that describe the same concept, are replete within the causal literature (e.g., Atkin, 1983; Atkin, Greenburg, Korzenny, & McDermott, 1979; Baker & Ball, 1969; Bandura, Ross, & Ross, 1963). Convergence is an important part of the causal argument. Without it, the argument begins to dissemble. If that's true, and it is, then why don't causationists definitively dispel the over-reach of convergence and set up causally designed studies? The answer (we suspect) is that the case for causality has long ago been made. But when was that case made? Convergence makes finding the definitive study impossible because there is no definitive study; things just kinda, sorta came together over time. And this is dangerous because without a definitive study, or even a finite set of studies that one can cite, causation is presumed.

Consider, for instance, the Huesmann et al. (2003) study. It's particularly interesting because of the notoriety it received from some causationists after its publication. The noted UCLA media scholar Neil Malamuth, for instance, declared the Huesmann study "the missing link in media violence research," the link that, once and for all, illustrates the connection between the long-suspected and all-but-proven exposure to media violence and its cause of aggression later in life (*Morning Edition,* 2003). But here's the problem, and the irony, of the Huesmann study. It presumes that the case for causality has already been amply demonstrated: "The evidence is already substantial that exposure to media violence is [a] long-term predisposing and short-term-precipitating factor [in motivating social aggression]; "Evidence from field studies has clearly shown that the amount of TV and film violence a child is regularly watching is positively related to the child's aggressive-ness"; "[O]ver the past several decades, the correlation between TV-violence viewing and childhood or adolescent aggression has been unambiguously demonstrated." And these assertions by Huesmann and his colleagues come *before* the data are presented, analyzed, and interpreted. Clearly, then, Huesmann and colleagues see their task as going beyond the documentation of a casual link between media violence exposure and social aggression. That has already been established. Rather, they see their task as providing the cap-stone study: a study that definitively shows what havoc media violence can inflict on the general population. In other words, they simply presumed it, just as many dozens of scholars before them have presumed it (J. Anderson, in press). And that's the problem with convergence. The causationists have a vouchsafe of sorts. Convergence is their assurance that everything is OK in the causal realm. This is particularly irksome to those of us who wish we could see something that looks like definitive empirical evidence in support of causality—a study, for instance? The irksome part is that no one study has had to bear the accountability of demonstrating that media violence causes social aggression. Rather, the causal hypothesis accreted, it evolved, it gradually progressed—in the fullness of time—toward acceptance. Thus, causationists simply rely on *presumed causality* without having to go to the trouble to point to specific evidence for it.

Convergence, as a general principle, is not without merit. Glymour, Glymour, and Glymour (in press) correctly point out that the concept taps into a well-regarded Bayesian calculus, which asserts that multiple studies, using different independent and dependent variables, which produce the same outcome—across studies and over time—suggest a high statistical probability that a causal relationship exists among the variables of interest. Certainly, smoking-and-cancer studies, in which causal experiments were not possible, bore out the hazards of smoking. Why, then, shouldn't the same principle be allowable for media violence studies? The answer isn't that there's something wrong with the convergence principle—that is, the Bayesian-inspired definition of convergence. Rather, few of the "rules" one must follow to make Bayesian convergence work are properly followed by the causationists (Grimes & Bergen, in press). Causationists commit a cluster of errors, which all fall under one rubric: They misconceptualize the most important variables that are run through the Bayesian calculus. Therefore, the calculus is powerless to make improper conceptualizations of variables that produce valid statistical predictions. So let's look at the most egregious example of this problem, the operationalization of aggression.

As we pointed out earlier, Huesmann and colleagues (2003) defined aggression as including "calling a person names," "belittling a person's physical abilities or looks," "shoving," "[giving] the finger to others," and even possessing a driving record that has moving violations. This variety of behaviors was included with more traditional definitions of aggression such as pushing or shoving someone in anger. Now consider the work of Johnson, Cohen, Smailes, Kasen, and Brook (2002), who defined aggression as physical fights resulting in injury, which is a reasonable definition. But they also included as a definition "any aggressive act against another person." The problem with definitions that do not include prima facie manifestations of aggression, such as physical assaults that can or do result in injury, is that aggression is then defined through the idiosyncrasies of one's own time and place. Thus, the idea that aggression is something we all recognize *and, as a result,* stands as an inert concept that need not be operationalized (when it is allowed to be defined as "any aggressive act against another person") does not take into account the inherent cultural contingency of the construct.

The famous series of studies, often referred to as the doll studies, gave juvenile participants an object against which to demonstrate aggression (e.g., Bandura et al., 1963). After children were shown a media stimulus, the way in which they interacted with the doll, or a similar target of aggression, was used to calibrate how aggressive they were as a result of having watched a violent media message. It was left up to the investigator to define what constituted aggression-motivated-by-media violence. That is, "aggression" was simply assumed to be whatever the investigator defined it as being. The notion that there would be serious questions as to what constitutes aggression never arises in these studies. And this view of aggression—I know it when I see it—is part of the reason we believe causal hypothetical studies have such little predictive value.

For instance, Savage (2004) states unequivocally that "the body of published, empirical evidence on this topic does not establish that viewing violent portrayals causes crime." Cantor and her research colleagues, on the other hand, although acknowledging that measures range from the trivial to the serious, holds that it is well established that media violence leads to higher levels of *antisocial* behavior (Cantor et al., 2001; Cantor & Mares, 2001). So what are we actually talking about? It appears that we are talking about nearly anything that can be considered not nice, from "hostile thoughts" to "flipping off" one's fellow drivers to more active play in a contact sport. In other words, any meaningful notion of aggression is dissolving before our eyes.

If there is a consistent objection we've gotten from anonymous reviewers to our work (e.g., Bergen & Grimes, 1999; Grimes & Bergen, 2001; Grimes et al., 2004; Grimes, Vernberg, & Cathers, 1997), it is the objection to our making the definition of aggression "so complicated." Aggression is aggression. We all know it when we see it, we're told. There's no reason to make the operationalization of aggression any more difficult. The inescapable consequence of such an operationalization—I know it when I see it—is that a researcher can define any behavior as aggressive if that researcher can convince peer reviewers to accept that researcher's definition. The problem, then, is that the operational definition is not necessarily valid. Our review of the causal literature shows that the great majority of operationalizations of aggression are paper-and-pencil measures, taken from participants, that are interpreted by researchers to be aggressive. Consider why this is problematic. For instance, in epidemiology studies, such as smoking-and-cancer studies, the criterion measures were actual deaths from cancer and confirmed diagnoses of cancer. As we stated in Chapter 4, they were not higher scores on self-report items such as "I believe I have lung cancer" or in peer reports such as "I believe he is sicker than I."

Let's take this argument a step further. The three authors of this book (Grimes, Anderson, & Bergen) confess to imitating the slapstick antics of *The Three Stooges* in their relationships with elementary school classmates. Does this mean that Grimes, Anderson, and Bergen were made aggressive by watching episodes of *The Three Stooges*? Or—were we behaving like the doll participants, except in this case, we were set off by *The Three Stooges*? Should our behavior have worried the adults who were, at the time, charged with our supervision? Forget the doll participants for the moment. Is the process that motivated us to behave in the way we did the same *general* process that motivated Ronnie Zamora to murder his elderly neighbor, Elinor Haggart, except that our behavior was lower on the aggression scale? Zamora stood trial in 1977 in Florida for the murder of Haggart and offered a defense in court that argued that his exposure to media violence caused him to commit the murder. (That didn't fly with the jury, by the way.)

The innocent bump, the deliberate body slam, and the Stooges and Zamora illustrations all show how behavior creates potential interpretational problems for investigators. Without ascertaining the motivation behind a person's behavior, the behavior itself tells us little about that person.

Egregious behavioral aggression such as murder or malicious assault, of course, gives us a reliable insight into a person's mental state. But when aggression is sliced so thinly that a moving traffic violation is defined as aggression, then motivating mental states become paramount in determining whether such behavior is psychopathological. Surely any behavior that simulates aggression, or could remotely be defined as such, cannot be defined as harmful. Otherwise, we find ourselves in a similar position to that of the dramatic irony dilemma we described earlier. If *any* behavior possesses characteristics of behaviorally poor judgment where agitation or hostility is judged harmful, then we find ourselves in another ontological conundrum and one that, by its nature, describes a society that doesn't exist as we three authors understand it. That is, aggregating a multitude of divergent behaviors into one category labeled as "harmful" is a fatuous, simplistic designation that takes a complicated behavior, one with a multidimensional sociological, cultural, and psychological profile, and trivializes it. It's trivialized by the know-it-when-you-see-it operationalization used by so many causationists—the lack of a serious attempt to connect it to a psychological state.

A Comeback (Maybe) for Behaviorism

Now here's an interesting twist: Behaviorism, of a sort, may be making a comeback, at least in communication circles. Psychophysiologists, who have a healthy skepticism when it comes to inferring internal psychological states, have developed ways to try to get around the ineffable black box of cognitivism. Acted-out behavior can be misinterpreted by a researcher on several dimensions, not to mention the cultural dimensions we described earlier. Thus, some psychophysiologists have developed what they believe to be a more reliable measure of aggression (Dodge, Bates, & Pettit, 1990; Dodge & Frame, 1982; Dodge & Tomlin, 1987; El-Sheikh, Ballard, & Cummings, 1994). That is, aggression is defined as a behavior that is preceded by physiological changes that must be present for an acted-out behavior to be deliberately used to inflict harm on one's self or others (Ekman et al., 1972).

Because aggression is such an important variable in measuring the effect of media violence on society, we used some of these same measures in the series of studies we conducted at the Menninger Clinic in Topeka, Kansas (Grimes et al., 2004). Our intention was to employ measures to infer behavioral intent or potential for aggressive behavior. This way, we could get around the nettlesome problems posed by idiosyncratic operationalizations of aggression. So we used accepted psychophysiological behaviors such as variations in vagal heart tone (Grimes et al., 2004; Porges, 1992), skin conductance (Grimes et al., 2004), and facial expressions (Ekman et al., 1972), which provide a more objective method of inferring the behavioral effect of media content on those who watch it. *Objective*, in this sense, means substituting one's judgment as to whether most behaviors are aggressive for an agreed-to standard of physiological responses to a stimulus that precede aggressive behavior.

We found that a number of juveniles with a disruptive behavior disorder (DBD) diagnosis did not display acted-out aggressive behavior in the presence of violent media materials that were presented to them (Grimes et al., 1997; Grimes et al., 2004). Nonetheless, these people did manifest instances of anger and psychophysiological aggression as defined by fluctuations in salivary cortisol levels (i.e., the fight-or-flight hormone, which is secreted into the bloodstream when external threats to safety are perceived), galvanic skin response, heart rate, and involuntary facial expressions—all of them changes generated in response to violent media messages. Had we used the we-know-it-when-we-see-it definition of aggression, we would have concluded that this category of participant was unaffected by media violence *because the participant never actually engaged in an acted-out behavior.* Yet, we found that children with a DBD diagnosis and a companion diagnosis of psychopathy (Grimes et al., 1997; Grimes et al., 2004) are quite sensitive to the arousing effects of violent media messages. And once aroused, the psychophysiological aggression that results, if left untreated, could eventually translate into behavioral aggression that can harm the aggressor or those to whom the aggression is directed.

But wait. Things may seem to be getting out of alignment: Is aggression a culturally defined concept as we earlier argued or is it not? Does cultural relativism have a role in defining aggressive behavior or not? If cultural relativism does have a place, then what's this notion about aggression having an objective, physiological/biological grounding? In other words, from the psychophysiological perspective, aggression would, indeed, seem to be an inert, immutable concept, which is not culturally contingent or relative.

We think an omnibus notion of aggression can be both; one conceptualization of aggression is culturally contingent, and the other conceptualization of it has a foundation in biophysiological processes. One is a cognitive definition, and the other is a behavioralistic definition. So . . . what gives? Well, this is what we think is happening: Most media researchers are actually using the culturally contingent definition of aggression, but they are trying to define it as a psychophysiological process and do not acknowledge the heavy cultural contingency that influences *their* conceptualization of aggression. Therefore, what may look like confusion as to what aggression is or is not may be an opportunity, here and now, to get matters straightened out.

Culturally contingent definitions of aggression should be clear. When Johnson and colleagues (2002) decided to define aggression as "any aggressive act against another person," nothing could be more overtly culturally contingent: Aggression then becomes whatever I think it is, based on my knowledge of the culture, what sort of behavior is acceptable, and what sort of behavior is offensive.

Our point, of course, is that it is incontrovertibly a culturally contingent notion when one asserts that aggression can be defined as "criticizing someone's looks," "giving someone the finger" in traffic, or piling up a lot of moving violations in a car (Huesmann et al., 2003). Would you describe those actions as instances of "aggression"? Are they instances of misbehavior? Or are they spunky? Might giving someone the finger be a case of chutzpah? Or might it be considered déclassé and hostile? Is the answer dependent on circumstances? Or is giving someone the finger always a bad thing? Yet, because these manifestations of aggression are not linked to a psychological state, which can be identified as pathological, that does not mean they are not instances of aggression. What it means is that the definition of aggression, as it relates to these sorts of operationalizations, is a cultural, not a psychophysiological, definition. If media researchers who broker in this definition of aggression wish to acknowledge that, then a new definition of aggression has emerged, a form of "cultural aggression" (for lack of a better way of putting it). It is a type of aggression that must develop its own theories and methods. But to develop those theories and methodologies, the developers must first acknowledge that they're dealing with a cultural phenomenon, not a psychophysiological/medical/epidemiological/clinically oriented construct.

What we're arguing here is not a radical notion. Indeed, it matches up quite nicely with that portion of media effects research that, we believe, does have currency and cachet. That is the area of effects research that examines the cultural erosion that is presumably taking place with the appearance of television programs such as *Beavis and Butt-Head, South Park, Jackass,* and all the other low-culture forms of entertainment that have arisen in the digital age (as described by Campbell, Martin, & Fabos, 2005). Perhaps the culture is less well off since the mass media have made some scatological terms safe for public airing, or sexually and hygienically oriented subjects safe for distribution as humor. Perhaps increased instances of giving someone the finger or disparaging someone's appearance are emerging attributes of changes in the culture brought on by the mass media. *But are those attributes psychopathological instances of aggression?* We think not. And we also believe that scholars who deal with forms of aggression that, to us, fall into a cultural category rather than a psychophysiological category might do well to drop the idea that they are dealing with that form of aggression that psychophysiologists and clinical psychologists examine. These media researchers might also consider the idea that increased levels of aggression are not the result of media violence consumption as much as the consumption of the cheeky, culturally subversive entertainment that can lead to wide acceptance of such behaviors.

We believe that most, perhaps all, causationists view the cultural aggression that they study as harmful, potentially dangerous, as associated in some way with pathology. They have taken instances of cultural aggression and "science-tized" them, made them the object of laboratory experiments, the positing of hypotheses; they have hinted or outright proclaimed them to be forms of illness. That is, aggression as they view it is a medical-psychological problem. And that's where the confusion about this issue originates. We three authors' juvenile antics, precipitated by watching *The Three Stooges,* were likely obnoxious, disruptive, and otherwise banal behavior. It is probably what *The Three Stooges* have done for millions of American children: made them insufferable. But that's a cultural-sociological problem (if it's a problem at all).

Aggression, as clinicians define it, is something else altogether. If we are examining pathological aggression, not cultural aggression, then the fundamental issue becomes one of attaching a behavior to a motivating psychological state, a psychological state that media violence has created.

Summary

The study of social science includes the study of politics. Media violence—the way it interacts with the culture—is inherently a political process. And so it's only reasonable that, as part of the complicated equation that renders media violence a debatable social construct, media violence may be defined by contemporary political climates. The generalizations we've made here about the White, middle-class nature of the people who conduct much of the causal research are, admittedly, sweeping. Nonetheless, *something* happened toward the end of the 20th century to recast the way media violence, as well as its effect on society, was conceptualized by a number of researchers. *Something happened.* Just what it was that happened may never be clear other than the fact that nothing changed in the broad conceptualization of social science or medical theory (e.g., clinical psychological theory, cognitive theory, psychiatric theory) that warrants the dire predictions of the causationists. But whatever changed in *communication theory,* it appears to have muddled and confused the issue and resulted in an overbuilt hulk of a causal framework, with all sorts of unnecessary moving parts.

Note

1. Were such measurement precision attainable in either the medical or social sciences, the method by which that calculus emerged would, in itself, be a stunning scientific discovery.

7

The Biggest Cultural Variable of All

The Child

When Grimes's and Bergen's rotting and dilapidated deck needed to be replaced last year, they wanted desperately to finish it off with a snazzy new railing of horizontal copper tubes running between upright redwood posts. Years of reading *House & Garden* magazine and a month of perusing the deck design books at the local Home Depot inspired an expensive, contemporary railing that would max out the home equity loan and make us the envy of the neighborhood. But then our contractor told us just how dangerous, irresponsible, and illegal such a design would be, ending any further discussion of a railing with a ladder-like design. Indeed, local building restrictions prohibit any design, posing anything remotely resembling a potential climbing hazard for children. Forget that there are no children living in our household. Ignore that the drop off from this deck is not more than 20 inches. Horizontal rails are illegal in our town, for apparently no more reason than it looked like a good idea to a policy maker interested in protecting children.

Of course, it's not hard to recognize this all-too familiar rationale for "the ladder effect" because it's the unassailable argument that we must protect our nation's children from any potential harm, whether it be from the possibility of a short fall from a private backyard deck or from the content of our media.

This view of children and childhood both justifies and simplifies the job of policy makers who, while policing railings, may fail to address the real reasons for social problems. What role does our understanding of "the child" fill in this discussion about the supposed harmful effects of media violence? We should be exceptionally cautious about allowing our assumptions around the notions of *children*, of *media*, and of *harm* to determine that this relationship must be self-evident. As we have diligently tried to show in previous chapters, it is this aggravating/pesky/infuriating notion of "self-evidence" that short circuits critical thinking that should be applied to the media violence issue. That is, if we could get causationists to unpack their assumptions about media violence, it might become clear how far they have taken the media-violence-causes-social-aggression argument past anything that is empirically and culturally reasonable. Thus, the purpose of this chapter is to inform this discussion around children and media violence so that we can better sort and evaluate the evidence available.

Assumptions about children have constrained and determined outcomes of social scientific inquiry in many disciplines. What is assumed about children—that they are innocent, vulnerable, in need of protection, uncontrived, poised to "become" rather than possessing a kind of currency, in time or place—seems to dictate the nature of the inquiry and the questions one asks as well. Why are children at the center of this debate? Why are we not equally focused and concerned with the effects of media violence on adults? Are children really the concern, or rather, are they simply the most convenient and justifiable access point for moralists who would impose limitations on anyone and everyone in society, from children to adults, if they could? Furthermore, what do we mean when we use terms like these to describe different life stages of development—adults and children, toddlers and teens, tweens, adolescents, even *adultolescents?*

Is childhood something that exists in a fixed state, defined by conventional markers such as age or physical characteristics, or is it understood to be a social construction, one that is fluid and refined as a function of both time and space? If childhood is understood to be a process, at what point does one emerge from that process? Is adulthood the destination? Can childhood be understood without also examining it in relation to adulthood? And how do notions about development, about stages of progression leading to higher and higher levels of maturity, contribute to the idea that media violence is perceived to be such a threat to those who occupy one place in this progression? To understand our contemporary fears about the power of media images and messages, we should consider first how our contemporary view of childhood anchors the focus of this discussion.

This chapter tries to accomplish that by contributing a social, historical, cultural, political, and economic context for posing the question about media violence and putative harm to children and justifies why so much research, so much political capital, so much moral fervor has been directed at the issue and why it is so instrumental in framing the results of research about media violence. We do so by examining our notions about children, about adults, about harm, and about fear.

Childhood Is a Multipurpose Construction

Children embody both our greatest hopes and our deepest fears about the future. For at the same time that we can imagine children to be innocent, vulnerable, and precious, there also exists an alternate and troublesome view of children embodying all that is corrupt and disordered about our social world, a vision that is so powerful that children can be seen not just as the symptom of social disorder but even as the *source* of much larger economic, political, and social concerns. This is the view of children that's grounded in our inability to understand them, to be afraid when we see two or more of them gather at the mall, dressed in black with a piercing or two, listening to music through ear buds connected to an MP3 player, music we imagine to be downloaded illegally, music (if it can be called that at all) that lacks both a beat and a tune.

This ambiguity about children, about what constitutes the qualities and characteristics of the child, allows for a juncture point around which the agendas of a number of influences can converge at the point that is occupied by children. Children serve a useful function in neutralizing the ideological agendas of those who seek to influence and constrain what happens in the private realm. As a means to an end, children and concerns about their welfare provide legitimizing means to bring about a goal that, if stated boldly and forthrightly, might be seen for what it is, an attempt to manipulate, censor, and control some separate and autonomous social group. Children provide a kind of neutral conduit between the public realm and the private world, an entrée point for government and for other public institutions, to enter into the private confines of the family. Historical examples abound of a clear pattern of intrusion by government into the realm of the private lives of citizens through regulation and control of their children. How better to explain the institution of child labor laws, which function not as a means to prohibit abuse of children so much as they remove from the workforce a significant group whose earnings might benefit their families, yet might also prevent the illusion of full employment of adults in society at the time?

Historical Notions of Childhood

The idea that children and youth require a special protection from the power of all manner of potential moral harms—from artistic expression, to violence, to sex—has existed at least since the notion of childhood innocence and vulnerability emerged as a 16th-century phenomenon. Although it wasn't until the 19th century that the notion of protecting youth through censorship truly gained ground (Heins, 2001), the assumptions about children render social constraints about them both justifiable and rational. Childhood is a concept historically and culturally bound, identified by historians and sociologists who see the notion of "childhood" as a new, modern phenomenon, one that is determined now less by biology than by social construction. Children are conceptualized as more natural, more biologically pure and innocent, possessing an inherent beauty or aesthetic with a greater similarity to plants, to animals, certainly more in common with things such as these than to the adults they will become. The perception legitimizes them as the subjects of inquiry, directs the focus of testable questions about them, questions about human behaviors, focuses directly on them as subjects of inquiry, and justifies the research on social, cultural, and biological grounds.

In a sense, this is the pathologizing of childhood, of adolescence in particular. We can identify a string of ways in which the behaviors of children are pathologized, criminalized, or mythologized. Consider the increase in *DSM-IV* (American Psychiatric Association, 1994) diagnoses of behavioral disorders such as attention-deficit hyperactivity disorder (ADHD), for example.

Adult anxiety about children in the modern world is based on a kind of ambivalence about them as active agents. The status of children is little more than just "adults in waiting," a construction that makes it possible to embrace any policy that will limit and constrain them, keep them in their rightful and subordinate roles as inferiors to adults. Adults are also engaged in a negotiation through children with their own childhoods—either to re-create an idealized and happy childhood or to prevent the harms of a troubled one. The desire to provide either a similar experience for their own children or to avoid the pitfalls of a terrible one drives both visions for a hopeful future and a challenge to their own fears of what lies ahead.

Our contemporary view of "childhood" is grounded in historically paternalistic, conservative constructs. Children are valued not for anything intrinsic within them but primarily for how they may eventually grow up and become adults and assume stature and presence in the real world. They are idealized as innocent, vulnerable, and passive, situated in subordinate roles outside of adult space. This idealized role for children is necessary to legitimize the need for adults to maintain control over children. Power is the central issue, as it is something that can be exercised by one group in society over another. Thus, the power that adults hold over children is legitimized by this idealized role for children (Jenkins, 1998; Scheper-Hughes & Sargent, 1998; Wyness, 2000).

This kind of thinking has consequences for the autonomy of children, as well as for the ways that society creates both opportunities and limits for children. By denying children and adolescents certain rights to engage as autonomous and active social agents, their dependency on adults is extended and their relationship with adults is reinforced. With such a definition, children can only exist in a subordinate role, devoid of autonomy, devoid of social agency. Do children have a stake in their own futures, or are they dependant wholly on adults? Constraints on childhood remind us that our society is increasingly organized around notions of age, cohorts created by marketers, by social groups, and by government policies and eligibilities based on age. In addition, children have never been afforded the means through which they might shape their own identities, and so adults have created social, political, and historical constructs that define them and the boundaries that separate them from adults.

Given this image of the child, the task of looking out for the best interests of children is an admirable thing under a paradigm that defines them as innocent, vulnerable, and in need of such protection. If the child is not perceived as an active social agent, then someone else must act to maintain his or her integrity. This image fits nicely with the desires of a multitude of social actors to extend their power, influence, and control. Affecting the lives of children is not the end but merely the means to an end.

Some scholars (Wyness, 2000) even argue that a "crisis of childhood" forces us to consider the idea that children are somehow "out of position," an idea that indicates that children either don't know or don't accept their relative place with regard to adults. Children's position relative to adults is either a protectionist one, one in which adults maintain authority and are obliged to provide for and protect, or an autonomous one, with rights for self-determination, where children choose, act independently, and may make decisions that even run counter to the ones adults would have made for them. This kind of autonomy granted to children can't but by definition threaten the traditional protective and paternalistic obligations of adults.

Wyness (2000) applies the concept of citizenship to the place that children occupy in society—as a minority group within the larger political and economic landscape, a designation for systematically viewing social strata not unlike more traditional and recognizable dimensions, such as race, gender, and class.

In *Channel Surfing*, his 1997 book on the crisis in American youth, Henry A. Giroux describes how representations of American youth in popular culture contribute to an ambiguous redefinition of the meaning of youth and are indicative of the devaluing nature of perceptions of young people. Children are constructed in media portrayals by conflicting images that, on one hand, offer "hope for the future" while, on the other, present a "threat to the existing social order." Young people become symbolic of the decline in democracy, social responsibility, and the obligations of citizenship.

Having it both ways legitimizes the devaluing and indifference that adults pay to adolescents while justifying subordination, censorship, and repression of young people's behaviors, personal expressions, and media choices. Giroux (1997) observes that political decisions of the 1990s served to undermine support for education, social services, and economic opportunities for young people and families challenged by poverty, unemployment, and a lack of health care. These decisions create what he calls "a new form of representational politics," one that is expressed in media depictions of youth defined as "criminal, sexually decadent, drug-crazed, and illiterate" (p. 40). This portrayal of young people perpetuates the notion that they threaten the social order; indeed, youth become the focus of adult fears and serve as scapegoats for society's ills.

To conceptualize childhood only in relations to another group—adulthood—we are defining the discussion about childhood as an encounter between two groups, rather than a continuous framework for development. This has implications and consequences for the question at hand, the notion of media violence and putative harm.

The Moral Crisis of Contemporary Childhood

Aiken (2001) examines how and where the "current moral crises of childhood" are constituted. He observes that by defining or distinguishing children from adults by focusing on what they lack—situating them in juxtaposition to adults based on their nonadult status—this creates a binary construction that reduces the complex nature of children's lives to a simplistic model. It forces an "us-them" constraint on any transaction between members of the two groups, and it maintains the inherent conflict that lies at the heart of the media violence/harm to children debate.

Aiken (2001) explores ideas about how social scientists (and geographers in particular, his own discipline group) "encounter" young people in their social scientific work, a phenomenon that he observes began in the mid-1980s. This "crisis of representation" among social scientists grappling with both appropriate theory and appropriate methods for approaching the relationship between observer and subject created a reliance on an artificial and politically contrived conceptualization of young people. The issue becomes most clear around terms used to describe them, what Aiken (p. 6) calls the "plasticity of terms" that include *children, teenagers, adults, childhood, adolescence,* and *adulthood.* Aiken's arguments focus on the social construction of meaning around young people through time and across space, in which he suggests that the Western ideological construction of childhood is:

> a privileged private domain of innocence, spontaneity, play, freedom and emotion in opposition to a public culture of culpability, discipline, work, constraint and rationality.... The creation and expansion of the modern antimony of child/adult, like the female/male dichotomy, is crucial to setting up hierarchical relations upon which modern capitalism and the modern nation-state depends. In what sense does this antimony help engender a status quo that reduces the lives and practices of young people to something from which corporations can profit? Put another way, how are the constraints on young people's lives also about how to make adult lives more comfortable? (p. 7)

Adolescence, Adulthood, and Childhood Characterized

If childhood can only be understood in a continuum of progress toward something based on maturity, if that destination is a place called "adulthood," and if media violence constrains both the progress toward that destination and is described and constrained by those others who have attained that destination, it seems to be a requirement that we examine the nature of these relevant stages to adulthood as well. What is a child? What is an adolescent? What is an adult? In his book *Arrested Adulthood,* author James E. Côté (2000) observes that the concept of adulthood is as troublesome and difficult to define as is childhood and that, indeed, the notion of adulthood is tied for its meaning based in the concept of maturity to a notion of childhood that is based on a characteristic of immaturity. Furthermore, he observes that adulthood tends to be described in ways not characterized by what people actually *do* as adults but rather as "prescriptive attempts to characterize what people 'ought to do'" (p. 51).

The media/violence/aggression construction is consistent with and helps to reinforce a conventional view of childhood, adolescence, and emerging adulthood that prevails in America today. For children, those youngest people prior to about age 9 or 10, we find a much greater degree of agreement about what is age-appropriate media content. At issue for the youngest children is the kind of reaction to inappropriate exposure to media content—the paternalistic idea of protecting children from violence, sex, or other content.

The Ontological Crisis

Where we find the larger social and political disagreements and concerns develop are around the issue of what is appropriate content for young people who fall into our category of adolescence. If adolescence is a hormonally based concept, one that begins with puberty and ends with adulthood, there is little to contest its beginning, at least. Adolescence, like other concepts created by social scientists to categorize people for the purpose of investigation, is a social construction that intends to reflect some essential characteristic or quality of human development. But some scholars have observed that the social construction itself can shape the lives of the people who experience it. Robert M. Galatzer-Levy (2002) writes of this phenomenon in and identifies the consequences of allowing young people to believe in the myths about them. These constructions about young people that limit their own views of themselves contribute to an increased inability to move beyond childhood into adulthood and tend to place greater and greater constraints on young people through restrictions on access to things such as media violence, restrictions that, in their limitations on personal autonomy, tend to have the reverse effect, leading to immaturity, lack of civic engagement, and a confusing view of adults who seem irrational because of their reactions to seemingly harmless things.

Images of childhood and images of adulthood are changing and blurring the line between what it means to occupy a space in either camp. Contemporary scholars have begun to recognize and identify the dimensions of uncertainty with regard to adulthood as a destination, the end point of childhood as a process of becoming something else. Adult life may be more unpredictable, less stable, and harder to determine than ever before. And this uncertainty about adulthood threatens the traditional balance between one and the other. Childhood has been defined primarily in terms of its dependant relationship to adulthood—a process of becoming or arriving at a destination. If adulthood as historically and culturally construed is no longer attainable as the destination, then childhood begins to lack its purpose and structure as well.

As policy makers, religious leaders, educators, parents, and others seek to stem the onslaught of social change and uncertainty about the uncoupling of society from its traditional institutions of government, church, schools, and families, the maintenance of an idea of childhood is a chance to retain one foothold in the traditional and familiar structure.

The divisions between developmental phases are marked by ambiguity and must rely on external attributes to define and retain them. Traditional markers or indicators of transition from one phase to another are even more difficult at the beginning of the 21st century to identify or to rely on. When does adolescence begin, for example? At age 11 or at age 13? Does it start when children enter middle school? At the beginning of puberty, an event occurring at an ever earlier age, especially for girls? And when does adulthood begin? At age 18? Or at age 21? When one moves out of a parent's house and begins earning a living? What about the person who lives at home but earns a living? Is one an adult when one finishes school? High school? College? A graduate degree? When one marries? Has children of her own? Buys a vacuum cleaner?

Consider the following:

> Whether it's reconverting the guest room back into a bedroom, paying for graduate school, writing a blizzard of small checks to cover rent and health-insurance premiums or acting as career counselors, parents across the country are trying to provide their twentysomethings with the tools they'll need to be self-sufficient—someday. In the process, they have created a whole new breed of child—the **adultolescent.** (Tyre, 2002)

And so now we have even begun to identify a new stage in the life cycle that helps to extend the idea of childhood and its inherent absence of legitimacy and maturity even further. The notion that past childhood, past adolescence, and yet still before adulthood, we have a stage called *emerging adulthood,* the term used by psychologist Jeffrey Jensen Arnett (Arnett & Tanner, 2006). This is a life stage that literally *extends* human development into another stage of transition from childhood to maturity, a new period identified between being an adolescent and being "a grown-up."

The young people who themselves fall into this new category may take umbrage with the notion that they are somehow less than mature at a certain age that qualified their parents for full membership in an adult world. Or they may actually prefer the sophisticated and clinically sounding label of "emerging adult" to others we've heard recently—terms such as "kidults" (for adults who buy and enjoy games designed for children) or "twixters" (the *Time* magazine term to describe those caught "betwixt" adulthood and childhood), or terms with worse connotations, such as "slacker," which emphasizes underachievement, or others that pathologize young people as sufferers of "Peter Pan Syndrome" or the "Wendy Dilemma," even more derogatory terms that have served in the recent past to label and degrade that constituency of young adults.

An idea such as "adultolescence" requires somebody older (dare we call them adults?) to ignore their own shortcomings or contribution to the creation of such a construction. Could such "helicopter parents" be so paranoid about letting go of control over their offspring that they are complicit in this odd denial for allowing freedom and self-identity to emerge? The MacArthur Foundation, an organization of significant prestige, is funding research to look carefully at this phenomenon of transition to adulthood and to examine the public policy implications of these changing patterns of human development. Sociological interest in childhood, adolescence, and now early adulthood promises to begin to challenge the traditional and limited images we have held about these stages and can help to inform the nature of inquiries about media influences at each level. There are at least two reasons why a redefined notion of childhood can begin to untangle the media-violence myth. One, it's a question of science. Social science inquiry in particular relies on the idea that children are an appropriate subject pool and that their behaviors, feelings, and opinions can be influenced by media messages and images in large part because they are easy to influence.

Two, a redefined notion of childhood recognizes the breadth of children's autonomy and their rights to make independent choices about the kinds of media (and other) experiences, which they engage. A rejection of the paternalistic relationship between adults and children recognizes that children are not *less than* adults, somehow of value only because they are on their way to becoming adults, and that they warrant status as an equivalently empowered human subgroup as legitimate as groups separated by differences of race, gender, or nationality. We routinely hear and act on ideas that children are *worth less* than adults. That they are less able than adults to make autonomous choices that affect their own lives.

A generational subset that is not defined hierarchically by chronological age is a difficult notion to embrace, not the least because chronology appears to advance hierarchically. Setting that idea aside allows for a vision of children and adults that is grounded in a reality of human dignity and respect. Such a position is far easier to describe, however, than to advance throughout society. But social scientists ought to be first to embrace the approach because to do so empowers the results of their work tremendously in terms of the validity of the inquiry and the usefulness of their findings.

Moral Panics and the Focus on Children

The ambiguous and disconnected notions that we hold about childhood seem to inform and to feed the frenzy of fear and concern that society reserves for issues around media violence and the putative effect it has on children. On one hand, the construction of childhood innocence violated feeds concerns about the overwhelming harm that media must certainly impose on impressionable children. On the other, we observe an equally misplaced and unverifiable fear of the harm posed to society by disaffected youth, inspired by their consumption of media violence, and rampantly violating the social order with deviance and abnormal behaviors.

This issue of media violence and its supposed harmful effect on children is always portrayed and construed first as a *social* problem. Concerns about it are situated in adult fear, in adult misremembering and misunderstanding of youth behavior, behavior that is so incomprehensible that it can only be understood as aberrant, only explained as deviant, only recognizable as abnormal. The concern about media violence always centers on the harm it will generate by influencing the behaviors of children, whose actions so inspired will lead to significant consequences with implications for social order. The problem of media violence is sometimes defined as a health risk, later it becomes a moral concern, and frequently it's cited as a correlate of criminal behavior. But always, these concerns are outwardly directed, public issues with social consequences and little grounding or relevance in private or personal experience.

The attributes and characteristics of the media violence issue as a social problem fit nicely with theory building surrounding the notion of *moral panics*. The model of a moral panic is a useful social construction, a model for understanding the way societies transform and process challenges to social moral order. Scholars who have identified and used the notion of a moral panic to explain such social phenomena identify that they occur as a kind of public hysteria, featuring an irrational fear of something (witches, video games, child abductions, fill in the blank here) that is of little concern to *you* but poses an overwhelming threat to everyone else, whose moral, economic, cultural, and ideological characteristics are questionable (and certainly different from your own). Such panics frequently have children as their focus, tend to arise when society is in flux, and are fed by media attention, misrepresentations, sensationalizations, and simplifications.

The concept of a moral panic is a useful heuristic for examining and understanding the nature of social reactions to threats that are perceived with a level of fear that is entirely out of proportion to the actual risk they represent. How do social issues come to be perceived as concerns so great that they require some formal and official response? How do social issues become "moral panics"? And how might understanding a model help us to better understand the public nature of the media violence myth?

The work on moral panics originated with British sociologist Steven Cohen's work in the early 1970s to try to explain the mass hysteria that arose after two small groups of British youths—the Mods and the Rockers—had, in 1964, clashed violently in an isolated incident at a seaside resort. Cohen's (1973) examination of the ensuing phenomenon of media, parental, and political reaction led to his seminal work, *Folk Devils and Moral Panics: The Creation of the Mods and Rockers.* The concept of moral panic helps to explain how people can be led to believe something that is not true and suggests clearly how it might serve as a valuable heuristic for understanding the perpetuation of the media violence-aggression myth. In *Moral Panics and the Media,* Charles Critcher (2003) examines the role of the media in contributing to the creation and legitimization of moral panics by examining a series of cases to determine whether they, indeed, fit the two prevailing models, the first articulated by Cohen and a second model later suggested by Erich Goode and Nachman Ben-Yehuda in 1994 with their book *Moral Panics: The Social Construction of Deviance.*

A moral panic model is most often applied by sociologists and criminologists on a case-by-case basis to one of any social problems that either share a set of common characteristics or attributes or move through a process distinguished by progress through a set of stages or emergent episodes. The five key elements of a moral panic suggested by Goode and Ben-Yehuda's (1994) attributional model, for example, include a high level of *concern* about the behaviors of a certain identifiable group; a level of *hostility* toward the group because its behavior can cause harm to the moral fabric of society; *consensus* about the threat within society at a sufficient level or within a certain visible subset of society (such as by a vocal special interest group) that legitimizes the threat as real; the defining quality of *disproportionality,* which is the center of the moral panic model, the notion that reactions to a perceived threat are wholly out of proportion to the actual risk; and, finally, a dimension of *volatility,* that the phenomenon erupts quickly and without warning, may subside and reemerge, and each subsequent episode builds on the last, although individually such episodes tend not to be sustained significantly over time.

As Critcher (2003) examines a series of British examples to see if the cases meet the definitions of a moral panic, he examines the British concern around "video nasties," among others, and suggests some intriguing modifications of the model. For one, he finds that concern and consensus (two features of the attributional model) need not reside fully in the public but that sufficient concern generated among elites in the media and politics is enough to raise the phenomenon to qualify as a moral panic. Two, he finds that hostility need not be directed toward a folk devil but, as in the case of horror films as the focus of the panic in Britain over video nasties, a moral panic needs only an object representing the threat.

Critcher (2003) proposes an explanation for the focus on childhood in every moral panic he examined. The key concern in a moral panic is to protect children from some threat generated by adults, and that requirement to regulate the adult propensity to violate childhood innocence and vulnerability requires an image of childhood that justifies the limits on adult autonomy.

The role the media play in moral panics is significant. Critcher (2003) observes that the media have the ability to "instigate moral panics on their own" (p. 152). Journalists have been quick to buy into the "playing-video-games-caused-Columbine" explanations for complex events. Furthermore, the impact of media on children is an issue frequently portrayed in the popular media as one of morality rather than of science, where both academic and popular discussions are polarized around conflict over youth, human nature, freedom, autonomy, authority, and control.

On the other hand, should the media attempt a balanced reporting of media effects, they are accused by effects advocates of failing to report "the actual state of scientific knowledge" (Bushman & Anderson, 2001). Moral panic clearly has value for a particular social agenda and may be instigated to advance it.

As part of the cultural struggle, we see the conflict but are uncertain about how to respond. Need we respond? Is there yet some view that embraces the world as it is should be and as it is without irrational fear of nonthreats but identification of problems that require our collective social focus?

Every Cloud Has a Silver Lining

Reruns of old *Saturday Night Live* episodes are a welcome companion when one is up at 3 a.m. with a cranky baby. Your keyboardist once sat cross-legged on the floor in front of a television set at such an hour, nursing a sleepless daughter who must have been about 13 or 14 months old at the time. (Observations about the appropriate length to nurse a child are reserved, thank you very much, for texts in baby and childcare, but not here.) The object of this story is the *SNL* episode, which featured Steve Martin as host and a particular skit in which he appeared as the grand arbiter of cowardice among fellow cast members, crew, audience members, and anyone who happened to be within the studio confines. The gist of the skit was for Martin to walk from one person to the next, down the hall backstage, meeting each person with a look in the eye and then to declare them to be either a "coward" or "not a coward" and proceed to the next person. This particular routine relied both on stupidity and on repetition to succeed, and 10, 12, maybe as many as 15 people were summarily ascertained to be either a coward or not a coward. Those deemed not to be cowards were spared, but everyone declared a coward got the slap. Suffice it to say, there was a fair amount of face slapping going on.

Meanwhile, baby Anna eagerly nursing away, was perfectly positioned to watch the entire antics of Martin on the television screen. Anyone who has nursed a child until a certain age will recognize that everything is a distraction and almost anything can be accommodated while a daughter is so engaged. Yet there was still that moment of surprise when the precious child, barely older than a year, not yet talking beyond the prewords of *mama* and *dada* and *kiki* (for cat), looked Mommy carefully in the eye, took a deliberate pause from eating, and reached up with her tiny hand and slapped Mother across the face.

One of the problems with the media violence connection is that all of us are experts in popular culture. It's hard not to make the logical case for what seems self-evident. Many of us have experienced or observed similar situations of media effects, immediate, imitative, playful. How many times did we jump off the brick wall with an open umbrella, hoping to fly like Mary Poppins? How often did we re-create television shows or advertisements we saw, like the Zest test we ran and reran in our parents' bathroom, determined to show that only Zest comes clean when you dip your eyeglasses in it, but the other soap leaves a soapy buildup? We know the media have effects on children because we observe it. We live it. Seems a logical next step to assume that the media cause normal people to engage in harmful and criminal behavior? Perhaps not, as any critical analysis will start to unravel the threads that hold this myth together.

Concerns about media violence and its effects have generally centered on behaviors, on feelings, and on beliefs. It's useful to think in terms of these distinctions when we start to examine the range of ideas and claims so often made in the public discussion about the effects that media may or may not have on children. What is our concern about media violence and children? Is it only the idea that children will imitate what they see? And even when they do, of what consequence is it? In the hierarchy of effects, the implication that behaviors trump feelings or beliefs most certainly prevails. But what of the feelings and ideas that are generated from exposure to media, the ideas that emerge from watching, engaging, and observing media narratives that may or may not include violence? And certainly this discussion has tended to focus on the negative effects, rather than the positive. Consider, for example, the work done by Karen Sternheimer, one of a handful of American scholars who have begun to address the idea that there may, indeed, be alternate interpretations for the media violence myth. In *It's Not the Media: The Truth About Pop Culture's Influence on Children*

(2003), she identifies those contemporary fears that drive the abiding cultural belief that media have serious and negative effects on children. Sternheimer, who teaches in the sociology department at USC, posits that the media have come to symbolize society and our national unease with recent change in our political, social, and economic lives. Couple that with our fear of what the future holds and it's easy to see why the media, popular culture, and children captivate our attention.

Sternheimer (2003) argues that what lies behind the American fear of media culture is really anxiety about an uncertain future. This fear is deflected onto children, who symbolize the future, and onto media, which symbolize contemporary society. Sternheimer then makes the case for why the media aren't the culprit but a convenient social and political diversion from real and difficult problems we ought to try to solve—problems such as poverty, gun control, access to quality child care, and affordable education and decent health care. Furthermore, Sternheimer observes that it is the affluent and the middle class who are the first to blame the media for harming children and generating social violence. Poor people, on the other hand, have firsthand experience with real social problems and recognize that media wield an insignificant impact on their life struggles. Much of this argument resonates with the lived experiences of young people, who can readily identify that their own experiences with media and popular culture tend to belie the inanity of the conventional wisdom. Indeed, Sternheimer and others have begun to finally examine the value that popular culture brings to a young person's life to compare this to the hypocrisy and ignorance of adults when it comes to understanding youth media culture.

It's Not the Media is not your father's media effects handbook. Indeed, Sternheimer (2003) dismisses most of what passes for media effects research, on grounds that the bulk of the work lacks rigor, validity, and generalizability. Hers is a compelling position that resonates with our own. Yet, you won't find many voices represent the other side of the media violence debate, although the momentum is growing (Barker & Petley, 2001; Buckingham, 1998; Fowles, 1999; Freedman, 1984; Heins, 2001; Jenkins, 1998; Jones, 2002; Katch, 2001; J. Katz, 1997). One dominant theme of all their work is the need to refocus the questions about media violence on some dimension of the issue that makes sense. These scholars are focusing on a more legitimate way to examine media violence by shifting the focus to *reception* rather than harm—in other words, why and how do people actually use and interact with violent media?

Their premise is that those who claim media violence causes harm are asking the wrong question. They're of the same school as those who insistently asked if human illness, the death of pigs, thunderstorms, and crop failures were the result of witchcraft. Indeed, Barker and Petley (2001) write that media violence is the witchcraft of our society. "You can only believe someone to be a witch if you believe there are 'witch-events.' The facts adduced only look like evidence and arguments if you are already within that frame of reference" (p. 43). But just like witchcraft, the claims about media violence serve crucial social and political functions that won't be easily abandoned.

Gerard Jones (2002), in a groundbreaking book titled *Killing Monsters: Why Children Need Fantasy, Super Heroes, and Make-Believe Violence,* was one of the first in a popular discussion about children's active interest in media violence to argue that instead of bashing media violence and prohibiting children from engaging with it, we should harness the power of fantasy to empower children to survive in a complex, complicated, violent world. He interviewed psychiatrists, pediatricians, family therapists, teachers, screenwriters, game designers, and parents. He talked with children and teens about their favorite movies, songs, stories, and games, collecting first-person accounts from young people about the benefits they've enjoyed from comics, action films, video games, and rap songs.

His commonsense arguments may resonate with parents who feel particularly ridiculous prohibiting behaviors they enjoyed themselves as children. He found young people "using fantasies of combat in order to feel stronger, to access their emotions, to take control of their anxieties, to calm themselves down in the face of real violence, to fight their way through emotional challenges and lift themselves to new developmental levels" (Jones, 2002, p. 6). Indeed, Jones (2002) suggests that parents actually confuse their children with regard to the difference between reality and fantasy when they react with dismay or concern over pretend violence and aggressive play. "We don't help children learn the difference between fantasy and reality when we allow their fantasies to provoke reactions from us that are more appropriate to reality," he writes.

> When a child is joyfully killing a friend who loves being killed, we don't make things clearer for them by responding with an anxious, "You shouldn't shoot people!" Instead we blur the very boundaries that they're trying to establish. We teach them that pretend shooting makes adults feel threatened in *reality,* and therefore their own fantasies must be more powerful and more dangerous than they thought. The result for the child is more anxiety and self-doubt, more concern over the power of violent thoughts, less sense of power over their own feelings, and less practice expressing their fantasies—a combination far more likely to lead either to behavioral problems or excessive timidity than safe self-enjoyment would be. (p. 56)

Jones (2002) argues further that such make-believe aggressive play provides opportunities for children to overcome their fears and to learn that such fears can be mastered. One reason that children crave fantasy violence, he suggests, is to prove to themselves they can be strong enough to overcome their fears. Their need for extreme fantasy violence—"raw, loud, and angry"—is a function of the intensity of violence both observed and presumed in reality, an intensity that has escalated in 40 years. Jones writes,

> What television news programs are willing to show, what parents are willing to discuss within earshot of their children, gives young people thoughts and images to grapple with that demand fantasy images just as potent. Being shocked by an image within the safe confines of fantasy can help them learn not to be so shocked in reality. (pp. 101–102)

Jones (2002) acknowledges that if young people grew up in a society less preoccupied with violence, they'd probably crave entertainment gore less and might be better off. But he argues it's unreasonable to expect them to be satisfied with "make believe that is more sanitized than their reality" (p. 103).

So, where are the voices of children on these issues of media violence? Mostly absent in the academic literature, the policy statements, and the news and entertainment media. But where children are free to express their views, their sensible approach to media violence rings true. Take a look at the Web sites where children engage in discourse about their favorite video games. Or read the reviews they write and post on Web sites such as Amazon.com for books that target their favorite entertainment as vile, harmful, and powerful enough to harm them. One example is this review of the book *Stop Teaching Our Kids to Kill: A Call to Action Against TV, Movie and Video Game Violence* (Grossman & Degaetano, 1999), posted July 24, 2001:

> I am 17 years old and have literally been playing video games longer than I remember. I've played some of the most violent, gory games ever created, such as Soldier of Fortune, which allows the player to actually blow limbs off of enemies, or Thrill Kill, an ultraviolet fighter that was canceled in the American and U.K. markets due to bad publicity just like this book. I've watched A Clockwork Orange several times—a film glorifying drugs, violence, and even rape. Sure, I've played Doom, and if I see vicious hellspawn rushing to impale me with their horns, I think I'd certainly shoot to kill. In reality, however, I scarcely believe I could shoot a squirrel unless my family was starving. I'm not a violent person, despite being subjected to violence in the media as described in this book. It's the responsibility of the parents to choose what their children see, and those kids that exhibit violent tendencies should be watched closely.

Video games can provide a visible outlet for these feelings, and might even provide early signs of instability. As for me, I'll go play tetris and hope the demons don't sneak up on me when I'm without my BFG. Stop blaming the corporations just because it's easier.[1]

We continue to grapple with the juxtaposition of what might be called enlightened ideas, ones that tend not to focus on the public and external notions of media violence but those that ring true for individuals, acting autonomously, within their own households, observing and engaging with their own children. But the fear factor continues in books such as one written by W. James Potter (2003) that purports to address the "myths" of media violence even while perpetuating them. In *The 11 Myths of Media Violence,* Potter might simply have borrowed the tag line "Be afraid . . . be very afraid" as a subtitle to this book. From Potter, we learn that four key players—the public, media producers, policy makers, and researchers—have defined the myths about violence through their adversarial grappling, by trading in misinformation, misperception, and misunderstanding. The 11 myths range from assumptions about who is vulnerable to media violence (children, of course, but even people who don't watch television) to who is culpable (producers, society, the marketplace, the genre of fiction) to how to solve the problem (ratings and V-chips are *not* the answer, but media literacy might help). Potter's position is that media generate significant negative effects in insidious and undetectable fashion. Indeed, he argues that even people who don't watch violence on television or film are harmed by such violence because, as we have noted before, simply knowing that such violence in film exists in your culture is enough to perpetrate a coarsening and degrading of your own existence. Start with Sternheimer and work through Potter to grasp the passion that each brings to the debate. Both provide deeply introspective narratives yet opposite worldviews about the impact of popular media. How can such disagreement occur? What is the context for such dramatically oppositional interpretations?

We know our own children. We know what they have watched, and perhaps despite what they have watched, we have seen their successful transitions through the many life stages we choose to invent. Our children and even our neighbor's children have somehow managed the gauntlet of media and growing up. But as has always been the case, some children have not. In an earlier age, we would have sought the source of that failure in the circumstances of the child. Through the 20th century, however, as our history of effects shows, we have increasingly favored the media—from the motion picture, to the radio crime drama, to the comic book, to television, and now to video games—as our explanation of choice. It's comforting to know that it is not our fault. In the next chapter, however, we turn back the clock and once again take up the circumstance of the child as the preferred explanation.

Note

1. "Speaking from experience"—Steve Edwards from Stockbridge, Georgia. Last accessed from Amazon.com on February 3, 2003, at http://www.amazon.com/exec/ obidos/tg/detail/-/0609606131/qid=1044823052/sr=2–3/ 102–4266701–2018560?v=glance&s=books.

8

The Role of Psychopathology in the Media Violence/ Aggression Equation

There is more than simple obdurate opposition in our resistance to the certainty of the causationists. There is a good bit of science as well. This science involves a return to an adaptive conditional argument, which was prevalent in media violence research up until the 1970s. This is the argument that redefines media violence from that of a clear and present social danger to an environmental stimulus that has differential effects, which are conditional to the sort of people who are exposed to media violence. Most especially, the conditional nature of media violence's effect is as dependent on the endogenous psychological and psychoneural characteristics the viewer brings to media violence as that which media violence brings to the viewer.

That Better Hypothesis

A more plausible hypothesis is one that asserts that exposure to media violence cannot, itself, induce aggression. There must be both the presence of social-environmental variables that interact with a psychological predisposition to aggression as well as the absence of suppressor variables (such as internal and external behavioral control variables) for the relationship between exposure and aggression to appear. This model is generally called a third-variable model, even though more than just one additional variable is likely involved. This is a quite different and more modulated hypothesis than the position of the causationists. And it is much more in line with our own experience with media content and with ethnographic studies of media audiences.

Note that this is not an ostrich position, which denies the existence of a relationship or one that claims that media content is without effect. But to use the drug metaphor of which causationists are so fond, multiple forms of media content (including violent content) are like alcohol, which vast numbers of people use without social consequence but also for which some uses by some individuals have grave social consequences and, by some people, should not be used at all. (As we pointed out earlier, we may consider the causationists to be our modern-day Temperance Unionists whose moral outrage has taken them beyond their science.)

Assume that our position is correct—that causationists have overreached. But . . . do we have the causationists to thank for alerting us to the notion that media violence *can* cause aggressive behavior in some individuals, if not in most individuals, as the causationists claim? In other words, hasn't the causal position provided some good? We regret to appear to be uncompromising—but no, the causationists have not helped matters one bit. The idea that media violence would cause a subset of people to behave aggressively and not others is derived from clinical psychological and psychophysiological research (which we will outline shortly). As rigid as it might sound—and we don't want to appear to be rigid—the work of the causationists has only muddled things. Had social scientists who are interested in this area of research only hewed to carefully crafted clinical and psychophysiological work, we don't think that communication theory would have gotten so far out of alignment with the available empirical evidence generated by the clinical and psychophysiological disciplines. Here's why. The idea that a set of "third variables" must be in play to elicit aggressive behavior is not a new idea. Other investigators came up with this notion some time ago (e.g., Atkin et al., 1979, and even Huesmann, Lagerspetz, et al., 1984). But we believe that clinical and psychophysiological theory provides a more precise explanation for why a predisposing third-variable set is present.

We have argued, based on established cognitive, clinical, and psychophysiological theory (Grimes et al., 2004), that for media violence to activate a series of cognitions and behaviors that result in a general rise in the magnitude of behavioral aggression, a psychiatric and neural framework must be present to allow that to happen. That is, a psychiatric predicate would have to exist before the type of sociopathic behavior that causationists claim takes place actually could take place; media violence, in and of itself, can't generate the conditions necessary to make most people behave in a sociopathic way. But the psychiatric and neurological literature, irrespective of the issue of media violence, does not posit the existence of such a framework. And so perhaps it's no coincidence that the causal camp has offered up very few clinical or neural explanations for why media violence causes social aggression.[1] And there most certainly isn't psychological or neurological evidence to sustain the assertion, attributed to Huesmann (Mifflin, 1999), that each instance of a person's exposure to media violence increases the risk of subsequent aggressive behavior. Thus, for communication researchers to argue that long-term exposure to media violence can lead to a more aggressive society not only posits a set of implied assumptions about human psychology that don't appear to exist but also posits assumptions about the way that civilized society has organized itself that doesn't appear to be met by sociological theory (which we will also explore). So the theoretical patchwork that some communication researchers have had to create to make the causal hypothesis work has resulted in rather inelegant and unconvincing psychological and behavioral models.

Causal Inelegance

We want to unpack all of what we've argued so far. So let's begin by examining some implications of the causal hypothesis for existing psychiatric models. Causationists have come up with a surprisingly few number of models that precisely and exactly describe how media violence motivates aggressive behavior (irrespective of whether such a model is actually valid). What models are extant are based on old and unsophisticated cognitive models. Our point is that, rather than build theory, many causal studies make a cursory acknowledgment of theories that *might* be applicable to the causal hypothesis and then proceed to demonstrate, in a controlled laboratory setting, that media violence has caused aggression among study participants.

For instance, consider learning theory. This claim asserts that very young children, 2 to 4 years of age, "learn" violent behavior as a result of watching it on television or in the movies (e.g., Bushman & Huesmann, 2001). As the child gets older and more discerning, so the theory goes, aggressiveness learned early on is reinforced in a number of different ways that sum to make it more difficult for the child to disabuse himself or herself later in life from the use of aggression as a social tool (Huesmann, Lagerspetz, et al., 1984). Thus, when these children encounter a social obstacle in which aggressive behavior would address the problem, they will behave aggressively because they have learned the value of such behavior and thus are habituated to its use. Although we have been able to trace this notion, as applied to media violence, as early in the literature as a 1963 study by Bandura and colleagues, we have not seen an attempt to experimentally connect the prediction to a clinical psychological mechanism that would drive behavioral aggression. Indeed, the contrary has been the case.

Suppressor Variables

A considerable amount of research explains why most healthy people will *not* do what advocates of learning theory in particular, and the causal hypothesis in general, predict. It revolves around the behavioral inhibition system (Grimes et al., 2004, p. 156) and other behavior-moderating theories such as the violence inhibition mechanism (Blair, 1995, 1999). All of these psychiatric processes militate against sociopathic behavior within healthy personalities, but it might be acquired. In other words, just as the common cold is no more than an annoyance for a healthy person, so it appears that media violence is sloughed off by healthy personalities. Just as the common cold can be fatal for people with certain co-occurring illnesses, media violence, we will argue, can be quite troublesome for people with certain psychopathologies—those psychopathologies being the third variable to which we referred earlier.

In any event, the core problem is that the mere enunciation of any one of several predictive theories that have been used to justify the causal hypothesis (Huesmann et al., 2003)—learning theory, excitation transfer theory (Zillmann, 1979, 1983), arousal theory (Berkowitz, 1993)—does not explain *why* the array of behavioral inhibition systems that psychologically well people carry with them through life would be repeatedly overridden by the effects of long-term exposure to media violence. To graft, convincingly, one of those theories to the aggressive behavior of a child or adult, one would have to engage in a series of laboratory experiments that employ a tight causal design. But most of the media violence research we have reviewed doesn't do that. To the contrary, it "topically applies" theory to paper-and-pencil protocols or simulated behavior. This topically applied theory does little more than speculate that theoretically framed psychological processes *can* account for observed behavior. It does not build the empirical/clinical/medical/neural links that undergird the processes that advocates of the causal hypothesis argue are extant.

Building a Better Model

So what *do* we assert that we know? To begin with, as both commonsense and empirical research shows, witnessing real violence can have important consequences for one's psychological health, especially if a person is exposed to real violence over a long period of time. Certainly, the many thousands of American soldiers in Iraq, who are exposed to the most gruesome examples of human cruelty, sadly illustrate this principle in the posttraumatic stress they must manage when they return to this country. As Grimes et al. (1997) have suggested when they reviewed the psychophysiological literature, long-term exposure to *genuine* murders and assaults can permanently turn on fight-or-flight hormones that, over time, cause psychological harm. Specifically, the hormone cortisol, which helps people flee dangerous situations, can harm structures in a developing (i.e., juvenile) brain if it is in a person's system more or less constantly. Too much cortisol over too long a period of time can create a variety of psychological conditions that can make it difficult for a person to control his or her aggressive tendencies or accurately read routine social cues. Gunnar and Donzella (2002), for example, have suggested that people who have high levels of cortisol in their systems, for long intervals, can become chronically angry and may view aggression as an acceptable social tool when they deal with other people or find themselves in stressful situations. (Armchair psychiatrists, noting the accusations made against United State Marines in Haditha, Iraq, in November 2005—their alleged wanton murder of civilians in response to the death of a fellow Marine—have repeatedly invoked this model.) These psychological conditions can create situations in which, what most of us recognize as dramatic or comedic entertainment, a person with a psychological impairment would misinterpret to be threatening. And that could lead to aggressive behavior. In other words, something has to interrupt or sidetrack normal message cue processing for media violence to lead people to behave aggressively.

The Role of Behavioral Disorders

More specifically, children who are diagnosed with attention-deficit hyperactivity disorder, oppositional defiant disorder, and conduct disorders are included within a cluster of disorders known as disruptive behavior disorders (DBDs). Children with these disorders show psychopathic symptoms that can include less emotional concern for victims and the ability to tolerate greater levels of violence than do children who do not have psychopathic symptoms (American Psychiatric Association, 1994). DBDs are among the most common undiagnosed (in their milder manifestations) emotional disorders suffered by children and young adults (Grimes et al., 2004). There may be as many as 5% of the juvenile population who suffer from DBDs and who are undiagnosed (Grimes et al., 2004). Often, children with a DBD diagnosis are viewed by public school counselors and perhaps even parents as cranky, moody, idiosyncratic—but "normal." Indeed, being viewed by parents as cranky, yet normal, may be why most of these children never receive the clinical help they need. If there is a risk that media violence provokes antisocial behavior, it is this group of children who, we believe, would be most vulnerable.

We are interested in DBD-diagnosed children not only because of their ubiquity in the population but also because they appear to behave *exactly like* the causationists predict the population at large behaves after long-term exposure to media violence. These children seem to track exactly the route the causationists imply the general population takes when it is exposed to media violence. But the problem, of course, is that these children with a DBD diagnosis have an entirely different psychological and neural prism through which they view media violence. We strongly suspect it isn't the prism through which well children view media violence, which, we would argue, is the reason well children are unlikely to be harmed psychologically by the media violence they consume.

Children with a DBD diagnosis, on the other hand, process certain social cues differently than children who don't have a DBD diagnosis. Children who have a DBD diagnosis occasionally see threats in everyday social interactions when those threats aren't actually present. Apparently, because these children don't get much useful social information from environmental cues, they seem to attend to fewer social cues than children who don't have a DBD diagnosis. Psychologically well children encode all or most social cues and therefore respond in ways appropriate to the social setting (Dodge, 1993; Dodge & Frame, 1982).

In fact, there is some evidence that children with a DBD diagnosis are actually attracted to displays of aggression. This may be because many of these children have an underlying chronic anger that pervades their view of the world in which they live (Compas, Connor, Saltzman, Thomsen, & Wadsworth, 2001). The reason for that anger may be the result of child abuse or because many of them have lived in a hostile and threatening environment that can permanently turn on a child's fight-or-flight instincts, raising the likelihood of aggression. (We hasten to add that the environment *doesn't* include a lot of TV or movie violence.)

In clinically well personalities there appears to be a balance between a psychological inhibition and activation system that governs how they manage anger (Newman, 1987; Newman & Schmitt, 1998; Patrick, Culbert, &

Lang, 1994; Quay, 1993). A behavioral inhibition system (BIS) seems to reside in most psychologically well children and adults. When people with a fully functioning BIS feel aggressive, the BIS seems to inhibit aggression. To best illustrate this phenomenon, most of us would acknowledge that, at one time or another in our lives, we have all "scared ourselves" in our reaction to provocations and have pulled back before we did something irrevocably harmful to ourselves or to others. That is an example of a functioning BIS. People who do not have a normally functioning BIS have few, if any, other psychological tools to help them reflect on the consequences of their actions, few psychological resources that will pull them back from the brink. The BIS is what likely pulls us back from the brink. On the other hand, a behavioral activation system (BAS) activates aggressive behavior. The interaction between the BIS and the BAS is what most communication researchers (and most people, for that matter) define as "behavior," and it is that behavior that researchers often label and report (Quay, 1993).

Violence Inhibition

Blair (1995) describes another process, which he calls the violence inhibition mechanism (VIM). It's activated by seeing an aggressor who's suddenly in distress. It suppresses a person's tendency to launch an attack against that now humbled aggressor. Blair suggests that as children develop, the VIM becomes paired with schemas formed through empathizing with people who are in distress. This pairing, then, eventually becomes so automatic that even the thought of someone in distress can elicit an empathic response. A psychopathic individual, according to Blair, probably has an underdeveloped VIM, whereby distress cues have not elicited empathetic responses, leading in turn to a relative inability to feel empathy toward another person's distress and thus making the likelihood of aggressive behavior greater.

The upshot is that people who don't pick up the usual environmental social cues that well people use to help them navigate through life are unlikely to activate the BIS or any other appropriate psychological mechanisms that mediate aggression. Indeed, some studies have shown (Patrick et al., 1994) that people who don't pick up these environmental social cues probably don't think about the social consequences of their subsequent acted-out behavior because their BIS was not activated. In other words, that's why they don't pull back, why they don't get a hold of themselves. So it's not difficult to understand how children with a DBD diagnosis might react when they are exposed to media violence. And the media, ironically, may make these personality disorders worse.

Unlike what we all experience in real life, movies or TV dramas employ production techniques that truncate time frames. Story lines are often exaggerated to enhance the viewer's entertainment, so there is a greater variety and intensity of odd circumstances that arise in the movies or on television. The pleasure of watching a well-written and well-produced TV or movie drama is often triggered by the fantastical juxtapositions of characters and portrayal of emotions, not to mention dramatic feints and creative deceptions that often run through story lines. So if a child has difficulty interpreting everyday environmental social cues as it is, media portrayals may make such interpretations even more difficult. And that can lead to all sorts of psychological mix-ups in how those children interpret and cope with what they are seeing.

Psychopathy and the Absence of Empathy

Benson and his colleagues (Benson, Vernberg, Grimes, & Fonagy, 2006) have narrowed the culprits that may be psychiatrically responsible for the interpretational problems that DBD-diagnosed children have with routine social cues. The culprit, they suspect, is psychopathy. Psychopathy is not a stand-alone illness. It always accompanies other illnesses such as DBDs. Among its characteristics is the psychopath's inability to experience empathy. That is, children with a diagnosis of psychopathy have difficulty, or are incapable of, understanding how other people feel. Under certain circumstances, they can't intuit it, sense it, or may not even be aware of it. That stipulated, Benson et al. found that overt, extreme suffering by people who were portrayed as being the victims of violence was noticed by children with a diagnosis of psychopathy, just as it was noticed by children without a diagnosis of psychopathy. But more subtle forms of suffering were not noticed by the psychopathic children Benson and his colleagues studied. And it may be those more subtle forms of suffering, when they are portrayed in entertainment media, are the ones that pose the most trouble. Consider the following experimental evidence.

Benson et al. (2006) data suggest that callousness to media violence is not the reason that empathy is not elicited when someone has been portrayed to be the victim of violence. Rather, the Benson data suggest that empathy is elicited on cue: portrayal of a teary face, a forlorn cry, the portrayal of suffering. We believe it goes too far to suggest that, in the absence of empathy where empathy *could or should* be elicited, no empathy is possible among viewers who have seen a lot of media violence in their lives. That explanation, which is used a lot in the causal literature (e.g., Huston et al., 1992), misses the point. Benson's data suggest that, where no one is shown suffering in a media portrayal, no empathy—from either psychologically well or DBD/psychopathically diagnosed children—is likely. For instance, participants in the Benson study were shown a scene from the movie *In the Line of Fire*. The protagonist, who was a would-be presidential assassin, shoots two duck hunters in the head as they came upon him. But in that scene, the duck hunters are facing away from the camera, and once the shots are fired, they fall down off-screen, where the viewer cannot see them suffering.

The fact, then, that suffering is not shown, and thus empathy was not elicited from Benson's psychologically well juvenile viewers, does not mean that those viewers are not capable of empathy or that they thought that shooting the duck hunters was somehow OK. It would be going too far to conclude that young viewers regard violence as a permissible social tool because (so these young viewers allegedly reason) nothing really bad happens when it's applied in the movies or on TV. It more likely means that empathy wasn't elicited from viewers with the appropriate social cues, and so none was offered. Furthermore, we have previously observed (Grimes & Bergen, 2001) that research that purports to show that children who consume a lot of media violence develop an "insensitivity" to it and thus become dangerously accepting of it (Murray, 1998) may simply be an acknowledgment that there is a lot of violence in TV programming.

We found that to be the case when we examined, in a clinical setting, psychologically well children who consumed large amounts of media violence (Grimes et al., 1997, 2004). Rather than attributing their ho-hum, what's-the-big-deal attitude toward media violence as a sign of pathology in the making, we accepted it for what it appeared to be: an acknowledgment by the children tested that, like comedy, tragedy, and other performance art forms, violence is part of the repertoire of the performing arts. Moreover, these children did not manifest any of the psychophysiological reactions to media violence that would suggest they were prepared to behave aggressively. Therefore, our interpretation that these children understood media violence to simply be a dramatic theatrical device such portrayals routinely use; that reasoning seemed justified. There's no reason to infer that media violence is a version of distance education in sociopathy. It's entertainment for most people, pure and simple. And they understand it as such. Why that simple fact is so difficult for the causationists to accept isn't clear to us.

The Benson research had more to tell us. Even participants with a DBD diagnosis show some sign of empathy when the media portrayal of suffering is in the extreme range. Examine the evidence: Participants were shown a short scene from the movie *Grand Canyon* in which the protagonist got out of his car. An assailant approached him and demanded the protagonist's Rolex watch. The protagonist misunderstood the aggressor's demand and gave the aggressor his car keys instead. The assailant, angered by the mix-up, shot the protagonist in the leg. The camera then zoomed in on the felled protagonist. It showed him vomiting, shaking with trauma, and urinating on himself.

This scene was so graphic that Benson et al. (2006) speculate that participants with a diagnosis of psychopathy clearly understood that the victim had been harmed and was suffering. Thus, this diagnosed group, like the undiagnosed group, could understand that what befell the protagonist was not pleasant. And so participants with a psychopathological diagnosis showed what the Benson research group called "concerned attention" for the protagonist. That is, the facial expressions of the children watching that scene—both psychopathically diagnosed and nonpsychopathically diagnosed children—showed concern and a clear indication that they understood that something had gone terribly wrong for the protagonist.

Nevertheless, the Benson data suggest that more subtle displays of psychological harm among protagonists went unnoticed by participants with a psychopathic diagnosis but were closely attended to in a concerned way by participants without a diagnosis. And it is these subtle messages that may do the most damage when they interact with the third variable, psychopathy. Let's examine a more subtle portrayal of distress and see how psychopathic children react as opposed to children without a diagnosis.

Both groups of participants were shown a clip from the movie *Regarding Henry,* in which the protagonist goes to a convenience store to buy a pack of cigarettes. He walks in on a robbery. The robber shoots the protagonist in both the shoulder and in the forehead. The protagonist does not show unusual distress until, upon attempting to leave the convenience store, the protagonist faints. The interpretation of Benson et al. (2006) was that, because the shooting scene in *Regarding Henry* portrayed less suffering by the protagonist than was the case of the shooting scene in *Grand Canyon,* a threshold must have been reached by the scene in *Grand Canyon,* which elicited concerned attention from both groups of participants. That threshold was apparently not reached by the shooting scene in *Regarding Henry,* at least for the group of participants with a psychopathic diagnosis. That group's psychophysiological responses to the scene made it clear that those with a diagnosis of psychopathy were not concerned by what they saw. That is, the cues that convey distress, pain, wrongdoing, and social chaos simply were not picked up by the group of children with a psychopathy diagnosis. The group without a psychopathic diagnosis was aroused psychophysiologically, which likely resulted in that group's manifestation of concerned attention as the scene was being played out before each member of the group in individual testing sessions. Just as the psychopathic group did not pick up on any of the social cues portrayed in the scene, the group without a psychopathic diagnosis did understand and process those cues.

Scripts and Rehearsals

In addition to what we have presented here, some research (Blair, 1995) also suggests that media violence can activate schemas in psychopathic personalities that cause them to rehearse in their minds past outrages, slights, and provocations. This, in turn, can create a fairly rapid and disruptive behavioral outburst. (We should note that Benson and his colleagues [2006] did not design their study to provoke and measure aggressive behavior.)

In any event, something isn't computing correctly within personalities that are afflicted with psychopathy. We know that because, if for no other reason, the children whom we (Grimes et al., 2004) identified as having a DBD/psychopathy diagnosis became violent—aggressive—merely because they had seen a violent movie segment. That simple unadorned fact, in itself, suggests that these children aren't correctly calculating the threat risk posed by a movie segment. To put it another way, well children simply don't behave like that.

To be clear, it is not enough to apply these different theories of behavior to some observed behavioral outcome that manifests itself in a laboratory. The hard work of piecing together behavior with the cognitive mechanisms that are suspected of driving that behavior is what most psychophysiologists try to do that, as best we can tell, very few media effects researchers do. To be fair to these researchers, few have clinical degrees or the state licensure that goes with those degrees, which would allow them to do the detailed personality inventories that are needed to connect behavior with motivating psychological states of mind. But that doesn't absolve media effects researchers from having to do that work. If they intend to make the claims they make about aggression and its effect on society at large, they're obligated to collaborate with licensed professionals so as to be able to authoritatively make the causal claims that they make.

Nonetheless, we don't know whether most investigators who posit the causal hypothesis are implying that mediated violence acts in the same way on the human nervous system that sustained exposure to real violence would affect the nervous system. The process that Huesmann et al. (2003) examined in a panel study spanning 15 years could just as well take place among a population of children, turned adult, who were exposed to violent and frightening *living conditions* for many years running rather than *media violence*. That notwithstanding, if children thought they had seen 8,000 mediated murders when they watched Roadrunner cartoons or the Bionic Woman, as causationists contend (Huesmann et al., 2003), then the outcomes that the causationists predict would likely obtain. We can say this with some confidence because there exists a psychological and neural theoretical framework that would account for the effect that media violence would be hypothesized to have on its consumers: That framework would assert that media violence invokes secretions of serum cortisol, which would slowly begin to affect one's ability to make sound threat assessment judgments. This would be backed up by psychophysiological measures of arousal as well as elevated levels of serum cortisol. But without that framework, or one very much like it, or the supporting data that would go with that framework, the causal hypothesis begins to fall apart because there's no psychological or neural evidence to support it.

A Summary of Psychopathology

In summary, what we know is that many of the predictions of the causationists are exhibited in people who have one or more psychopathologies, which seems likely to center on psychopathy. And our laboratory experience has told us so far that children who do not have a clinical diagnosis do not seem to be affected in any systematic way by the media violence we showed them. We assembled a control group that consisted of children who did not have sustained high levels of salivary cortisol and were diagnosed as not having a mental disorder; these children brushed off the media violence they saw with, in some cases, a ho-hum boredom (Grimes et al., 2004). Clearly—at least to us it was clear—these psychologically well children were able to categorize media violence as something that would not pose a threat to them. They viewed it as entertainment.

We certainly don't have every piece of the causal puzzle put in place. We, too, are speculating as to what processes are in play with respect to children with DBD diagnoses. But we believe we are closer than the causationists to understanding which populations are vulnerable to any pernicious effects of media violence. And we have some idea as to why they may be vulnerable, as we've outlined. The upshot is that directly experienced, first-order violence can do psychological harm (as common sense would tell us). But second-order violence, dramatically portrayed violence as offered up by the American entertainment industry, does not appear to inflict similar psychological harm

(Benson et al., 2006; Grimes et al., 2004). If that's true, then it is probably because psychologically well viewers know media violence is fictional. So it cannot create the system stresses on the nervous system that genuine violence can create. At least this is what makes sense to us: If media violence, consumed at sustained levels for the long term, creates behavioral aggression of the sort that a variety of causationists insist is happening, then the only psychiatric and neural way we can account for that would be that media violence increases sustained levels of serum cortisol in viewers.

Our big point is that you have to account for pathological behavior using some established behavioral model, which modern psychiatry and clinical psychology have provided us. One can't just make up an explanation for a behavior that doesn't comport with established psychiatric theory. And for whatever faults it may have, our work hews closer to psychiatric theory than does the work of most of the causationists we study. Everything comes together with respect to psychologically compromised children and adults—and the causal hypothesis. This is the population we ought to be worried about, not psychologically well children and adults.

Note

1. There has been some work in this subject area that does try to make a clearer connection between exposure to media violence and hypothesized psychopathologies. For instance, John P. Murray, one of the most staunch advocates of the causal hypothesis, has begun a program of research, using a functional magnetic resonance imagery methodology, that he asserts will result in the creation of a neural map that will show how media violence affects the neurological system (Murray, 2006). However, that research program has just begun and has so far not yielded the empirical evidence necessary to make a case for a neurological etiology for aggressive behavior. Craig Anderson and Brad Bushman (2002b) have developed a comprehensive model of media violence cognition called the general aggression model (GAM). The GAM carefully pieces together the psychological processes that must be present to motivate people to be aggressive as a result of having consumed media violence.

9

The Attempt to Make an Ideology a Science

The media scholar, George Comstock (2006), asserts the traditional causal hypothesis but adds that "certain factors" can also put a media violence consumer at risk for social aggression. Those certain factors, according to Comstock, fall under the category of a predisposition (what Comstock calls a "dispositional link") to media violence. We interpret those predispositions to be emotional and other psychiatric disorders.

The certain factors explanation, indeed, is a kind of conditional lite. It tries to do what the conditional explanation does better. Yet, it allows the preservation of the primacy of content and its putative pervasive effect on society. The certain factors seem to create a social-psychological context that renders media violence *especially* toxic (at least, that's the benefit we infer from the "certain factors" explanation). Consequently, certain factors seem to actually enhance media violence's social toxicity, not merely render it an influence that blends into the many other environmental influences that may—or may not—predict human behavior.

Our point, of course, is that it would make a lot more sense if the media violence conceptualization were rearranged to accommodate the condition of the individual first. That is, conceptualize it as a kind of equation: a predisposing psychopathology + media violence = sociopathic behavior. For the sort of aggressive behavior, exhibited among psychologically ill people who we've studied in our labs (Grimes et al., 1997, 2004), to take place within the population of well people, media violence would have to be the social analog of asbestos or benzene. For instance, everyone is vulnerable to the pathology created by exposure to asbestos and benzene. It's probably safe to say that humans, as a species, have no defense against these agents' toxic effects. In much the same way, media violence would have to exploit a fundamental, universal weakness in the human psyche the way toxic substances exploit human biology. We three authors, and we presume most social and biological scientists, need—indeed *must*—understand what that fundamental psychological weakness is—its structure, function, and psychological/neural etiology. And that's what the causationists cannot or will not provide. As best we can tell, they don't see a need to provide that information (we assume) because the generalized social effects of media violence are presumed. Perhaps a causationist, cloistered somewhere in a university office, has plans to eventually address the subject. Perhaps someone is already addressing it. It would do our hearts great good if this were the case (our publisher's feelings about the disconfirmation of this book's hypothesis notwithstanding). Our book be damned, we say! The revelation of the psychological/neurological etiology of humanity's vulnerability to media violence would be a great contribution to social-psychological understanding of how the human species operates within a social context.

But as things stand today, no such study has come forth, and matters are even more muddled than we have so far portrayed. Here's why: We have previously speculated (Bergen & Grimes, 1999) that many of the participant samples that causationists use to conduct laboratory experiments are actually convenience samples, not random samples. This is an important distinction because, to make inferences to the population at large, an experimenter must use a random sample of the population. That is, everyone in the population under study (however that population is described) has to have an equal probability of being chosen to be tested. Therefore, a sample of such people has a high likelihood of being like the much larger population they're supposed to represent. However, Potter, Cooper, and Dupagne (1993) have speculated that only about 5% of published communication research in this area allows generalization to the population due to sampling problems.

OK. We need to be fair to the causationists: Very few behavioral science experiments use true random sampling to compose the two or more groups that the investigator wishes to then test. Most of the time, especially in laboratory-based research, genuine random selection is too expensive and time-consuming. So most laboratory experiments employ the procedure of *random assignment*. Random assignment takes a group of people, systematically selected (usually because it's convenient to do so), and randomly assigns each person to one of the two or more groups to be tested.

So if random assignment works for most behavioral science studies, why shouldn't it work for media violence research? This is not an easy question to answer because random assignment can work for media violence research if certain assumptions are made. But if the wrong assumptions are made, random assignment experiments just dig the hole deeper for investigators who are already headed in the wrong direction. Allow us, then, to take out a few paragraphs to explain why random assignment, the preferred method of sampling for causationists, doesn't work.[1]

When random assignment works (as opposed to random selection from the population under study), it works for the following reason: The characteristics of biological systems are distributed more or less equally among all such systems. That is, each individual, being a biological system, has a range of behaviors that she or he can manifest. Therefore, if a researcher applies a stimulus to a group of participants to see how they will behave, and if they behave in the way the researcher predicted they would behave because of the stimulus that was applied to them, then the researcher can conclude that the stimulus caused the participants to behave in a particular way. Now, let's look at an experiment in which random assignment was a prominent feature.

Bergen, Grimes, and Potter (2005) wanted to run a memory and attention experiment to determine whether certain production techniques would enhance viewers' memory for TV news messages. Bergen and her colleagues drew their sample from a university course titled "Mass Communication and Society." Because, in this example, differential memory and attention processes are an inherent component of the "biological systems" in that class, Bergen and her colleagues could test different methods of getting her study participants to remember different presentational formats for TV news messages. If one of those methods works, then that method could be inferred to *cause* the participant to remember the TV news message to which the participant is exposed.[2]

People randomly remember and forget things, and they randomly attend to and don't attend to dozens, perhaps thousands, of environmental stimuli many times each day. So, because a particular method of helping people attend to and remember TV news, developed by Bergen and her colleagues (2005), increased participants' memory for TV news messages, then she could conclude that this method *caused* the participants in the study to better remember the TV news stories they were shown. But she and her colleagues went further than that: They could assume that methods they tested in her experiments would likely affect the general TV-watching population in the same way had that population been participants in the Bergen et al. experiments. The only thing she and her colleagues could not determine, precisely because they did not employ random selection, is the *proportion* of television viewers within the population who would have responded as her participants responded in their random assignment experiments. That's because the participants in the study were not randomly selected from the population of all TV news viewers. But—because *all people* are believed to have an inherent ability to remember, to forget, and so on—Bergen and her colleagues could be confident that the results of their experiments, gathered as they were from an intact group such as a large lecture class, would likely apply to a random sample of the population had one been collected.

True, to know that for sure, participants would have to be randomly selected from the television-viewing population at large. But because the variations in memory and attentional processes that were tested in the experiments that Bergen and her colleagues conducted manifest themselves in all TV news viewers, Bergen and her colleagues (2005) would at least have justification to confidently continue down this research path so as to better understand what makes TV news more memorable.[3]

So why shouldn't the same set of assumptions hold for TV violence research? Why shouldn't causationists be able to conduct an experiment the way Bergen and her colleagues conducted their research, using random assignment, and arrive at a valid and reliable conclusion about the ability of TV violence to *cause* aggressive behavior? Why can't causationists benefit from the same sampling efficiency that most other social psychologists benefit from?

Although *some* people are more susceptible to aggressiveness when they are exposed to media violence, such as psychologically ill people, *all* people must be susceptible to aggressive behavior in response to media violence. And this is where things break down for the causationists. Our position is that, unlike the universal human ability to remember and attend to messages well, poorly, or in between, there is no such universal susceptibility to aggression in response to media violence among the psychologically well population. Except with respect to psychologically ill people. There the evidence strongly suggests that children with a diagnosis of psychopathy, which is characterized by an inability to appropriately read routine social cues, will act aggressively to all sorts of environmental and even internally generated stimuli. In other words, they constitute a "biological system" in which aggression is a background component that colors their generalized behavior patterns. (We will discuss this in more detail later.) They therefore would seem to be a likely study target, which could be studied using random assignment methods.

So the trap that causationists get into when they engage in random assignment of participants is threefold. First, they assume that aggression in response to media violence is universal in the population. Psychiatric and clinical psychological evidence strongly suggests otherwise, as we will outline later. Second, because few causal hypothetical studies have engaged in random selection, it is impossible to make a behavioral inference to the population from those studies. Third, most causationist studies appear to be sampling from the most biased of participant pools: the public schools. As we have previously pointed out (Grimes & Bergen, 2001), there are few institutions in America that are more segregated by race, class, and even psychopathology than the nation's public schools. Of all places from which to draw a sample "of the nation's youth," the public schools would be among the last places, unless some pretty serious demographic and psychiatric work were undertaken to determine the representativeness of the population that is being examined. For instance, were one to go into a poor, urban public school, chances would be good that whatever sample comes from that school might have an overrepresentation of various psychopathologies, which might skew the sample toward susceptibility to aggression. The reason, of course, is that many of the children from those schools likely have seen their share of neighborhood, domestic, and school violence; may have suffered from physical abuse; and may have experienced other personality-warping events in their lives.

In any event, the only proper way to deal with these problems is to engage in random selection of study participants. Causationists must select from a participant pool such that everyone in the population has an equal chance of being included in their participant sample. In that way, and in only that way, will they be able to convincingly determine how vulnerable "the population" is to the putative harm they ascribe to media violence.

To reiterate our point, causationists assume that the human susceptibility to media violence, as a cause for subsequent aggression, is universal. If it is, then it doesn't matter much what group of people one selects for study. The findings can be reasonably generalized to apply to the population. If susceptibility isn't a universal characteristic of being human, as we have argued—if, instead, that susceptibility is attached to a variety of psychopathologies—then the findings do not generalize to the population. They apply only to those who meet the conditions of susceptibility. The correlational evidence that is generated if humans are universally susceptible to media violence constitutes the relative strength of association between media violence and aggression—which is what the causationists claim. That same correlational evidence would only suggest the *rate of occurrence* of the condition of susceptibility in an ordinary population, which is what we claim. That is, the correlational evidence, between exposure to media violence and aggression, would only suggest the proportion of the population that is susceptible to media violence as a source of aggression—assuming that a random selection experiment is conducted. Estimates of psychopathology within the general population range between 5% and 10%. We would guess, therefore, that were the causationists' media violence studies random selection studies, rather than random assignment studies, they would likely find that between 5% and 10% of the population is susceptible to media violence as a source of social aggression. That is, with proper sampling procedures and measurements, we believe that the findings concerning the putative media violence-aggression link would change from all of us being susceptible to a subset of the population.

Causationists have made it quite clear that there is a social urgency to doing *something* about the violence on television, in the movies, and in video games—violence that is hopping up our population and making it more aggressive as a result ("Neurological Research," 2003). Therefore, the causationists are representing the convenience samples they use as being representative of *us*. They are we. The causationists are telling us what's happening to us as a nation because of our obsession with violence as an entertainment medium. So it's important that the causationists get it right. We believe that there's a high likelihood that they aren't getting it right on this dimension, the sampling dimension, as well on the other dimensions we've reviewed up to this point.

OK. If random assignment in experiments can't be used to infer what the population is like, then how is it that all these causal studies show statistically significant differences between the aggression levels of people who watch a lot of media violence and those who don't? Those differences are allegedly being demonstrated through comparison to a probability distribution of the population, which is called a sampling distribution. Well, the dumb answer is that statistical computer programs don't know whether a group of participants in a laboratory experiment was randomly selected or randomly assigned. They don't know whether the variables "violent media" or "aggression" were properly conceptualized by the researcher. Those statistical programs don't know anything more than the numbers a researcher entered into the program. So the person doing the statistical analysis isn't going to see a flashing "TILT!" sign on the computer screen when she or he calls for a statistical analysis of nonrandom samples.

Now here's the smart answer, and it's a bit more complicated. Because many of the samples used in causal studies are flawed for the reasons we've outlined, and therefore can't be compared to a population of any kind— well people, ill people, or anything in between—the study results that many causationists are generating are based on a fantasy. And precisely because there are no "TILT!" signs that pop up when a researcher wants to make a flawed inference, the error they're making tends to feed on itself.

Regretfully, random selection isn't a panacea. Even it poses problems. For instance, even if an investigator were to use random selection, the fact that an investigator *can* make normal children measure as sociopathic on various dimensions, if only temporarily, could describe a population that exists—but only in the lab. (We're not conceding that psychologically well people can be made temporarily sociopathic by media violence. Rather, we're using this notion as an illustration.). That is, the "hothouse" effect of the laboratory, described nicely by Tavis MacBeth (1996, 1997), which he claims *can* cause most children to evince something that looks like aggressive behavior, does not mean that those same children *do* evince such behavior outside the laboratory. This is roughly similar to those famous studies we've all read about where lab rats are fed five times their body weight in synthetic sweetener for 3 straight months—then they get cancer and die. (Who, in the real world, would eat five times their body weight in synthetic sweetener for a month? Well, if you can get cancer in a lab when you eat that much of a synthetic sweetener, do you really get cancer outside the lab when you eat that sweetener in normal proportions?)

The problem, then, is that MacBeth's (1996, 1997) can/does effect, duplicated over hundreds of experiments, may create a body of results that misleads investigators into thinking that media are more harmful to young well people than is the case. We have previously asserted (Bergen & Grimes, 1999) that, with a powerful enough stimulus array, one *can* agitate, excite, and otherwise arouse most anyone with violent television programming—or humorous, exciting, or sad TV programming; not just violent TV programming. The challenge, as Freedman (1986, 1988) has asserted, is to take those *can* outcomes, derived from the hothouse atmosphere of an experimental laboratory, and replicate them in people's homes, schools, and everyday venues of life outside the lab. *Does* what happens in people's homes, over years of television and movie viewing, match what *can* be initiated with powerful stimuli in the laboratory?

The principal claim of this chapter is this: Who is watching is more important than what is being watched. An individual, psychopathically predisposed to aggression, can use whatever resources are available to fulfill that predisposition. The previous chapter presented strong evidence for the case of psychopathology. This chapter has shown that the evidence the causationists claim as their own can be better understood by a conditional model that places the viewer first. This conditional model directs us away from understanding social behavior in the terms of media content and directs us toward the people who act in ways society finds injurious.

But are we three authors guilty of the very attribute we're accusing the causationists of possessing? Do we believe that we are simply correct in our view, and nothing the causationists can do can dissuade us of our noble correctness?

That is, is it true that none of the research the causationists have executed is any good because most of it is based on a faulty statistical premise—random assignment? Is it true that, the hothouse laboratory environment can make anyone crazy if you psychologically poke and probe the poor devils sequestered in a room at a university with a bunch of researchers perpetrating who-knows-what on them? In other words, we've trashed our causationist colleagues such that nothing they do is right. So we're the heroes. We win by default.

There's no blinking at the fact that we don't think much of the causal position. And yes, much of the causal literature is so flawed that there's very little left of value. But we're not offering an equally bodacious hypothesis. To the contrary, we counsel caution and awareness of the social-cultural influences that affect the way we all plan experiments and interpret results. And mostly we counsel hewing closely to established clinical psychological-psychiatric personality and neural theory for guidance to what is and isn't likely with respect to generalized media effects. Yes, dear reader, we may yet be shown to be wrong. The crucial set of causationist data that proves us so may still be delivered. But until it is, how could anyone object to a counsel to caution?

This caution has powerful implications for policy—the topic we take up next.

Notes

1. The first author gives credit to his colleague, Arthur Glenberg, a professor of psychology at the University of Wisconsin–Madison, for helping him reason through this idea. His e-mail and telephone counsel, plus the ideas presented in his statistics textbook (Glenberg, 1988), helped the first author with the explanation that you are reading here. In addition, consulation with Jerome Frieman, professor and chair of the Department of Psychology at Kansas State University, helped produce the wording that appears in this chapter, which differentiates the effects of random selection from random assignment.

2. Because the behavior of biological systems is inherently random, that inherent randomness meets some requirements of inferential statistics that make it possible for the experimenter to say, with confidence, that the new method of helping people remember TV news messages actually does help—that it wasn't just random chance that it helped the participants in the experiment to better remember TV news messages. Inferential statistics require that the reaction of a participant to a stimulus be independent and not influenced by any other reaction the participant might evince to the stimulus. Therefore, the inherent randomness of the human species' attentional and memory processes fits quite nicely with the requirements of inferential statistics (Glenberg, 1988).

3. The plain fact is that most good mass media researchers would likely conclude that the enhanced memory technique that the researcher used in this experiment will likely apply to most everyone who watches TV news. This would especially be true if other researchers, using the same technique, replicated the same results several times over. Inferential statistical techniques can't be used to arrive at that conclusion, unless random selection of participants is used. But because most people who watch TV news have the inherent ability to remember, most good communication researchers would not doubt that the results apply to the population of all TV news viewers.

10

To Legislate or Not to Legislate Against Media Violence

W e noted at the beginning of this book that, in the history of most mass media, there has been a sociology that has converged to create public worry—a moral panic of sorts—about the putative effects of the mass media. We argued that the first traceable piece of legislative public policy, reflecting moral panic, was promulgated in 1912 with the passage of the Sims Act, which banned the importation of boxing films.

The moral panic of 1912 was instigated by an African American boxer, Jack Johnson, who demolished one great white hope after another. Johnson fled the United States, fought overseas, and recorded some bouts on film, which led to the nonimportation rule of his films. Given the cultural context of the time, there was concern that films of a Black boxer defeating a White boxer would offend most White audiences or lead them to racial violence. Today that sounds crazy, not to mention offensive. Although the fear of violence was not based on a series of lab experiments—thus providing "objective" verification that the fear was justified—it does suggest the political, social, and cultural power of moral indignation to warp, refract, and reinterpret, within a cultural context, reality. We suggest that's part of what's going on within the causationist literature. True, the causationists back up their position with what they claim is empirical evidence for their position. But one does wonder if moral outrage (i.e., moral panic) motivates the concern about media violence in the first place.

In any event, the prescription for engaging in a little moral panic today is somewhat different than in Jack Johnson's era. Today, moral panic has this structure: (1) A pervasive threat—in this case, media violence—is connected to a widespread social concern—in this case, violent crime (even if just by implication). (2) The threat has no interest groups that support it and no accountable culprit that one can attribute to the threat (other than the amoebic "media" or even the more fuzzy and out-of-focus "contemporary culture"). The absence of an accountable person or identifiable business or corporation constituting the threat makes it less risky to go all out in opposition to the threat—no one gets hurt, no one can sue, no one can campaign against the threat's opponents. Thus, opposition toward the threat is a popular position without having to take a costly moral position. (3) Action against the threat is consistently deferred, until "technical issues" are resolved (say, for example, the First Amendment). This structure was repeatedly displayed in the testimony in one of the most recent media violence/media decency hearings in Congress (*Open Forum on Decency*, 2006). Although the causationists don't constitute a cabal that deliberately describes a threat that it can exploit for moral or political purposes (even we aren't that cynical), media violence does present the perfect straw man against which to rage. No on gets hurt, no one is held accountable, one can (in the process of raging against the demon) reaffirm sacrosanct principles—the special position of the child in society, the injury to cultural normatives that media violence inflicts, and the role one can play as that of the upright, concerned, and responsible citizen. To reiterate, we don't want to appear cynical or mocking of causationists. But . . . a crusade against media violence, the protection of children, and the salvation of our culture through that crusade must rank as one of the best feel-good civic acts one can engage in. In other words, fighting against media violence can be as self-reaffirming a behavior as one can engage in. The crusade itself is an uplifting and psychologically rewarding experience. Thus, there's a powerful psychological incentive to keep the crusade going, irrespective of countervailing social science.

However, that does not mean there are no public policy implications with respect to media violence research. The crusade against media violence doesn't just play out in its own universe without implications—and complications—for the rest of us. That's because, irrespective of what social and medical science may have to say about the subject and irrespective of how impotent public policy threats against the media may actually be, special interest groups will continue to hammer the subject. Therefore, we have some conclusions and recommendations that both public interest groups and legislators might consider.

- *Media violence almost certainly does not have epidemiological implications for psychologically well people. But that implication will still be advanced by the ardent.*

For special interest groups to pathologize media violence—and then to advance arguments for controlling it as an epidemiological pathogen—creates a hypostatization that's chasing its tail. Media violence causes personality disorders among psychologically well viewers (the hypostatization), so there's a need to "do something" about the production and distribution of media violence on account of its *psychological* harm (this is the tail-chasing part).

Although one of the populations most vulnerable to media violence is that with a codiagnosis of psychopathy (Bergen & Grimes, 1999; Grimes et al., 1997, 2004), media violence may be the least of that population's problems. Children and adults with certain mental disorders, which include a companion diagnosis of psychopathy, confront a confusing and threatening world every day they wake up. For those who are diagnosed, medical care has been established to try to help these people cope with the different manifestations of their illness. In other words, there's a protocol in place for people with diagnosed psychopathological ailments.

Grimes and his coauthors (Grimes et al., 1997, 2004) found that talking to children with a psychopathy diagnosis—by making sure they understood that the media stimuli they were shown were not real and did not pose a danger to their well-being—calmed them down sufficiently so that they posed no danger of acting aggressively. Although this postviewing discussion with these children was conducted by staff psychiatrists and clinical psychologists, the content of those discussions could easily be engaged in by parents. There was no special knowledge conveyed by the psychiatric or clinical psychological staff. Just a reassurance that what the affected child has seen was not real and was nothing to worry about.

If the focus were to be shifted from *control* of content to a new focus on *care* of the diagnosed, policy makers would not have to participate in the problematic and certainly culturally embedded science of the causationists. Furthermore, such a legislative focus is positive, affirmative, and more effective in reducing the presence of aggression. Social aggression is not a normal curve distribution (that is, the well-known bell curve) where the majority of us can be "turned" to its dark side. Social aggression has a power curve distribution (like a hockey stick or a check mark) where a small percentage of individuals are loaded into one small portion of the curve and who account for most of the problem. Spending huge sums of money on a censoring bureaucracy to control outcomes in the massive middle will not affect this small percentage. Focused allocations on those most at risk will.

- *Media **violence** and media **indecency** are often commingled in public policy forums. This leads to an ill-defined, intellectually confused locus of concern.*

This principle is no better illustrated than by two congressional hearings on the media violence/media indecency issue. The Senate Commerce Committee held hearings in November 2005 and January 2006, which examined—and this is the confusing part—*decency* in the mass media (*Decency*, 2005; *Open Forum on Decency*, 2006). Media violence, sexually explicit programming, and countercultural programming that thumbs its nose at prevailing cultural values were lumped together as equivalent problems. This, in turn, led to a spurious—in our opinion—blending together of the three types of programming, which resulted in making equivalent the three message types that simply are not equivalent. To the extent that media violence, sexually based programming, and countercultural programming are problematic, they pose different problems with different solutions. But, when they're lumped together, what is already a sociologically and psychologically tough study area to begin with becomes uninterpretable and so muddled that any conversation about them is rendered meaningless.

For instance, one witness, Jeff McIntyre, the legislative and federal affairs officer of the American Psychological Association, defined indecency as being media violence, whereas other witnesses, at both the 2005 and 2006 hearings, defined it as mostly sexually or counterculturally based programming, with less frequent references to media violence but references to it nonetheless. McIntyre's definition of indecency is different from the claims made by witnesses, who defined indecency as that related to sexually explicit programming. For instance, Brent Bozell, president of the Parents Television Council, defined indecency primarily as that programming that appears on many FX network and Comedy Channel programs. In particular, he referred to sex orgy scenes within an FX network program, as well as a scene in which an animated character on the Comedy Channel stuffs a pineapple up an animated female's vagina (*Decency*, 2005, pp. 8–9).

We can't read Mr. Bozell's mind, of course. But referring to vaginas and pineapple insertions in a U.S. Senate hearing surely must have been intended to shock the panel and thus demonstrate, right then and there, the revulsion such references on television must evoke among some viewers and thus the putative harm done. The inclusion of religious leaders among the panel of witnesses (*Open Forum of Decency*, 2006), such as Frank Wright, president of the National Religious Broadcasters Association, extends the problems that the media create into that of the countercultural. Their testimony provides evidence that the blasphemy portrayed on television, in itself, has the potential to offend a number of different constituencies and that a hypothesized, causally derived behavior is not necessarily the focus of their concern. Thus, the injury—the harm—is not found in a transitively conveyed behavior such as aggression but rather in intransitive psychological states such as revulsion or umbrage.

To further this notion, none of the witnesses, who defined indecency primarily as that which is sexually oriented or counter to "decent" cultural values, made explicit predictions as to a transitive effect, such as rape or an increase in sex crimes, or the disrespect of parents or of government or religious leaders. Although witnesses in the past, and over the years, have made such predictions, it is nonetheless interesting to note that this set of hearings (*Decency*, 2005; *Open Forum on Decency*, 2006) seemed focused on the intransitive effects of indecency. The graphic descriptions of the programming to which several witnesses objected appeared, in and of themselves, to be self-evident as constituting harm. On the other hand, McIntyre's presentation reiterated the Huesmann metric for calculating the effect of media violence on society: Each viewing instance increases the likelihood that a child will become aggressive later in life (*Decency*, 2005, p. 3). This is a clear transitive effect.

So one form of indecency, media violence, has a calculable effect on society many years after exposure: aggression. Under this construction, aggression can be defined, and its proliferation within society can produce actuarial estimates of harm. Yet, another form of indecency, sexually graphic programming, is ipso facto harmful; no calculus of harm needed here. Even more so than media violence, sexually graphic and countercultural programming—a Virgin Mary–like animated character, portrayed on the Comedy Channel, is shown with blood pouring from between her legs, at which point a pope-like character jokes about "chicks" and their reproductive organs (*Open Forum on Decency*, 2006)—is repulsive, offensive, and otherwise disgusting. The "harm" it does must surely be one's revulsion to it.

Psychologically healthy people can be offended, disgusted, and repulsed. And they can justifiably ask for remedies, even legislative, to counter the exposure of such programming to their children (the constitutionality of such remedies notwithstanding). But here's what is important for public policy formulators to remember: The commingling of three very different forms of program content, as well as our reactions to them, is fraught with all sorts of confusion. It's the offensiveness of *South Park, Beavis and Butt-Head, Jackass,* Howard Stern, and *Girls Gone Wild* that helps lead to the invalid and non sequitur–like connection to media violence. That is, there's an intellectual sloppiness imbued in the commingling of media violence and sexual-cultural offensive messages that simply doesn't withstand intellectual and legislative scrutiny. If one wishes to pursue legislative remedies to offensive media messages, at least we all know what such remedies are designed to remediate: one's outrage at offensive portrayals. But manufacturing a societal-level psychopathology to complement one's own offended sensibilities is going too far, and that's exactly what the causationists are doing with respect to media violence. Bozell's obvious outrage and hurt at the desecration of Catholic iconography (*Decency*, 2005) is all that's required to justify a social response to that desecration. Like the cartoons that so outraged Islam in 2006, it's the ipso facto, face-valid proof of harm.

Now, whether you or we think a legislative remedy for such blasphemy is appropriate, in itself, is a legitimate basis for a public policy debate. Neither you nor we would dispute the fact that many thousands, perhaps millions, of Americans would be disgusted by the mockery of revered religious symbolism. That settled, we can then move on to the public policy debate as to what to do about it and all other forms of countercultural or sexually offensive programming, which is under the purview of the national legislature. What we three authors *cannot* countenance is an attachment of a reified pathology to an otherwise simple case of viewer disgust. This is especially true when media violence can be parsimoniously grouped with the other flotsam and jetsam of American popular culture. Simply declare media violence distasteful and manage it the way *South Park* and *Girls Gone Wild* would otherwise be managed were public policy responses sought.

- *Within traditional American culture, competing ideas have always contested one another in perpetuity. Such a contest is an organic part of a democracy. Manage media violence the way democracies manage all manner of competing ideas.*

The pattern for coping with unsavory ideas, at least in this culture, has not been to repress them but to dominate them through a higher order understanding of core principles. Some core principles are communally shared as, for instance, many (but not all) rulings of the Supreme Court. Other core principles have been differentially shared, such as the principles of competing political parties. We, in the United States, are engaged in a continual effort at trying to live with one another, at tolerating one another's preferences, at trying to come to accord on overarching principles that will allow us to abide social, political, and cultural differences.

Our nation has strong philosophical roots in the Enlightenment, roots that gave us a democratic civil government and a court system grounded in reasoned action. From this intellectual tradition comes the potential management strategy of a raucous, sometimes unnerving, but always edgy mass media. Media literacy, the ability to think critically about media messages and to understand the commercial, cultural, political, and literary dimensions of those messages, fits the American way of socially managing the detritus of a democratic state. The attempt to come to an understanding of something that is, at first, disorienting or troubling is a core principle of the Enlightenment's methodology—of the American cultural tradition.

The idea behind media literacy, of course, is to teach children that the messages they view are constructed to reach a goal, such as to sell products or persuade viewers to think or believe some idea or another. With that in mind, the messages don't go away. But they become tolerable, are understandable, and seem to fit into the democratic cacophony that constitutes latter-day American society. This method, to us, seems like a far more reasonable response to a media panoply than trying to craft some legislative top-down control of the bumptious mass media. (Of course, there's no law that says media literacy courses can't be legislatively mandated. The state of New Mexico has done just that.)

But there's a not-so-savory side to media literacy programs. The curriculum is variously taught in schools, in after-school programs supported by churches and parents groups, targeted at low-income groups or others deemed particularly "at risk" to the power of media messages. But these programs are all generally embraced because they provide an inoculation effect, mitigating the harm that media messages purportedly cause when children are exposed to them. It is a way to teach about media in order to inoculate against a pathology. Although the approach may incorporate teaching about production techniques and the "media messages as text," the approach is primarily designed to expose and vilify the corporate media structure, the commercial motivation and profit orientation for generating media messages, and the harm that comes from being exposed to messages about drugs, sex, violence, and all other cultural and social harms portrayed in the media.

This protectionist approach is consistent with the notion that children (and we are thinking here particularly of adolescents, not very young children) are devoid of the ability to make active and informed choices and decisions about their media without help from adults. By teaching teenagers in formal media literacy curricula that their favorite television programs, video games, Internet sites, music, and films can harm them sets up a ludicrous relationship between teens and adults over the issue of media and harm. To suggest to young people in a formal educational setting that exposure to media will lead to negative effects helps to call into question the entire enterprise of public education, at least from the point of view of an adolescent. It's yet another version of the "You'll grow hair on the palms of your hands!" argument. Adolescents engage in the behavior—in this case, the consumption and enjoyment of media violence—and then intuitively know it isn't harming them. Quite the contrary, it's entertaining! Therefore, to be taught that it can make you sort of, kind of, go nuts (i.e., sociopathically aggressive) just won't wash with this cohort.

Renee Hobbs (1998), a Temple University associate professor and media literacy scholar, has noted that teachers at both university and K–12 levels find their students don't respond to the notion that they are somehow help-less in the face of media influence or that they must be "rescued from the excesses and evils of their interest in popular culture." A better approach is one that embraces the ability of young people to fully engage with, appreci-ate, and enjoy the products of popular culture while recognizing that media culture can be approached critically. This approach offers a positive social, cultural, literary, and artistic menu *as well as* messages that are unpleasant, offensive, and sometimes degrading to those who consume them.

- *The fractured, balkanized nature of mass communication makes any legislative remedy ineffectual.*

What, precisely, might we gain if we *do* impose some form of utopian leg-islation on a corner of the mass media? One should look no further than February 1, 2004, when Janet Jackson's right breast appeared on the CBS Television Network's coverage of the Super Bowl. Hell broke loose the next day. The Federal Communications Commission (FCC) commissioner, Michael Powell, called for an investigation of CBS. CBS apologized later in the week for the breast exposure. Yet, that same week, other Viacom prop-erties (Viacom owns CBS), the Comedy Channel and MTV, were cranking out countercultural, some would say indecent, programming by the hour. Yet, not a peep: no apologies, no FCC investigations threatened, no outcry. What gives? The television sets in our houses that delivered the Jacksonian breast that appeared on the CBS broadcast network also delivered to our liv-ing rooms the scatological irreverence of *South Park*. The breast: oh no, fine CBS. The comedic discussion on *South Park* of the use of the word *shit*: That's OK. There is a certain craziness about it all. So what does give?

What gives comes in two parts. The first is that CBS was using what has traditionally been considered a public resource—the broadcast spectrum. Its use is to be in the public interest, convenience, and necessity. It is a resource with a regulatory history of content control, particularly of sexu-ally inflected content (the "seven dirty words rule"). That famous breast might have been delivered via cable or satellite to more than half of U.S. homes, but it originated on regulated public airwaves. This is old school: The public has to be protected from disruptive and disturbing content in its various forms of entertainment. This perspective comes from a period of time when it was possible to restrict access to such content because the com-mercial sources were few, high production costs eliminated the amateur, and distribution was easily controlled. Close off distribution by revoking a license, denying a postal permit, and refusing an import certificate and the content disappears, buried under its costs of production.

New school is that production costs can be recouped by even small underground audiences that receive the content through point-to-point sales, as demonstrated by the continuing success of the EC horror comic book. An even newer school holds that production costs are so low they no longer matter, and as YouTube.com demonstrates, content is firmly in the hands of all the people. We are also rapidly moving away from the use of traditional public resources to deliver content. That move eliminates the whole protectionist argument and undercuts our ability to regulate. The FCC as a content regulator is an anachronism. If its control of halftime entertainment significantly lessens the audience, the Super Bowl will simply move off broadcast television, or as we saw in 2006, cable will offer counterprogramming during halftime and audiences will switch.

Then there's convergence. Not the definition of convergence of evidence that we discussed earlier. Rather, this is a use of the term to denote a process whereby boundaries of content, medium, and delivery system are erased. *Desperate Housewives,* a hit television program broadcast on ABC, is available on memory chip or for download onto one's video iPod. The rule is fairly simple: If you want it, you can get it in whatever format is most convenient for you. Bits are bits (digitally encoded content); they go anywhere in increasingly smaller packages.

Convergence has an interesting countereffect on audiences. Convergence homogenizes technology, but it atomizes the audience. That, in turn, has ameliorated the offensive, the indecent, the unsavory by making it easier to ignore. So, on that February Sunday in 2004, we saw a kind of matter-antimatter clash between the centuries-old analogical era, when all media were mass, and the barely decade-old digital era, when most media are more akin to point-to-point communication. You might not care if we three authors set up a Web site and distributed topless content to subscribers—a method of message dissemination that far exceeds what the over-the-air CBS Television Network could have ever hoped to achieve. Yet, were we to do the same thing using an analogical point-to-mass medium, there would be hell to pay, not to mention fines.

Although there have been calls for the FCC to regulate cable and satellite TV just as it regulates over-the-air television (e.g., *Open Forum on Decency,* 2006), it seems to us that the era of "calls to action" by Congress may be, if they are not already, an anachronism. If Congress could get regulatory authority over cable, satellite, the Internet, and other digital distribution mechanisms, then the porous digital world would surely nullify what might be left of congressional regulatory authority by dint of sheer numbers of media pathways. Indeed, we have argued that "regulation" is an analogical concept. Because analogical media are structurally best suited for point-to-mass distribution, because the means of distribution is easily controlled, and because they must take into account mass taste, mass tolerance for, and the mass appeal of the messages carried by those media, they are targets for regulation (whether they should be or not).

But digital media simply don't fit a regulatory model—with respect to content. And not just because they architecturally aren't suitable for content regulation. We contend that it's not what Janet Jackson and Justin Timberlake (who performed with her at Super Bowl halftime) did; it's the striking, sharp contrast their actions gave to the sexuality and scatology that cascades from the various cable television networks. Although there have been and continue to be calls to do something about the Low Culture of cable and the Internet (e.g., *Open Forum on Decency*, 2006), the explosive outrage that the halftime show ignited demonstrates that, as audiences atomize through convergence, the opportunity for focused public outrage dissipates. The fact that digital media don't elicit such calls strongly suggests that the digital delivery of messages may lower the temperature for perennial calls to "do something" about indecency, countercultural programming, and media violence.

Policy Maker to Social Scientist

PM: OK, let's review some things here. It sounds like you are saying that congressional hearings on media violence are just posturing. I can assure you they do important work.

SSI: I certainly agree with you, but the work is not so much to find a solution, which you know is not only difficult but also fraught with its own unintended consequences. The work is sometimes something else. You, of course, are familiar with symbolic politics theory.

PM: Sure, where at least some of what we do is important as much for its symbolism as for its outcomes.

SSI: Exactly. The symbolism here is that "we are concerned; we are trying to find the answer, but it's hard." None of us can give up being concerned even if we think the current direction of that concern is misguided.

PM: You seem to be arguing that aggression in society is not the problem causationists make it out to be. They clearly think that media
violence has a lot to do with aggression. And I can tell you that a
lot of what we worry about in Congress has to do with violence
and aggression and the fallout from them in health care, education,
employment, and so on.

SS3: There were a little over a half million arrests for violent crime in
the United States in 2004, the last year I could get full figures. That
is 2 tenths of 1% of the population. Now we can argue whether
arrests equate to incidents, but even if the number of crime events
was 10 times greater than the arrests, that is still only 2% of the
population. It's a big number of people, approaching 6 million, but
miniscule in relation to the 294 million who do not commit violence. Here's my point: The causationists are directing their concern
toward 294 million people who aren't aggressive or aren't aggressive enough to create a social problem. Some of these 294 million
people may give someone the finger in traffic occasionally, or collect
a speeding ticket, or say something tacky about a coworker and so
on—all measures that some causationists have listed as "aggressive."
But the causationists appear to ignore, or don't seem to aim their
research at, the 6 million who have a darned serious problem with
aggression. I would argue that the guy who mocks a coworker's appearance is no one to worry about. The whole debate, it seems to me, is
simply bassackwards, as we might say in Kansas.

PM: All right. Stop where you are. You're starting to aggravate me. I see
what you're up to here and I don't like it. You've created a protective cordon around media violence by stripping it of its pathology.
So, if it's not pathological, just offensive, then what you've done is
that you've made it not worth worrying about. And anyone who
does worry about it is an idiot.

Media violence is a gnat that, you claim, various public officials and
concerned constituencies are trying to shoot down with an F-16
fighter when all they have to do is wave it away or, better yet, just
forget about it. That has the effect, then, of making it untouchable;
it's still a concern for a lot of parents but one they can't do anything
about because it's not *worth* doing anything about. See how your

(Continued)

(Continued)

argument has, in a sense, shielded media violence from being addressed by people who are still worried about it, whether or not you're worried about it, whether or not you respect the motives of the people who worry about it?

SS2:   Touché, as the old cliché goes. Look—legislators, policy makers, and public interest groups can propose all the legislation, rules, and whatever else they want to propose to manage media violence. The only thing we're advocating is this: Don't make a rule, a law, a regulation that's predicated on the idea that media violence can make psychologically well people sick. Create legislation that funds media literacy studies in all the nation's public schools. Refine the TV ratings system that activates a parentally programmed V-chip or remote control. But don't hang any of that on the urgency of preventing illness. The chances are so slim that media violence makes well people sick that to worry about *that* really is a waste of time.

PM: Well, wait. You social scientists have also argued that it's becoming difficult, and will soon be impossible, to regulate much of what appears on television anyway . . . what with digitalization, which has expanded some cable and satellite TV offerings to 400 channels and more. You're also saying that all the content that's generated is distributed over too many different transmission devices, such as iPods, which makes it technically impossible to regulate what goes out to the public. And then you argue that nearly anyone can create and distribute this content anyway. In other words, you can see how a critic might believe that you social scientists have triangulated your argument such that you've tied up the causationists like Gulliver.

SS1:   Look at it this way: It's not that we're shills for the media industry or that we're advancing some sort of clever design here to shield media violence from any regulation whatsoever. No, what we're arguing is that there's plenty of reason to examine regulation of analogical and digital communications, but not on the content level. Congress may always feel a need to hold a hearing now and then to let complaints be registered. But the selectivity media consumers can apply to digital communications is already dramatically apparent, even in this transitional world between the digital and the analogical. And, we hasten to add, our view that media violence doesn't make psychologically well people ill is gaining scientific credibility steadily. Those two facts, the scientific assessment of media violence and the sociology that digital communications bring with them, will bring tranquility to the media violence argument eventually. Add to that policy initiatives in education and in health care and you have both a reduction in public pressure and effective programs that reduce the likelihood of harm.

PM: Sounds like a win-win to me. However, I checked with my staff on media literacy. It's not all what it is cracked up to be.

SS2: Like any educational program, its promise outreaches its outcomes. Children and adults can learn critical approaches without necessarily applying them in decision-making situations. And there is some concern that what is learned in school stays in school (sort of the Las Vegas rule). But overall, the research says that trained individuals make use of more complex decision rules than untrained folks. Remember, the "fine child" exception to the universal and immutable laws of cognition? Let's be in the business of providing the resources that each child can be that fine child. Media literacy can be one small part of those resources. At the same time, don't forget your far larger responsibilities for opportunity, equality, and social justice.

PM: Fine children, one and all.

References

A. C. Nielsen. (1976). *Nielsen television 76*. Northbrook, IL: Author.

Abelman, R. (1999). Preaching to the choir: Profiling TV advisory ratings users. *Journal of Broadcasting and Electronic Media, 43*(4), 529–550.

Aiken, S. C. (2001). *Geographies of young people: The morally contested spaces of identity*. New York: Routledge.

American Psychiatric Association. (1994). *Diagnostic and statistical manual of mental disorders* (4th ed.). Washington, DC: Author.

Anderson, C. A. (2000). *Violent video games increase aggression and violence*. Retrieved April 1, 2005, from http://www.psychology.iastate.edu/faculty/caa/ abstracts/2000-2004/00Senate.html

Anderson, C. A., Berkowitz, L., Donnerstein, E., Huesmann, L. R., Johnson, J. D., Linz, D., et al. (2003a). Authors' note. *Psychological Science in the Public Interest, 4*(3), ix.

Anderson, C. A., Berkowitz, L., Donnerstein, E., Huesmann, L. R., Johnson, J. D., Linz, D., et al. (2003b). The influence of media violence on youth. *Psychological Science in the Public Interest, 4*(3), 81–110.

Anderson, C. A., & Bushman, B. J. (2001). Effects of violent video games on aggressive behavior, aggressive cognition, aggressive affect, physiological arousal, and prosocial behavior: A meta-analytic review of the scientific literature. *Psychological Science, 12*(5), 353–359.

Anderson, C. A., & Bushman, B. J. (2002a). The effects of media violence on society. *Science, 295*, 2377–2378.

Anderson, C. A., & Bushman, B. J. (2002b). Human aggression. *Annual Review of Psychology, 53*, 27–51.

Anderson, C. A., Bushman, B. J., & Groom, R. W. (1997). Hot years and serious and deadly assault: Empirical tests of the heat hypothesis. *Journal of Personality and Social Psychology, 73*, 1213–1223.

Anderson, C. A., & Dill, K. E. (2000). Video games and aggressive thoughts, feelings, and behavior in the laboratory and in life. *Journal of Personality and Social Psychology, 78*(4), 772–790.

Anderson, C. A., & Huesmann, L. R. (2003). Human aggression: A social-cognitive view. In M. A. Hogg & J. Cooper (Eds.), *The Sage handbook of social psychology* (pp. 296–323). Thousand Oaks, CA: Sage.

Anderson, J. A. (1996). *Communication theory: Epistemological foundations.* New York: Guilford.

Anderson, J. A. (2006, February). *The production of media violence and aggression research: A cultural analysis.* Paper accepted for presentation at the Western States Communication Association Convention, Palm Springs, CA.

Anderson, J. A. (in press). The production of media violence and aggression research: A cultural analysis. *American Behavioral Scientist.*

Anderson, J. A., & Baym, G. (2004). Philosophies and philosophic issues in communication 1995–2004. *Journal of Communication, 54,* 589–615.

Anderson, J. A., & Meyer, T. P. (1987). *Mediated communication: A social action perspective.* Thousand Oaks, CA: Sage.

Anderson, J. A., & Ploghoft, M. E. (1981). Receivership skills: The television experience. *Communication Yearbook, 4,* 293–307.

Anderson, K. B., Anderson, C. A., Dill, K. E., & Deuser, W. E. (1998). The interactive relations between trait hostility, pain, and aggressive thoughts. *Aggressive Behavior, 24,* 161–171.

Arnett, J. J., & Tanner, J. L. (Eds.). (2006). *Emerging adults in America: Coming of age in the 21st century.* Washington, DC: American Psychological Association.

Aschaffenburg, G. (1913). *Crime and its repression* (A. Albrecht, Trans.). Boston: Little, Brown. (Original work published 1903)

Atkin, C. K. (1983). Effects of realistic TV violence vs. fictional violence on aggression. *Journalism Quarterly, 60,* 615–621.

Atkin, C. K., Greenburg, B. S., Korzenny, F., & McDermott, S. (1979). Selective exposure to television violence. *Journal of Broadcasting, 23*(1), 5–13.

Baker, R. K., & Ball, S. J. (1969). *Mass media and violence: A staff report to the National Commission on the Causes and Prevention of Violence.* Washington, DC: Government Printing Office.

Ball-Rokeach, S. J. (2001). The politics of studying media violence: Reflections 30 years after the violence commission. *Mass Communication & Society, 4*(1), 3–18.

Bandura, A. (2001). Social cognitive theory of mass communication. *Media Psychology, 3,* 265–299.

Bandura, A., Ross, D., & Ross, S. (1963). Imitation of film-mediated aggressive models. *Journal of Abnormal and Social Psychology, 66,* 3–11.

Barker, M., & Petley, J. (2001). *Ill effects: The media/violence debate.* London: Routledge.

Bell, R. Q. (1979). Parent, child and reciprocal influences. *American Psychologist, 34*(10), 821–826.

Belson, W. A. (1967). *The impact of television: Methods and findings in program research.* Hamden, CT: Archon Books.

Benoit, W. L., Pier, P. M., & Blaney, J. R. (1997). A functional approach to televised political spots: Acclaiming, attacking, defending. *Communication Quarterly, 45*(1), 1–20.

Benson, E. R., Vernberg, E. M., Grimes, T., & Fonagy, P. (2006). *Empathy-related processing differences between children with and without a disruptive behavior disorder when viewing violent movies scenes.* Unpublished manuscript, University of Kansas.

Bergen, L., & Grimes, T. (1999). The reification of normalcy. *Journal of Health Communication, 4*(3), 211–226.

Bergen, L., Grimes, T., & Potter, D. (2005). How attention partitions itself during simultaneous message presentations. *Human Communication Research, 31*(3), 311–336.

Berkowitz, L. (1986). Situational influences on reactions to observed violence. *Journal of Social Issues, 42*(3), 93–106.

Berkowitz, L. (1993). *Aggression: Its causes, consequences, and control.* New York: McGraw-Hill.

Blair, R. J. R. (1995). A cognitive developmental approach to morality: Investigating the psychopath. *Cognition, 57*, 1–29.

Blair, R. J. R. (1999). Responsiveness to distress cues in the child with psychopathic tendencies. *Personality and Individual Differences, 27*, 135–145.

Bloom, R. W. (2002). On media violence: Whose facts? Whose misinformation? *American Psychologist, 57*, 447–448.

Blumer, H. (1933). *Movies and conduct.* New York: Macmillan.

Blumer, H. (1946). Collective behavior. In A. M. Lee (Ed.), *New outline of the principles of sociology* (pp. 167–222). New York: Barnes and Nobel.

Boffey, P. M., & Walsh, J. (1970). Study of TV violence: Seven top researchers blackballed from panel. *Science, 168*, 949–952.

Bogart, L. (1972–1973). Warning: The Surgeon General has determined that TV violence is moderately dangerous to your child's mental health. *Public Opinion Quarterly, 36*(4), 491–521.

Bremner, G., & Fogel, A. (2001). *Blackwell handbook of infant development.* Malden, MN: Blackwell.

Brett, G. (1996). Communication research, the Rockefeller Foundation, and mobilization for the war on words, 1938–1944. *Journal of Communication, 46*(3), 124–148.

Brockmeier, J., & Harré, R. (2001). Narrative: Problems and promises of an alternative paradigm. In J. Brockmeier & D. Carbaugh (Eds.), *Narrative and identity: Studies in autobiography, self, and culture* (pp. 39–58). Amsterdam: John Benjamins.

Brook, J. S., Whitman, M., & Gordon, A. S. (1981). Maternal and personality determinants of adolescent smoking behavior. *Journal of Genetic Psychology, 139*, 185–193.

Buckingham, D. (1998). Children and television: A critical overview of the research. In R. Dickinson, R. Harindranath, & O. Linne (Eds.), *Approaches to audiences: A reader* (pp. 131–145). New York: Arnold.

Bushman, B. J., & Anderson, C. A. (2001). Media violence and the American public: Scientific facts versus media misinformation. *American Psychologist, 56*, 477–489.

Bushman, B. J., & Huesmann, L. R. (2001). Effects of televised violence on aggression. In D. Singer & J. Singer (Eds.), *Handbook of children and the media* (pp. 223–254). Thousand Oaks, CA: Sage.

Campbell, R., Martin, C. R., & Fabos, B. (2005). *Media and culture: An introduction to mass communication*. Boston: Bedford–St. Martin's.

Canguilhem, G. (1989). *The normal and the pathological*. Cambridge: MIT Press.

Cantor, J. (2000). Media violence. *Journal of Adolescent Health, 27*(Suppl.), 30–34.

Cantor, J., Bushman, B., Huesmann, L. R., Groebel, J., Malamuth, N. M., Impett, E. A., et al. (2001). Some hazards of television viewing: Fears, aggression, and sexual attitudes. In D. G. Singer & J. L. Singer (Eds.), *Handbook of children and the media* (pp. 207–307). Thousand Oaks, CA: Sage.

Cantor, J., & Mares, M. L. (2001). Effects of television on child and family emotional wellbeing. In J. Bryant & J. Alison (Eds.), *Television and the American family* (2nd ed., pp. 317–332). Mahwah, NJ: Lawrence Erlbaum.

Cantor, J., & Wilson, B. J. (1984). Modifying fear responses to mass media in preschool and elementary school children. *Journal of Broadcasting, 28*(4), 431–443.

Carey, J. W. (1983). The origins of the radical discourse on cultural studies in the United States. *Journal of Communication, 33*(3), 311–313.

Carnagey, N. L., & Anderson, C. A. (2004). Violent video game exposure and aggression. *Minerva Psichiatrica, 45*(1), 1–18.

Cavanagh, J. R. (1949). The comics war. *Journal of Criminal Law and Criminology, 40*(1), 28–35.

Ceci, S. J., & Bjork, R. A. (2003). Editorial: Science, politics, and violence in the media. *Psychological Science in the Public Interest, 4*(3), i–iii.

Cohen, S. (1973). *Folk devils and moral panics*. St. Albans: Paladin.

Collins, W. A., Sobol, B. L., & Westby, S. D. (1981). Effects of adult commentary on children's comprehension and inferences about a televised aggressive portrayal. *Child Development, 52*(1), 158–163.

Compas, B. E., Connor, J. K., Saltzman, H., Thomsen, A. H., & Wadsworth, M. E. (2001). Coping with stress during childhood and adolescence: Problems, progress, and potential in theory and research. *Psychological Bulletin, 127*, 87–127.

Comstock, G. (2006). *A sociological perspective on television violence and aggression*. Unpublished manuscript.

Côté, J. E. (2000). *Arrested adulthood: The changing nature of maturity and identity*. New York: New York University Press.

Couldry, N. (2004). Theorizing media as practice. *Social Semiotics, 14*, 115–132.

Critcher, C. (2003). *Moral panics and the media*. Philadelphia: Open University Press.

Culley, J. D., Lazer, W., & Atkin, C. K. (1976). The experts looked at children's television. *Journal of Broadcasting, 20*, 3–22.

Davis, R. E. (1965). *Response to innovation: A study of popular argument about new mass media*. Unpublished doctoral dissertation, University of Iowa, Iowa City.

Decency: Hearing before the U.S. Senate Committee on Commerce, Science and Transportation, 109th Cong. (2005).

Dinsmoor, J. A. (2004). The etymology of basic concepts in the experimental analysis of behavior. *Journal of the Experimental Analysis of Behavior, 82,* 311–316.

Dodge, K. A. (1993). Social-cognitive mechanisms in the development of conduct disorder and depression. *Annual Review of Psychology, 44,* 559–584.

Dodge, K. A., Bates, J. E., & Pettit, G. S. (1990). Mechanisms in the cycle of violence. *Science, 21*(250), 1629–1788.

Dodge, K. A., & Frame, C. L. (1982). Social cognitive biases and deficits in aggressive boys. *Child Development, 53,* 620–635.

Dodge, K. A., & Tomlin, A. (1987). Utilization of self-schemas as a mechanism of interpretational bias in aggressive children. *Social Cognition, 5*(3), 280–300.

Dorr, A. (1981). Television and affective development and functioning: Maybe this decade. *Journal of Broadcasting, 25,* 335–345.

Dubow, E. F., Huesmann, L. R., & Boxer, P. (2003). Theoretical and methodological considerations in cross-generational research on parenting and child aggressive behavior. *Journal of Abnormal Child Psychology, 31*(2), 185–192.

Edelman, M. J. (1964). *The symbolic uses of politics.* Urbana: University of Illinois Press.

Edelman, M. J. (1971). *Politics as symbolic action: Mass arousal and quiescence.* Chicago: Markham.

Ehrler, D. J., Evans, J. G., & McGhee, R. L. (1999). Extending the Big-Five theory into childhood: A preliminary investigation into the relationship between Big-Five personality traits and behavior problems in children. *Psychology in the Schools, 36,* 451–458.

Ekman, P., Liebert, R. M., Friesen, W., Harrison, R., Zlatchin, C., Malmstrom, E. V., et al. (1972). Facial expressions of emotion as predictors of subsequent aggression. In G. A. Comstock, E. A. Rubinstein, & J. P. Murray (Eds.), *Television and social behavior: Vol. 5. Television's effects: Further explorations* (pp. 22–58). Washington, DC: Government Printing Office.

El-Sheikh, M., Ballard, M., & Cummings, E. M. (1994). Individual difference in preschoolers' physiological and verbal responses to videotaped angry interactions. *Journal of Abnormal Child Psychology, 22,* 303–320.

Eron, L. D. (1982). Parent-child interaction, television violence, and aggression of children. *American Psychologist, 37*(2), 197–211.

Eron, L. D. (1987). The development of aggressive behavior from the perspective of a developing behaviorism. *American Psychologist, 42*(5), 435–442.

Fairclough, N. (2003). *Analyzing discourse: Textual analysis for social research.* New York: Routledge.

Federman, J. (Ed.). (1997). *National television violence study* (Vol. 1). Thousand Oaks, CA: Sage.

Federman, J. (Ed.). (1998). *National television violence study: Vol. 3. Executive summary.* Santa Barbara, CA: Institute for Social, Behavioral, and Economic Research.

Felson, R. B. (1996). Mass media effects on violent behavior. *Annual Review of Sociology, 22,* 103–128.

Fergusson, D. M., & Horwood, L. J. (1999). Prospective childhood predictors of deviant peer affiliations in adolescence. *Journal of Child Psychology and Psychiatry, 40,* 581–592.

Fisherkeller, J. (1999). Everyday learning about identities among young adolescents in television culture. *Anthropology and Education Quarterly, 28*(4), 467–492.

Foucault, M. (1961). *Folie et de raison; histoire de la folie a l' age classique* [Madness and civilization: A history of insanity in the age of reason]. Paris: Plon.

Fowers, B. J., & Richardson, F. C. (1993). A hermeneutic analysis of Huesmann and Eron's cognitive theory of aggression. *Theory & Psychology, 3*(3), 351–374.

Fowles, J. (1999). *The case for television violence.* Thousand Oaks, CA: Sage.

Freedman, J. (1984). Effects of television violence on aggression. *Psychological Bulletin, 96,* 227–246.

Freedman, J. L. (1986). Television violence and aggression: A rejoinder. *Psychological Bulletin, 100,* 372–378.

Freedman, J. L. (1988). Television violence and aggression: What the evidence shows. *Applied Journal of Social Psychology Annual, 8,* 144–162.

Freidson, E. L. (1953). Adult discount: An aspect of children's changing taste. *Child Development, 24*(1), 39–49.

Frey, L. R., Botan, C. H., & Kreps, G. L. (2000). *Investigating communication: An introduction to research methods.* Needham Heights, MA: Allyn & Bacon.

Galatzer-Levy, R. (2002). Created in others' eyes. *Adolescent Psychiatry, 26,* 43–72.

Garbarino, J. (2001). Violent children: Where do we point the finger of blame? *Archive Pediatric Adolescent Medicine, 155,* 13–14.

Gerbner, G. (n.d.). *Rethinking media violence.* Retrieved April 1, 2005, from http://www.ciadvertising.org/sa/spring_03/382j/kimberly/page2.html

Gibson, K. R. (2000). Corroboration. *American Psychologist, 55,* 271–272.

Giroux, H. A. (1997). *Channel surfing: Race talk and the destruction of today's youth.* New York: St. Martin's.

Glenberg, A. M. (1988). *Learning from data: An introduction to statistical reasoning.* San Diego: Harcourt, Brace, Jovanovich.

Glymour, B., Glymour, C., & Glymour, M. (2006). *Watching social science.* Unpublished manuscript.

Glymour, B., Glymour, C., & Glymour, M. (in press). Watching social science. *American Behavioral Scientist.*

Goode, E., & Ben-Yehuda, N. (1994). *Moral panics: The social construction of deviance.* Oxford, UK: Blackwell.

Graham, H. D., & Gurr, T. R. (1969). *Violence in America: Historical and comparative perspectives: A report to the National Commission on the Causes and Prevention of Violence.* Washington, DC: Government Printing Office.

Greenberg, B. S., & Wotring, C. E. (1974). Television violence and its potential for aggressive driving behavior. *Journal of Broadcasting, 18*(4), 473–495.

Greene, J. O. (1984). A cognitive approach to human communication: An action assembly theory. *Communication Monographs, 51,* 289–306.

Grieveson, L. (1998). Fighting films: Race, morality and the governing of cinema, 1912–1915. *Cinema Journal, 38*(1), 40–72.

Grimes, T., & Bergen, L. (2001). The notion of convergence as an epistemological base for evaluating the effect of violent TV programming on psychologically normal children. *Mass Communication and Society, 4*(2), 183–198.

Grimes, T., & Bergen, L. (in press). The epistemological argument against a causal relationship between media violence and sociopathic behavior among psychologically well viewers. *American Behavioral Scientist.*

Grimes, T., Bergen, L., Nichols, K., Vernberg, E., & Fonagy, P. (2004). Is psychopathology the key to understanding why some children become aggressive when they are exposed to violent television programming? *Human Communication Research, 30*(2), 153–181.

Grimes, T., Vernberg, E., & Cathers, T. (1997). Emotionally disturbed children's reactions to violent media segments. *Journal of Health Communication, 2*(3), 157–168.

Grigsby, J. (1994). Procedural learning and the development and stability of character. *Perceptual and Motor Skills, 79,* 355–370.

Grossman, D., & Degaetano, G. (1999). *Stop teaching our kids to kill: A call to action against TV, movie and video game violence.* New York: Three Rivers Press.

Gruenberg, S. M. (1935). Radio and the child. *Annals of the American Academy of Political and Social Science, 177,* 123–128.

Gunnar, M. R., & Donzella, B. (2002). Social regulation of the cortisol levels in early human development. *Psychneuroendocrinology, 27*(1–2), 199–220.

Gunter, B. (1985). *Dimensions of television violence.* New York: St. Martin's.

Gunter, B. (1988). The perceptive audience. *Communication Yearbook, 11,* 22–50.

Gunter, B. (1998). Ethnicity and involvement in violence on television: Nature and context of on-screen portrayals. *Journal of Black Studies, 28,* 683–703.

Gunther, A. C., & Storey, J. D. (2003). The influence of presumed influence. *Journal of Communication, 53*(2), 199–215.

Haefner, M. J., & Wartella, E. A. (1987). Effects of sibling coviewing on children's interpretations of television programs. *Journal of Broadcasting & Electronic Media, 31,* 153–168.

Hebb, D. O. (1960). The second American Revolution. *American Psychologist, 15,* 735–745.

Heins, M. (2001). *Not in front of the children: "Indecency," censorship, and the innocence of youth.* New York: Hill & Wang.

Hess, R. D., & Goldman, H. (1962). Parents' views of the effect of television on their children. *Child Development, 33*(2), 411–426.

Hobbs, R. (1998). The seven great debates in the media literacy movement. *Journal of Communication, 48*(1), 16–32.

Hoerrner, K. L. (1998). *Symbolic politics: An historical, empirical, and legal discussion of Congressional efforts and the issue of television violence.* Unpublished doctoral dissertation, University of Georgia.

Hoerrner, K. L. (1999). The forgotten battles: Congressional hearings on television violence in the 1950s. *WJMCR, 2*(3). Accessed April 10, 2007, at http://www.scripps.ohiou.edu/wjmcr/vol02/2-3a-B.htm

Hoerrner, K. L. (2000). Symbolic politics: Congressional interest in television violence from 1950 to 1996. *Journalism and Mass Communication Quarterly, 76,* 684–698.

Hoffner, C., & Buchanan, M. (2002). Parents' responses to television violence: The third-person perception, parental mediation and support for censorship. *Media Psychology, 4,* 231–252.

Hoffner, C., Buchanan, M., Anderson, J. D., Hubbs, L. A., Kamigaki, S. K., Kowalczyk, L., et al. (1999). Support for censorship of television violence: The role of the third-person effect and news exposure *Communication Research, 26*(6), 726–742.

Hoffner, C. A., Plotkin, R. S., Buchanan, M., Anderson, J. D., Kamigaki, S. K., Hubbs, L. A., et al. (2001). The third-person effect in perceptions of the influence of television violence. *Journal of Communication, 51*(2), 283–299.

Hogben, M. (1998). Factors moderating the effect of televised aggression on viewer behavior. *Communication Research, 25,* 220–247.

Hollis, E. V. (1940). The foundations and the universities. *Journal of Higher Education, 11*(4), 177–181, 230.

Holmes, J. L. (1929). Crime and the press. *Journal of the American Institute of Criminal Law and Criminology, 20*(1), 6–59.

Huesmann, L. R. (1973). Television violence and aggression: The causal effect remains. *American Psychologist, 28*(7), 617–620.

Huesmann, L. R. (1986). Psychological processes promoting the relation between exposure to media violence and aggressive behavior by the viewer. *Journal of Social Issues, 42*(3), 1986.

Huesmann, L. R. (1988). An information processing model for the development of aggressive behavior. *Aggressive Behavior, 14*(10), 13–24.

Huesmann, L. R. (1993). Cognition and aggression: A reply to Fowers and Richardson. *Theory & Psychology, 3*(3), 375–379.

Huesmann, L. R., & Eron, L. D. (Eds.). (1986). *Television and the aggressive child: A cross-national comparison.* Hillsdale, NJ: Lawrence Erlbaum.

Huesmann, L. R., Eron, L. D., & Dubow, E. F. (2002). Childhood predictors of adult criminality: Are all risk factors reflected in childhood aggressiveness? *Criminal Behaviour and Mental Health, 12,* 185–208.

Huesmann, L. R., Eron, L. D., Lefkowitz, M. M., & Walder, L. O. (1984). Stability of aggression over time and generations. *Developmental Psychology, 20,* 1120–1134.

Huesmann, L. R., Lagerspetz, K., Akademi, A., & Eron, L. D. (1984). Intervening variables in the TV violence-aggression relation: Evidence from two countries. *Developmental Psychology, 20*(5), 746–775.

Huesmann, L. R., & Malamuth, N. M. (1986). Media violence and antisocial behavior: An overview. *Journal of Social Issues, 42*(3), 1–6.

Huesmann, L. R., Moise-Titus, J., Podolski, C.-L., & Eron, L. D. (2003). Longitudinal relations between children's exposure to TV violence and their aggressive and violent behavior in young adulthood: 1977–1992. *Developmental Psychology, 39*(2), 201–221.

Huesmann, L. R., & Taylor, L. D. (2006). The role of media violence in violent behavior. *Annual Review of Public Health, 27,* 393–415.

Hunt, R. G. (1970). *Strategic selection: A purposive sampling design for small numbers research, program evaluation, and management.* Buffalo: State University of New York Press.

Huston, A. C., Donnerstein, E., Fairchild, H. H., Feschbach, N. D., Katz, P. A., Murray, J. P., et al. (1992). *Big world, small screen: The role of television in American society.* Lincoln: University of Nebraska Press.

James, W. (1890). *The principles of psychology.* New York: Henry Holt.

Jenkins, H. (Ed.). (1998). *The children's culture reader.* New York: New York University Press.

Jensen, G. F. (2001). The invention of television as a cause of homicide: The reification of a spurious relationship. *Homicide Studies, 5*(2), 114–130.

Johnson, J. G., Cohen, P., Smailes, E. M., Kasen, S., & Brook, J. S. (2002). Television viewing and aggressive behavior during adolescence and childhood. *Science, 295,* 2468–2471.

Jones, G. (2002). *Killing monsters: Why children need fantasy, super heroes, and make-believe violence.* New York: Basic Books.

Jowett, G. S. (1989). "Capacity for evil": The 1915 Supreme Court Mutual decision. *Historical Journal of Film, Radio & Television, 9*(1), 59–78.

Kamel, B. Z., Gardner, J. M., & Freedland, R. L. (1996, June). *Arousal modulated attention in neonates is not affected by maternal tobacco smoking.* Paper presented at the College on Problems of Drug Dependence, San Juan, Puerto Rico.

Kane, T. R., Joseph, J. M., & Tedeschi, J. T. (1976). Person perception and the Berkowitz paradigm for the study of aggression. *Journal of Personality and Social Psychology, 33*(6), 663–673.

Katch, J. (2001). *Under deadman's skin: Discovering the meaning of children's violent play.* Boston: Beacon.

Katz, E., & Foulkes, D. (1962). On the use of the mass media as "escape": Clarification of a concept. *Public Opinion Quarterly, 26*(3), 377–388.

Katz, J. (1997). *Virtuous reality: How America surrendered discussion of moral values to opportunists, nitwits and blockheads like William Bennett.* New York: Random House.

Kellerman, J. (1999). *Savage spawn: Reflections on violent children.* New York: Ballentine.

Kellner, D., & Share, J. (2005). Toward critical media literacy: Core concepts, debates, organizations, and policy. *Discourse: Studies in the Cultural Politics of Education, 26,* 369–386.

Kiesner, J., & Kerr, M. (2004). Families, peers, and contexts as multiple determinants of adolescent problem behavior. *Journal of Adolescence, 27,* 493–495.

Kim, S. J. (1994). Viewer discretion is advised: A structural approach to the issue of television violence. *University of Pennsylvania Law Review, 142*(4), 1383–1441.

Kobar, P. C. (2000). Policy news you can use: A federal funding update for NSF and NIH. *Psychological Science Agenda, 13,* 6.

Kochanska, G., & Aksan, N. (2004). Development of mutual responsiveness between parents and their young children. *Child Development, 75,* 1657–1676.

Kohut, A. (2005). *New concerns about Internet reality shows: Support for tougher indecency measures, but worries about government intrusiveness.* Washington, DC: The Pew Research Center for the People and the Press.

Kuhn, T. S. (1970). *The structure of scientific revolutions.* Chicago: University of Chicago Press.

Larroque, B., Kaminski, M., Lelong, N., Subtil, D., & Dehaene, P. (1993). Effects on birthweight of alcohol and caffeine consumption during pregnancy. *American Journal of Epidemiology, 137,* 941–950.

Latour, B. (1987). *Science in action: How to follow scientists and engineers through society.* Cambridge, MA: Harvard University Press.

Lazarsfeld, P. F., & Merton, R. K. (1948). Mass communication, popular taste, and organized social action. In L. Bryson (Ed.), *The communication of ideas* (pp. 95–118). New York: Institute for Religious and Social Studies.

Lee, N. (2001). *Childhood and society: Growing up in an age of uncertainty.* Philadelphia: Open University Press.

Lefkowitz, M. M., Eron, L. D., & Huesmann, L. R. (1978). Parental punishment: A longitudinal analysis of effects. *Archives of General Psychiatry, 35,* 186–191.

Lefkowitz, M., Eron, L., Walder, L., & Huesmann, L. R. (1972). Television violence and child aggression: A follow up study. In G. A. Comstock & E. A. Rubenstein (Eds.), *Television and social behavior: Vol. 3. Television and adolescent aggressiveness* (pp. 35–135). Washington, DC: Government Printing Office.

Levy, D. A. (2003). Neural holism and free will. *Philosophical Psychology, 16,* 205–228.

Liebert, R. M., & Sprafkin, J. (1988). *The early window: Effects of television on children and youth* (3rd ed.). New York: Pergamon.

Lo, V.-H., & Niu, L.-G. (2003). Third-person effect, self-esteem, and support for restrictions of media. *Mass Communication Research, 75*(1), 141–167.

Low blows. (1972, May/June). *Columbia Journalism Review, 11*(1), 4.

Luhmann, N. (1990). *Essays on self-reference.* New York: Columbia University Press.

Luhmann, N. (1995). *Social systems* (J. Bednarz Jr. with D. Baecker, Trans.). Stanford, CA: Stanford University Press.

Lutz, R. J., & Swazy, J. L. (1977). Integrating cognitive structure and cognitive response approaches to monitoring communications effects. In W. D. Perreault Jr. (Ed.), *Advances in consumer research* (Vol. 4, pp. 363–371). Atlanta, GA: Association for Consumer Research.

MacBeth, T. (Ed.). (1996). *Tuning in to young viewers: Social science perspectives on television.* Thousands Oaks, CA: Sage.

MacBeth, T. (1997). Quasi-experimental research on television behavior. In J. K. Asamen & G. L. Berry (Eds.), *Research paradigms, television, and social behavior* (pp. 109–151). Thousand Oaks, CA: Sage.

MacDonald, K. (1984). An ethological-social learning theory of the development of altruism: Implications for human sociobiology. *Ethology and Sociobiology, 5,* 97–109.

Martin, C. L., & Ruble, D. (2004). Children's search for gender cues: Cognitive perspectives on gender development. *Current Directions in Psychological Science, 13,* 67–70.

Mayer, V. (2005). Research beyond the pale: Whiteness in audience studies and media ethnography. *Communication Theory, 15*(2), 148–167.

McCormack, T. (1978). Machismo in media research: A critical review of research on violence and pornography. *Social Problems, 25*(5), 544–555.

Messner, S. F. (1986). Television violence and violent crime: An aggregate analysis. *Social Problems, 33*(3), 218–235.

Meyer, T. P., Traudt, P. J., & Anderson, J. A. (1980). Non-traditional mass communication research methods: An overview of observational case studies of media use in natural settings. *Communication Yearbook, 4,* 261–275.

Mifflin, L. (1999). Many researchers say link is already clear on media and youth violence. Retrieved December 19, 2005, from the *New York Times* electronic database.

Milavsky, J. R., Kessler, R. C., Stipp, H. H., & Rubens, W. S. (1982). *Television and aggression: A panel study.* New York: Academic Press.

Miller, M. C. (2001, September). Does violence in the media cause violent behavior? *The Harvard Mental Health Letter,* pp. 5–8.

Miller, N. (1939). Radio's code of self-regulation. *Public Opinion Quarterly, 3*(4), 683–688.

Mishler, A. L. (1955). Seduction of the innocent. *Public Opinion Quarterly, 19*(1), 115–117.

Morgan, C. L. (1894). *An introduction to comparative psychology.* London: W. Scott.

Morning edition [Radio broadcast]. (2003, March). Retrieved from http://discover.npr.org/features/feature/jhtml?wfId=1187559

Murray, J. P. (1998). Studying television violence: A research agenda for the 21st century. In J. K. Asamen & G. L. Berry (Eds.), *Research paradigms, television, and social behavior* (pp. 369–410). Thousand Oaks, CA: Sage.

Murray, J. P. (2006). *Media violence: The effects are both real and strong.* Unpublished manuscript.

Murray, J. P., & Wartella, E. A. (1999). The reification of irrelevancy: A comment on the "Reification of normalcy." *Journal of Health Communication, 4,* 227–231.

Nagel, E. (1961). *The structure of science.* London: Routledge & Kegan Paul.

National Commission on the Causes and Prevention of Violence. (1970). *To establish justice, to insure domestic tranquility.* New York: Praeger.

National Institute of Mental Health. (1982). *Television and behavior: Ten years of scientific progress and implication for the eighties.* Rockville, MD: Author.

Neurological research and the impact of the media. (2003, April 10). Retrieved December 19, 2005, from http://commerce.senate.gov/hearings/testimony.cfm?id=706&wit_id=1888

Newman, J. P. (1987). Reaction to punishment in extraverts and psychopaths: Implications for the impulsive behavior of disinhibited individuals. *Journal of Research in Personality, 21,* 464–480.

Newman, J. P., & Schmitt, W. A. (1998). Passive avoidance in psychopathic offenders: A replication and extension. *Journal of Abnormal Psychology, 107,* 527–532.

Nord, D. P. (1995). Reading the newspaper: Strategies and politics of reader response, Chicago, 1912–1917. *Journal of Communication, 45,* 66–93.

Nordlund, A. M., & Garvill, J. (2002). Value structures behind pro-environmental behavior. *Environment and Behavior, 34,* 740–756.

Norton-Meier, L. (2005). Joining the *video-game literacy* club: A reluctant mother tries to join the flow. *Journal of Adolescent and Adult Literacy, 48,* 428–432.

Open forum on decency: Hearing before the U.S. Senate Committee on Commerce, Science and Transportation, 109th Cong. (2006).

Paik, H., & Comstock, G. (1994). The effects of television violence on antisocial behavior: A meta-analysis. *Communication Research, 21,* 516–546.

Patrick, C. J., Culbert, B. N., & Lang, P. J. (1994). Emotion in the criminal psychopath: Fear image processing. *Journal of Abnormal Psychology, 103,* 523–534.

Pecora, N. O., Murray, J. P., & Wartella, E. A. (2007). *Children and television: Fifty years of research.* Mahwah, NJ: Lawrence Erlbaum.

Peters, C. C. (1933). The relation of motion pictures to standards of morality. *Journal of Education Sociology, 6*(5), 251–255.

Peters, J. D. (Ed.). (1996). Tangled legacies [Special issue]. *Journal of Communication, 46*(3).

Peterson, R. C., & Thurstone, L. L. (1933). *Motion pictures and the social attitudes of children.* Oxford, UK: Macmillan.

Poffenberger, A. T. (1921). Motion pictures and crime. *The Scientific Monthly, 12*(4), 336–339.

Popper, K. (1959). *The logic of scientific discovery.* London: Hutchinson & Co.

Porges, S. W. (1992). Vagal tone: A physiological marker of stress vulnerability. *Pediatrics, 31,* 498–504.

Potegal, M., & Archer, J. (2004). Sex differences in childhood anger and aggression. *Child and Adolescent Psychiatric Clinics of North America, 13,* 513–528.

Potter, W. J. (1988). Perceived reality in television effects research. *Journal of Broadcasting and Electronic Media, 32*(1), 23–41.

Potter, W. J. (2003). *The 11 myths of media violence.* Thousand Oaks, CA: Sage.

Potter, W. J. (2004). Argument for the need for cognitive theory of media literacy. *American Behavioral Scientist, 48,* 266–272.

Potter, W. J., Cooper, R., & Dupagne, W. (1993). The three paradigms of mass media research in mainstream communication journals. *Communication Theory, 3,* 317–335.

Preston, M. I. (1941). Children's reactions to movie horrors and radio crime. *Journal of Pediatrics, 19*(2), 148–167.

Prilleltensky, I. (1994). *The morals and politics of psychology: Psychological discourse and the status quo.* Albany: State University of New York Press.

Proctor, L. J. (2006). Children growing up in a violent community: The role of the family. *Aggression and Violent Behavior, 11*(6), 558–576.

Quay, H. C. (1993). The psychobiology of undersocialized aggressive conduct disorder: A theoretical perspective. *Development and Psychopathology, 5,* 165–180.

Reeves, B., & Nass, C. (1996). *The media equation: How people treat computers, television, and new media like real people and places.* Stanford, CA: CSLI Publications and Cambridge University Press.

Reynolds, C. R. (1999a). The inference of causality between smoking and low birth weight: Good science of good politics? *Journal of Forensic Neuropsychology, 1,* 55–86.

Reynolds, C. R. (1999b). Inferring causality from relational data and designs: Historical and contemporary lessons for research and clinical practice. *The Clinical Neuropsychologist, 13*(4), 386–395.

Robbins, R. W., Gosling, S. D., & Craik, K. H. (1999). An empirical analysis of trends in psychology. *American Psychologist, 54,* 117–128.

Roe, K. (1995). Adolescents' use of the socially disvalued media: Towards a theory of media delinquency. *Journal of Youth and Adolescence, 24,* 617–631.

Rowland, H. (1944). Radio crime dramas. *Educational Research Bulletin, 23*(8), 210–217.

Rowland, W. D., Jr. (1982). *The politics of TV violence: Policy uses of communication research.* Beverly Hills, CA: Sage.

Rowland, W. D., Jr. (1997). Television violence redux: The continuing mythology of effects. In M. Barker & J. Petley (Eds.), *Ill effects: The media violence debate* (pp. 102–124). London: Routledge.

Rubenstein, E. A. (1982). Introductory comments. In D. Pearl, L. Bouthilet, & J. Lazar (Eds.), *Television and behavior: Ten years of scientific progress and implications for the eighties: Vol. 2. Technical reviews* (p. 104). Rockville, MD: National Institute of Mental Health.

Salwen, M. B., & Dupagne, M. (2001). Third person perception of television violence: The role of self-perceived knowledge. *Media Psychology, 3*(3), 211–236.

Sampson, E. E. (1981). Cognitive psychology as ideology. *American Psychologist, 36,* 730–743.

Santayana, G. (1952). Hypostatic ethics. In W. Sellars & J. Hospers (Eds.), *Readings in Ethical Theory* (pp. 263–271). New York: Appleton-Century-Crofts.

Savage, J. (2004). Does viewing violent media really cause criminal violence? A methodological review. *Aggression and Violent Behavior, 10,* 99–128.

Scantlin, R. M., & Jordan, A. B. (2006). Families' experiences with the V-chip: An exploratory study. *Journal of Family Communication, 6*(2), 139–159.

Schecter, S. R., & Bayley, R. (2004). Language socialization in theory and practice. *International Journal of Qualitative Studies in Education, 17,* 605–625.

Scheper-Hughes, N., & Sargent, C. (1998). *Small wars: The cultural politics of childhood.* Berkeley: University of California Press.

Schnaitter, R. (1987). Behaviorism is not cognitive and cognitivism is not behavioral. *Behaviorism, 15,* 1–11.

Schorr, D. (1981, October). Go get some milk and cookies and watch the murders on television. *The Washingtonian,* pp. 190–196.

Schramm, W., Lyle, J., & Parker, E. B. (1961). *Television in the lives of our children.* Stanford, CA: Stanford University Press.

Shea, A. (1948, November). What are your children reading? *Book Bulletin of the Chicago Public Library*, pp. 163–164.

Simpson, C. (1994). *Science of coercion: Communication research and psychological warfare, 1945–1960*. New York: Oxford University Press.

Singer, J. L., & Singer, D. G. (1981). *Television, imagination, and aggression: A study of preschoolers*. Hillsdale, NJ: Lawrence Erlbaum.

Singer, J. L., Singer, D. G., & Rapaczynski, W. (1984). Family patterns and television viewing as predictors of children's beliefs and aggression. *Journal of Communication, 34*, 73–89.

Skinner, B. F. (1948). *Walden two*. New York: Macmillan.

Skinner, B. F. (1953). *Science and human behavior*. New York: Macmillan.

Smith, M. C. (1994). *Social science in the crucible: The American debate over objectivity and purpose, 1918–1941*. Durham, NC: Duke University Press.

Smith, S. L., & Donnerstein, E. (1998). Harmful effects of exposure to media violence: Learning of aggression, emotional desensitization, and fear. In R. G. Geen & E. Donnerstein (Eds.), *Human aggression. Theories, research, and implications for social policy* (pp. 167–202). San Diego, CA: Academic Press.

Sparks, G. G. (2006). *Media effects research: A basic overview*. Belmont, CA: Thomson.

Sternheimer, K. (2003). *It's not the media: The truth about pop culture's influence on children*. Boulder, CO: Westview.

Strasburger, V. (1989). Editorial comment: Children, adolescents, and television: The role of pediatricians. *Pediatrics, 83*(3), 446.

Strasburger, V. C. (1995). *Adolescents and the media: Medical and psychological impact*. Thousand Oaks, CA: Sage.

Strasburger, V. C. (n.d.). *Study says children watch too much TV: What's a parent to do?* Accessed April 11, 2005, at http://rileyhospital.healthology.com/childrens-health/childrens-health-information/article287.htm

Taylor, L. D. (2005). Effects of visual and verbal sexual television content and perceived realism on attitudes and beliefs. *Journal of Sex Research, 42*(2), 130–137.

Teglasi, H. (1998). Temperament constructs and measures. *School Psychology Review, 27*(4), 564–585.

Television and growing up: The impact of televised violence: Report to the Surgeon General. (1972). Washington, DC: National Institute of Mental Health.

Thurstone, L. L. (1926). The method of paired comparisons for social values. *Journal of Abnormal & Social Psychology, 21*(4), 384–400.

Thurstone, L. L. (1928). Attitudes can be measured. *American Journal of Sociology, 33*, 529–554.

Thurstone, L. L. (1929). Theory of attitude measurement. *Psychological Review, 36*, 222–241.

Thurstone, L. L. (1930). A scale for measuring attitude toward the movies. *Journal of Educational Research, 22*, 84–89.

Thurstone, L. L. (1931). Influence of motion pictures on children's attitudes. *Journal of Social Psychology, 2,* 291–305.

Tierney, K. J., & Smith, J. A. (1997). What are the reinforcers for cognitivism in behaviour therapy? In K. Dillenburger, M. F. O'Reilly, & M. Keenan (Eds.), *Advances in behavior analysis* (pp. 81–87). Dublin: University College Dublin Press.

Tolman, E. S. (1930). *"Insight" in rats.* Berkeley: University of California Press.

Tryon, W. W. (2002). Neural network learning theory: Unifying radical behaviorism and cognitive neuroscience. *Behavior Therapist, 25,* 53–57.

Tyre, P. (2002, March 25). Bringing up adultolescents. *Newsweek,* pp. 38–40.

Udry, J. R. (1994). Integrating biological and sociological models of adolescent problem behaviors. In R. D. Ketterlinus & M. E. Lamb (Eds.), *Adolescent problem behaviors: Issues and research* (pp. 93–107). Hillsdale, NJ: Lawrence Erlbaum.

U.S. Congress, House Committee on Interstate and Foreign Commerce, Subcommittee on the Federal Communications Commission, *Investigation of Radio and Television Programs,* 82nd Cong., 2nd sess. (1952).

U.S. Public Health Service. (1964). *Smoking and health: Report of the advisory committee to the Surgeon General of the Public Health Service* (PHS Pub. No. 1103). Washington, DC: U.S. Department of Health, Education, and Welfare, Public Health Service, Center for Disease Control.

Uttal, W. R. (2000). *The war between mentalism and behaviorism: On accessibility of mental processes.* Mahwah, NJ: Lawrence Erlbaum.

Vandell, D. L. (2000). Parents, peer groups, and other socializing influences. *Developmental Psychology, 36,* 699–710.

Vanderstraeten, R. (2000). Autopoiesis and socialization: On Luhmann's reconceptualization of communication and socialization. *British Journal of Sociology, 51,* 581–598.

Walder, L. O., Abelson, R., Eron, L. D., Banta, T. J., & Laulicht, D. H. (1961). Development of a peer-rating measure of aggression. *Psychological Reports, 9,* 497–556.

Watson, J. B. (1913). Psychology as the behaviourist views it. *Psychological Review, 20,* 158–177.

Wertham, F. (1954). *Seduction of the innocent.* New York: Rinehart.

Wyness, M. G. (2000). *Contesting childhood.* London: Falmer.

Zillmann, D. (1979). *Hostility and aggression.* Hillsdale, NJ: Lawrence Erlbaum.

Zillmann, D. (1983). Transfer of excitation in emotional behavior. In J. T. Cacioppo & R. E. Petty (Eds.), *Social psychophysiology: A sourcebook* (pp. 215–240). New York: Guilford.

Zubov, A. (2004). Formalization of the procedure of singling out of the basic text contents. *Journal of Quantitative Linguistics, 11,* 33–48.

Index

About the Authors

Tom Grimes is Professor of Journalism and Mass Communication at Texas State University. He earned a bachelor's degree in Philosophy and French Literature from the University of Arkansas and a master's degree in Journalism from Columbia University. He then spent 8 years in television news in his hometown of Dallas, Texas, from 1974 to 1982. He left television and earned a PhD in mass communication from Indiana University in 1986. He took academic appointments at the University of Wisconsin–Madison and Kansas State University, where he was the Ross Beach Professor of Journalism and Mass Communications. It was in Kansas, at the Menninger Clinic and the University of Kansas's Clinical Child Psychology Program, that Grimes, Lori Bergen, and colleagues conducted experiments, which challenged conventional assumptions about the psychological effects of media violence. He is married to Lori Bergen.

James A. Anderson, PhD, (Iowa) Professor of Communication, University of Utah, is the author/coauthor/editor of 16 books, including *Communication Research: Issues and Methods* (1987), *Mediated Communication: A Social Action Perspective* (1988), *Communication Theory: Epistemological Foundations* (1996), and *The Organizational Self and Ethical Conduct* (2001). His 100-plus chapters, articles, and research monographs are in the areas of family studies, cultural studies, media literacy, organizational studies, communicative ethics, methodology, and epistemology. He is a Fellow and past president of the International Communication Association. He has been the editor of *Communication Yearbook* and *Communication Theory,* associate editor of *Human Communication Research,* guest editor of *Communication Studies* and *American Behavioral Scientist,* and a member of the editorial board of seven other journals. He is currently executive editor of the *Rocky Mountain Communication Review.* His forthcoming titles from Sage include works on mediated communication research methods and theory.

Lori Bergen is Professor and Director of the School of Journalism and Mass Communication at Texas State University in San Marcos. She earned a PhD from Indiana University in mass communication and two degrees from Kansas State University, a bachelor's degree in history and political science, and a master's degree in journalism and mass communications. She is a journalist who has been on the faculties of Southwest Texas State, Wichita State, and Kansas State universities. Her research about newspapers, journalists, children, and television violence appears in the *Newspaper Research Journal, Journal of Health Communication, Human Communication Research, Journal of Advertising,* and *Mass Communication & Society.*